INDIANA : an Interpretation

INDIANA

An Interpretation

BY

JOHN BARTLOW MARTIN

With an introduction by James H. Madison

INDIANA UNIVERSITY PRESS
Bloomington and Indianapolis

The paper used in this publication meets the minimum requirements of
American National Standard for Information Sciences—Permanence of
Paper for Printed Library Materials, ANSI Z39.48-1984.

Manufactured in the United States of America

Library of Congress Cataloging-in-Publication Data

Martin, John Bartlow, 1915–1987.
    Indiana : an interpretation / by John Bartlow Martin ; with an
introduction by James H. Madison.
        p.   cm.
    Originally published: New York : Knopf, 1947.
    Includes bibliographical references and index.
    ISBN 0-253-33682-1.—ISBN 0-253-20754-1 (pbk.)
    1. Indiana—History.   I. Title.
F526.M25   1992
977.2—dc20   92-15855

1 2 3 4 5 96 95 94 93 92

CONTENTS

Contents

Introduction

JAMES H. MADISON

*I*ndiana: An Interpretation was written long ago. When it first appeared in the fall of 1947, there were no shopping malls, interstates, or McDonalds hamburgers in Indiana. A farm woman likely made her everyday dresses from feed sacks; a decent man always wore a hat; and nearly everyone gathered on the courthouse square on Saturday evenings. Few books written so long ago are worthy of being read today, particularly those commonly referred to as "regional" books. John Bartlow Martin's book about Indiana is an exception. While "out of date" in small ways, in many others it remains a modern and compelling piece of writing.

Martin's interpretation of Indiana was different. Nearly all that had been written about the state up to the end of World War II celebrated achievement and progress. The common narrative line was one of steady ascent. Popular writers focused on hardy, independent pioneers who created a civilization out of a wilderness; on their descendants, who marched forward on a Hoosier highway of progress; and on an Indiana "golden age," beginning near the end of the nineteenth century. Even much of the scholarly writing on Indiana fit this model, telling a story of a blossoming of pioneer democracy in the Hoosier forests and a flowering of business and culture in the prosperous towns and cities of the late nineteenth century. Most writers ignored the twentieth century or treated it as a simple extension of the "golden age."

Readers expecting such heartwarming and reassuring portrayals of the Hoosier state in this book should turn elsewhere. Rather than comfort, Martin offers challenge. Rather than passivity or easy assent, he provokes engagement, perhaps even disagreement. Some readers in 1947 resisted the book, as did the young Gene Pulliam, Jr., reviewer for the *Indianapolis Star*, who coolly labeled it "interesting and different as books about Indiana go." The unidentified reviewer in the *Indiana Magazine of History* had more to say, disagreeing vehemently with the "inaccurate and inadequate" interpretation that "hurls a bolt of lightning at the people of Indiana." Whether in agreement or disagreement, thoughtful readers today will find more passion in this book than in most of the "newer" volumes that sit on the regional shelves of their bookstores and libraries. And they will discover here a writer who could work magic with words, whose "idea of heaven," his son recalled, "was reaching a mass audience with a serious piece of writing."[1]

When he returned to Indianapolis in the summer of 1946 to write a book about Indiana, John Bartlow Martin was already a local boy deemed worthy of a newspaper story. Asked to explain his success by an admiring interviewer for the *Indianapolis Times* Martin responded, "Hell, I'm just a reporter."[2] He was indeed "just" a reporter, but one helluva reporter, his colleagues would have said. So good was he at his craft of writing by 1946, in fact, that he could make a comfortable living without the burden of holding a regular job at a newspaper or magazine. Some thought him the best freelance writer in America.[3]

John Bartlow Martin was born August 4, 1915, in Hamilton, Ohio. At age three, he moved with his parents to Indianapolis, where his father was a building contractor. Unlike many Hoosiers who have written reminiscences of growing up in Indiana, Martin later recalled that "most of my childhood memories are dark." He came of age, he remembered, on "a mean street in a mean city." Among his earliest recollections was a parade of the Ku Klux Klan around Monument Circle. His father, who had little understanding of the boy's bookish interests, prospered during the booming 1920s, only to fall to the blows of the Great Depression. And although Franklin D. Roosevelt's New Deal saved the family's house from mortgage foreclosure and gave his father a job in the Works Progress Administration, Martin's parents fought in a loveless marriage that eventually ended in divorce.[4]

Martin escaped to college at DePauw in Greencastle, Indiana, where he studied history, political science, and economics and edited the college newspaper. His vital energy broke free when he began reporting for the *Indianapolis Times* while still in college and then full time in 1937. His first assignment was working with Heze Clark, who covered the city police. In Martin's words, Clark was "probably the most thorough collector of facts on police cases I ever knew." Indeed, as Martin recalled, "in a few days he taught me all I needed to cover police. Years later, when I was teaching at Northwestern University's Medill School of Journalism, I marveled how a student could spend ten thousand dollars and a full year learning less than Heze Clark taught me in a few days free."[5]

In 1938 Martin left Indianapolis. Like generations of young Midwesterners, particularly those with literary ambitions, he moved to Chicago. There he began to write detective stories combining fact and fiction, doing this well enough to make a living for himself and for Frances Smethurst, whom he married in 1940. Soon he began writing "fact pieces," often dealing with crime but gradually shifting to other social and political issues. A break came when he decided to write a story on the mood of ordinary Americans on the World War II homefront. He went to Muncie, Indiana, to research the story and to do "true heavy-fact legwork" for the first time. *Harper's* published his article that summer. It was filled with telling details and direct quotations gathered from union leaders, newspaper editors, and the ordinary people of an ordinary American town trying to get through the hard times of war. In style and substance there was little of the sentimentally patriotic and far more of the dark shadows and hard edges that marked the *film noir* genre of the 1940s. The style matched the message—"strong declarative sentences and syntax that sped the reader's eye along the page."[6]

The Muncie article showed Martin's skills in combining the voices and stories of ordinary people, lots of carefully selected details, minimal editorializing, and a keen sense for a specific place—all carefully crafted to present a vivid and sometimes hard-edged portrait. It was a combination he would use again and again, most immediately, following service in the army, in a book about Indiana.[7]

Why Martin chose to write a book about Indiana is unclear. A quick reading might lead to speculation that it offered a chance to get even. Martin raised the possibility himself in his memoirs: "Since I had hated my childhood, one would have assumed I would hate Indiana and I was therefore surprised to find a certain affection suffusing parts of the book."[8] There is indeed a certain affection in the book, though the reader needs to look behind the disaffection and beyond the hard edges that are so central in Martin's interpretation of Indiana's past and present. His affection is of a different kind than the pap and whipped cream featured in the more romantic writing about the state. Martin's may in fact be a deeper affection in that he offers more substance even today for Hoosiers concerned about, and loving of, their state.

Martin's interpretation starts with "the Indiana idea"—the notion that the state is "a pleasant, rather rural place inhabited by people who are confident, prosperous, neighborly, easygoing, tolerant, shrewd." This Indiana idea, he finds, not only "contains a good deal of mythology" but also stands in the way of facing a past and a present that Hoosiers too readily avoided.[9]

The opening chapter shows immediately Martin's powers of description as he paints detailed images of visitors to the 1946 state fair and then takes the reader outward in different directions from Monument Circle in Indianapolis. With the stage set he then presents the pioneers, using as he always does particular individuals to carry the story line, in this instance, a story of beginnings and of growth. By the late nineteenth century Hoosiers had created a settled civilization and a vibrant capitalism that offered prospects of progress and prosperity. Martin's treatment of this part of the story is brief and less engaged and compelling than the later chapters that deal with the twentieth century. In his treatment of nineteenth-century Indiana Martin even drifts toward some of the more romantic portrayals he sets out to correct.

It is in presenting the period after 1900 that *Indiana: An Interpretation* comes alive. Here Martin's skills as a fact seeker and word painter are brought fully to bear. He adeptly weaves personal interviews and stories through the narrative. (The book's acknowledgment section contains a long list of Hoosiers he talked with, including many Indiana newspaper reporters.) The last two thirds of the book also shines with a spare prose style that pulls the reader into the story. Most important, it is here that Martin presents his original contribution, his interpretation, by arguing that in the twentieth century Indiana suffered a "hardening of the arteries" and "lost its way." After 1900 "the Indiana idea" no longer fit.[10]

Essential to understanding Martin's argument is the central place he gives to Eugene V. Debs. In his memoirs Martin admitted that "Debs almost ran away with the book." Most early twentieth-century Hoosiers considered the Terre Haute socialist either a softheaded idealist or a dangerous radical; in any event, he was surely a man best forgotten. Monuments to Debs in his hometown and elsewhere in the state were notable for their absence. Martin now stated the shocking proposition that Debs was "the most important figure Indiana has produced," and he proceeded to paint a portrait that warmly captured Debs's saintly qualities. Doubtless with intended irony, Martin quotes the Hoosier poet James Whitcomb Riley, not to celebrate frost on the pumpkin or old swimming holes, but in praise of Gene Debs's warm heart. Debs so appealed to Martin because the labor organizer and socialist questioned the direction of modern life, particularly capitalism. It is the voice of protest that Martin finds refreshing and essential, from Robert Owen to the Hapgood family, all refusing, like Gene Debs, to believe that what was had to be or should be. These voices outside the mainstream were the antidote for the hardening of the arteries, the cartographers who would lead Hoosiers away from smug contentment and toward progress.[11]

If Debs is the good guy there are bad guys to match. In the book's centrally important section, "Four Gentlemen from Indiana," Martin gives readers two bad apples, each a powerful voice of bigotry and intolerance.[12] In most accounts of Indiana this dark voice is represented by D. C. Stephenson, the grand dragon of the Indiana Klan of the 1920s.[13] Martin devotes a chapter to Stephenson. Although failing to ask why so many Hoosiers followed this charlatan, Martin's portrait encompasses the wonderful detail (for example, the traditional Thanksgiving rabbit hunt) and the compelling immediacy that derived from interviews with those who remembered "Steve." Less well known but perhaps even more interesting than Stephenson is Court Asher, the second "gentleman" from Indiana. Asher is a more convincing bigot than Stephenson, one more homegrown and more Hoosier than the puffed-up grand dragon, though here too there is a bit of exaggeration.

Martin employs Asher to display the dark side of Indiana most brilliantly when he follows him to a family reunion.

Martin sketches in more sympathetic tones the remaining two of the four gentlemen. His treatment of Ned Gorrell, the small-town newspaper editor, is perhaps the best chapter in the book. Here is "the outsider's idea of a Hoosier, an idea that is sadly out of date," Martin concludes. And with Ralph Gates, the governor of Indiana at the time, Martin illuminates "both the old and the new" and the good and the mediocre—if not the bad—in the peculiar world of Hoosier politics. It was Gates and his fellow politicos Martin condemned when he wrote, in an oft-quoted sentence, that "today Indiana is full of people who never see the economic or social ends of politics but are fascinated merely by the day-to-day business of vote getting, buttonholing, horse trading, drink buying—all the little trickeries that make Presidents and ward heelers alike."[14]

In the last two chapters Martin treats the present—his present of the Great Depression, World War II, and the immediate postwar era. It is an anxious and sometimes gloomy present, marked by the atomic bomb and the threat to peace and by widespread fear of a return to dark economic depression. Where was Indiana going? No one seemed to know. Too few Hoosiers, in Martin's view, seemed to care. Too many had lost their confidence, their vision. Rather than ask hard questions, too many folks hid behind a "self-conscious rusticity," retreating to an Indiana idea that no longer fit modern times.[15]

Some readers may find that Martin overstates his argument. Perhaps the nineteenth century was not nearly as golden as he suggests, the twentieth century not nearly as dark. Just as this book appeared, in fact, Indiana and the nation were heading toward a period of growth that would bring widespread affluence, marked, for example, by undreamed-of expansion of education from kindergartens to the state universities. There would be signs too of growing tolerance, as in Indiana's pioneering Civil Rights Act of 1963. Moreover, through the 1950s and beyond there were unmatched joys in such continuing Hoosier traditions as the state fair, the high school basketball tournament, and family reunions in a state park. Perhaps Martin got it all wrong.

And yet, from a perspective near the end of the twentieth century, it is possible to believe that Martin was on to something nearly fifty years ago, something that makes his writing resonate in our own time. Don't political campaigns of the 1990s, which seem to focus almost exclusively on promising no tax increases, continue the unhappy tradition of avoiding the most pressing social and economic challenges? Is it possible to argue that bigotry is no longer a feature of the state's culture, even if signs reading "We Cater to WHITE TRADE only" no longer hang in restaurant windows as they did in Martin's day? Is there today a selfishness and narrowness, a malaise of the spirit, as Indiana moves toward the bicentennial celebration of its birth? Will the year 2000 hold the promise that Martin found in 1900, or have we indeed lost our way? Will this generation of Hoosiers agree with Martin that at some point in our century "the wonder went out of all the wonderful things"? Finally, can we ask these hard questions with "a certain affection" for the Hoosier state?[16]

One wishes that John Bartlow Martin had returned to Indiana more frequently after writing *Indiana: An Interpretation*. He continued to write, mostly for the "big slicks"—*Life, Look, Saturday Evening Post*, and other mass-circulation magazines that presented serious writing for readers in the 1940s and 1950s. Living near Chicago and resisting lures pulling toward New York City, he continued to focus his pieces on the Midwest, "the locomotive of America," he believed. Place and a sense of place remained central to his writing. He wrote about labor, mental hospitals, race segregation, crime, and politics. He spent much of his time traveling across the Midwest, gathering the facts and the telling details that give such richness to his writing. He was tall and thin with short red hair, and "his pockets bulged with pencils and his brief case with railroad timetables, the requisites of the roving writer." He had, one newspaper reported, "the kinetic energy of a caged panther." He was, another said, "a modest, bespectacled man, whose diffidence belied great intensity."[17]

It was logical that Martin's interests would lead him to politics in general and to liberal Democrats in particular. He entered presidential politics as a speech writer for Adlai Stevenson in 1952 and again in 1956. He deeply admired Stevenson—so much, in fact, that he eventually wrote a two-volume biography of the Illinois

Democrat.[18] Martin worked also in the John F. Kennedy campaign of 1960. President Kennedy later appointed him ambassador to the Dominican Republic, a place to which Martin devoted a long-term interest.[19] And he joined the campaign of Robert Kennedy in 1968, which provided an occasion to return to Indiana and to play a role in the important Indiana primary. That spring campaign, Martin recalled, was "in many ways the climactic event of my life, bringing together writing, politics, and Indiana."[20] He mourned John F. Kennedy's assassination deeply, and the death of Robert Kennedy at the hands of an assassin, as Martin's son recalled, "broke the back of my father's spirit."[21] The political candidates he most admired were dead. After these years, he taught journalism at Northwestern, wrote books, and spent summers at his home in Upper Michigan, but his engagement was less intense.

John Bartlow Martin died January 3, 1987, at the age of seventy-one. *Time* magazine remembered him as a writer who "turned out a million words a year at his peak."[22] Many of those words still stand, still worthy of readers, including those in *Indiana: An Interpretation*. This reprinting will ensure that a new generation will have easy access to one of Indiana's most interesting writers.

NOTES

1. *Indianapolis Star,* November 9, 1947; unsigned review (possibly by the editor, John D. Barnhart), *Indiana Magazine of History* 44 (September 1948): 309, 308; John Frederick Martin, "John Bartlow Martin," *American Scholar* 59 (Winter 1990): 99. In 1987 the Pulliam family newspaper, the *Indianapolis Star,* carried an obituary of Martin that failed to mention the Indiana book. *Indianapolis Star,* January 5, 1987. Newspaper editors, historians, and others who write about the place in which they live and work may face special challenges in maintaining a critical perspective. It was doubtless this challenge that motivated the reviewer in *The New York Times* to write that "as a piece of regional writing . . . this book is a rare adventure into the field of self-criticism." *New York Times Book Review,* December 7, 1947. A similar point was made by reviewers in the *New York Herald Tribune Weekly Book Review,* December 7, 1947, and in the *Saturday Review of Literature,* January 10, 1948.

2. *Indianapolis Times,* July 31, 1946.

3. *New York Times,* January 5, 1987 (obituary); *Indianapolis Times,* March 4, 1962.

4. John Bartlow Martin, *It Seems Like Only Yesterday: Memoirs of Writing, Presidential Politics, and the Diplomatic Life* (New York, 1986), 18, 19. Much of the biographical information in this introduction comes from this source.

5. Ibid., 14.

6. Ibid., 44; John Bartlow Martin, "Is Muncie Still Middletown?" *Harper's Magazine* 189 (July 1944): 97–109; John Frederick Martin, "Martin," 97. See also John Bartlow Martin, "Middletown Revisited: Snapshots of Muncie at Peace," *Harper's Magazine* 193 (August 1946): 111–19.

7. Before he was drafted, Martin finished the book *Call It North Country: The Story of Upper Michigan* (New York, 1944), set in a part of the Midwest where he spent summers most of his adult life.

8. Martin, *It Seems Like Only Yesterday*, 49.

9. John Bartlow Martin, *Indiana: An Interpretation* (New York, 1947), viii, 277.

10. Ibid., 122, 270.

11. Ibid., 49, ix.

12. The feature of Martin's book that "dates" it more than any other is that he writes almost exclusively about white men. Women seldom play active roles. Nor do African Americans. While Martin conveys something of the extent of white racism in Indiana, he does not employ black Hoosiers as actors in his story.

13. Leonard J. Moore has shown recently how overemphasis on Stephenson has impeded an understanding of the Klan. See *Citizen Klansmen: The Ku Klux Klan in Indiana, 1921–1928* (Chapel Hill, N.C., 1991).

14. Martin, *Indiana*, 234, 273.

15. Ibid., 274.

16. For some of these sentiments, see David Hoppe, *Where We Live: Essays about Indiana* (Bloomington, Ind., 1989). Earlier and generally more optimistic views are presented in Donald F. Carmony, ed., *Indiana: A Self-Appraisal* (Bloomington, Ind., 1966).

17. Martin, *It Seems Like Only Yesterday*, 43; *Current Biography*, 1956, 416; *Indianapolis Times*, March 4, 1962; *New York Times*, January 5, 1987.

18. John Bartlow Martin, *Adlai Stevenson of Illinois* (Garden City, N.Y., 1977); John Bartlow Martin, *Adlai Stevenson and the World* (Garden City, N.Y., 1978).

19. See John Bartlow Martin, *Overtaken by Events: The Dominican Crisis from the Fall of Trujillo to the Civil War* (New York, 1966); John Bartlow Martin, *U.S. Policy in the Caribbean* (Boulder, Colo., 1978).

20. Martin, *It Seems Like Only Yesterday*, 277.

21. John Frederick Martin, "Martin," 98.

22. *Time*, January 19, 1987, 80.

Preface

THE purpose of this book, as set forth in the opening pages, is to interpret a state, Indiana, and the people who inhabit it. This requires explanation for it seems to imply that the book conforms to certain conventions of regional writing, and I don't believe the book does. For example, according to convention, regional writing should be rhapsodic, not critical. This, however, is not a book designed to advertise or praise (or, for that matter, to condemn) Indiana. Nor is it a tourist's guide; in that field the *Indiana Guide* (Oxford, 1941) will be found more satisfactory. Again, this book is by no means a complete work on Indiana or even a short, informal history; I have not treated George Rogers Clark and many others. This book is not history; it is journalism. It is one man's interpretation of Indiana—that is, the Hoosier character, the Hoosier thought, the Hoosier way of living.

I have included only such ancient history as seemed interesting, fresh, and necessary to an understanding of Indiana today (only about one eighth of the book deals with events prior to the Civil War). None the less I have tried to fill a gap. There is, so far as I know, no serious book for the general reader synthesizing the Indiana story. At least there is none bringing the Indiana story to date, and the traveler entering Indiana today, having read nothing since Tarkington and Riley, might not recognize the place. The book deals more with people than with events. The Grange is treated as the human experience of some farmers in trouble, not as a movement. Although the book contains (so far as I know) no fiction, it is basically a story. The people in it are all actual people. Some of them, including Debs, Morton, and Harrison, were national figures; others are almost unknown outside their home towns. In nearly every case they were selected because they threw some light on the ideas and the character of the Hoosiers. Probably "Hoosier" is better known in the United States than any locale nickname save "Yankee," but in Indiana it is used seriously only by editorial writers, Fourth of July orators, and chamber-of-commerce propagandists, and in his private life any of these would shoot like a dog a man who called him a Hoosier. Why does the Hoosier whisper diffidently that he is from Indiana (whereas the Texan bellows that he's from Texas)? This book inquires into the reasons.

A lot of things started in Indiana—the automotive industry, for one—and Indiana has produced a great many ideas, many wrongheaded and some downright wicked. Viewed one way, this book is a study of Indiana ideas, for threads run through it—the quest for the better life, bigotry, provincial protest. Viewed another, it is a study of an idea itself, the Hoosier, or Indiana, idea. By the "Indiana idea" I mean the idea of Indiana and the Hoosiers that is held by people elsewhere. It is a conception of Indiana as a pleasant, rather rural place inhabited by people who are confident, prosperous, neighborly, easygoing, tolerant, shrewd. We shall inquire into the origin of this Indiana idea and into its validity today.

It is customary for a writer of a regional book to claim that his chosen region includes all others. This usually is nonsense. Yet it is true that Indiana is a place where the American kind of capitalistic democracy grew up in its native form. In saying this I am not claiming that this book is a study of American democracy; I just want to say that in handling the material I kept discovering that some of it seemed not peculiar to Indiana but, rather, common to the United States. It was no accident that Mark Sullivan suggested early in his history of *Our Times* that the typical American of 1900 more closely resembled the inhabitant of Indiana than of any other place, or that the Lynds selected Muncie, Indiana, when they were looking for Middletown, U.S.A.

The book had to be extremely selective. The selection was made arbitrarily with, again, interest, freshness, and importance as the yardsticks. The emphasis will displease scholars, I fear. But I felt a need, for example, only to show Morton's tremendous force, not to treat him definitively. Again, Debs is treated at greater length than any other individual because I think it can be argued that Debs is the most important figure Indiana has produced, and surely he stood at apogee among all the good men who have searched in Indiana for the better life, yet he is not remembered that way (and besides, he made a good story). God has made few more unimportant Governors than Gates; but I have devoted a good deal of space to him because he is, really, extremely important. There are so many Hoosiers like him.

The plan is roughly chronological. Occasionally, however, some character, considered from beginning to end in a single chapter, intrudes on chronology. The outline is as follows:

The first section is a rapid survey of the subject, Indiana, as a whole, viewed within the framework of a Hoosier institution, the State Fair; the people and places, historical and contemporary, barely referred to in this chapter are dealt with in detail later on. This is a once-over-lightly.

The second section sketches the pre-Civil-War background.

The third section shows how the Civil War changed Indiana irrevocably; theretofore a neglected agrarian state on the frontier, it swiftly became a manufacturing state weighty in national affairs.

The fourth section covers the 1880's, 1890's, and early 1900's. Indiana did have a golden age, complete with a literature of its own.

The fifth section deals with Eugene V. Debs and the Hapgoods, who were men in revolt against the abuses of capitalism, the very capitalism, that is, which had produced the golden age.

The sixth section presents four representative or influential men who flourished in Indiana between one world war and another.

The last section makes a picture of Indiana during and just after the war of the 1940's.

Acknowledgments and bibliography appear elsewhere.

JOHN BARTLOW MARTIN

Highland Park, Illinois
April 1, 1947

PART ONE

Crossroads, U.S.A.

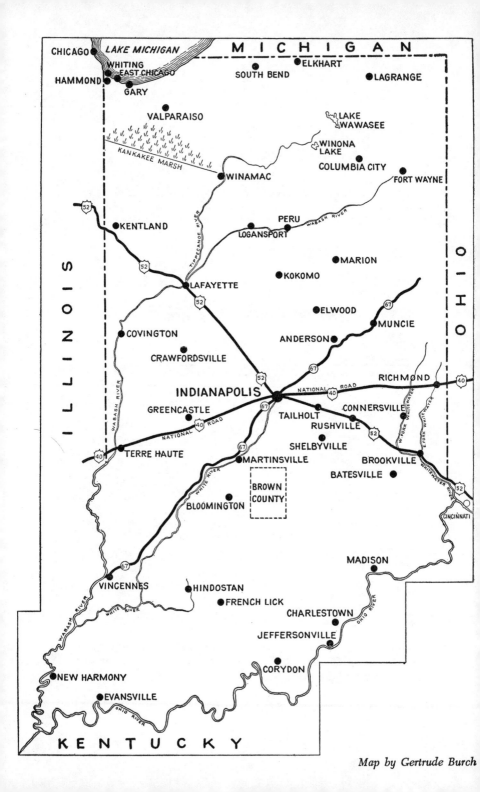

Map by Gertrude Burch

Chapter 1

STATE FAIR

THE boy stood out in front all alone beside his calf. His solemn face was impassive but his fingers were clenched tightly at the seam of his khaki pants. The judge, a large man in a round, hard Panama hat and white shirt with sleeves rolled up, walked slowly round the calf, stepping close to prod it exploringly, stepping back to ponder. Most of the men in the folding chairs on the tanbark watched silently. The judge waved his hand, the solemn boy led his calf back to the others, and the judge called another out. The other kids soothed their calves; they made a long line against the concrete wall of the arena. Above them hung bright bunting, and beyond, anonymous in the vastness of the Coliseum, sat their proud mothers and fathers, girl friends and boy friends. High up among the crossbeams dust motes swirled in the August sunlight that poured in through the windows. The judging went forward slowly, seriously. This was State Fair judging.

The judge, a godlike figure, slowly paced the row of calves, and as he touched each for new tentative rank, the rigid flank-to-flank line dissolved in swirling confusion. A man with overalls stuffed into rubber boots was saying: "You know how my corncrib sets, well—" but his friend was not listening, for the judge now put at the head of the line a calf he had heretofore overlooked, one owned by a grinning, freckled red-haired boy; and the girl he replaced kept rubbing her calf's back with a cane to hide her chagrin. Now at the judge's order the redhead and the solemn boy brought their calves out in front, side by side. Red cracked his gum, but the other boy stood rigidly and his face was morose. Yet it was his calf the judge finally chose as best of all, calling out runners-up and explaining his choice to the crowd: "Folks, they isn't a steer in this class just comes up like a bar of soap in a bathtub. Now, this girl's calf ain't built right from the head on back through the shoulders. This one here's a showy kind of a calf."

But already the boy who won had led his sleek black-and-white steer away, and Red had followed. They walked the length of the huge arena, emerged briefly into the bright white sunshine, and went on into the cool strong-smelling cattle barn, uproarious with bellowings. Here in their pens jet-black Angus cattle slept deep in straw, and from a wagon drawn by be-spangled horses an attendant pitched hay to the concrete floor; 4-H boys wrestled in the aisles; city people peered at the cattle with quick curiosity. Striding along, Red called to friends: "I got second," and waved, but the winner walked silent and alone, a boy with his calf in a big strange place. He was a slight dark-skinned boy of thirteen, with dark brown eyes and a pouty mouth. His calf's pen was at the far end of the building; he seemed glad to reach it, glad to take longer than he needed to bed down his Hereford, Shorty. Then sitting on a bale of hay, he talked a little about himself. His name was Jim Smoker. He lived on a farm in La Porte County near Wanatah, up in the northwest part of Indiana, and he was in the eighth grade at Clinton. He and his father and mother had brought four calves down to the Fair; this was their first trip.

A fellow in a sweat shirt said: "Nice goin', Jim," and Jim nodded solemnly. His father came along, a short, powerful, smiling man in blue suit and shined black shoes and soft, tan, expensive Stetson; only the deep mahogany color of his face and the way he wore his clothes indicated he was a farmer. He offered no congratulations, just said matter-of-factly that Jim had better go eat and get ready for the afternoon judging. Jim hurried off. His father, Dwight Smoker, said there was just enough time to grab a sandwich. He led the way rapidly up the street to a big rectangular lunch stand where he sat down on a stool and ate a hamburger and talked about farming and about

4

his boy Jim. True, this appeared to be simply a boy and his calf, but, like so many things in Indiana, that was deceptively simple. There was much more to it than that, as we shall see.

The main street of the fairgrounds was crowded now at noon. The day was hot. The feet of the crowd stirred up clouds of dust. This was August 30, 1946, in Indianapolis, the first day of the first State Fair after the war. The wandering people spilled off the sidewalk into the auto thoroughfare. On the grassy parkway in the center weary men sat leaning back stiff-armed, their aching legs stretched out flat. Ranged in a half-moon in front of the Administration Building the young uniformed band of the Patriotic Order, Sons of America, from Crawfordsville, tooted out march tunes and jazz, and on the sidewalk near by stood a little farm woman alone, listening seriously, head cocked, hands clasped, heels together, lips pursed, eyes unblinking behind rimless glasses, her graying hair caught tight in a net beneath a white knit cap; she wore black flat shoes and coarse stockings as loose and wrinkled as the skin on her face. She stood there a long time unmindful of the crowd that moved about her, and the sunlight in the maples made leaf patterns on the sidewalk. Flags billowed against the Administration Building's white columns; up above, white clouds drifted across the bright blue sky. On the porch some young publicity men in gabardine suits were planning the radio show of Hoosier talent—Olsen and Johnson, comedians; Hoagy Carmichael, the song writer who wrote *Star Dust;* others, like Cole Porter, a song writer from Peru, had sent regrets. A former governor, though no longer a candidate, was none the less shaking hands with a circle of clubwomen in flowered hats. Outside, a loudspeaker announced that a child was lost. Aging courthouse hacks in orange sun helmets were directing traffic officiously with canes. On a wooden bench an old man in high black shoes was saying to a young fellow wearing an Army field jacket: "I got a friend-got ten acres of rye up there." The crowd flowed past the Indiana Farm Bureau Building and up the sidewalk lined with stands and signs—"Church Members Relief Ass'n," "Popcorn and Peanuts," "Snowballs," "Cold Beer Hamburger and Hot Fish"—and the air was heavy with the smell of onions cooking. This year the draft-horse pulling contest was missing, not because the horse is vanishing but because electric bugs used by gamblers to spur the horses had aroused the wrath of anti-cruelty societies. An oblong, yellow school bus labeled "Henry County No. 7" stopped near the concrete grandstand and disgorged children. Grand-circuit harness racing was about to start. In the box seats sat paunchy horse breeders in Panamas, thin horsemen with skin loose on their throats, lean, tanned rich women and their men in sports jackets and bow ties. But when the race was close and the flying hooves thudded loud on the loam and the silks streamed by bright and fast, the crowd's roar came from higher up in the grandstand, where the farm folk sat in eighty-five-cent seats. (Ah, but now the farmers were rich from war years of high prices and good crops; they could afford the box seats if they wanted.) Presently, after the jugglers had finished their act, Governor Ralph F. Gates, a large, smiling, heavy-jowled man, presented a cup to the winner and posed for the photographers.

Far out in the distance you could see the swooping aluminum flash of the aerial rides on the midway. In a circus wagon the press agent said this was the best fair plant, the largest fair, in the country. The crowd listened cheerfully to the barkers but spent its quarters and half dollars—dimes no longer—warily. The belly shows were cleaned up for the Hoosiers, but the come-on remained: a girl in low-cut satin, a jazz tune. The other acts were comfortably familiar: "The Four-Legged Girl," "The Pygmy Fire Eater," "The Girl With the Iron Tongue," "Gang Busters" ("See the Killing of John Dillinger," and John was Indiana's own, a pride of the thirties).

Across the fairgrounds farmers, their hands in their pockets, walked slowly through a magic forest, the Machinery Field. They studied the huskers and trucks and threshers and combines and plows, all painted brilliant reds and yellows and greens, and they walked into the big staked-out tents. From one fluttered a pennon bearing the great name of Oliver; from another an amplified voice pleaded incessantly: "Come on in folks and enjoy a little rest at the Allis Chalmers tent, we have ice water in here, three hundred chairs, come in and send a post card to the folks back home"; a sign before a third proclaimed: *"What Indiana Farmers are doing thru their Farm Co-op Bureau to help themselves to help their community."*

6

Here the farmers watched the demonstrations of a clanking corn planter and listened to the co-op men talk: "You know what old Tom Marshall said when he was Vice President of the United States? You know what he said? He said: 'What this country needs is a good five-cent cigar.' Yes sir, and that's just what this country needs today." Or other talk: about how the wicked packers set prices, about the co-ops' great progress in manufacturing farm equipment as well as in selling it and in marketing farmers' produce. ("Yes sir, I hope it'll not be too many years till we make everything we sell.")

Close by was the Saddle Horse Barn, the cleanest, quietest place of all, a well-bred place of well-bred horses and well-bred people, with pretty red boxes lettered neatly "Knight Fairy," "Lovely Rose," and tonight in the Coliseum spotlights would appear ladies and gentlemen in jodhpurs and diamonds. Out near the gate the Manufacturers' Building displays little but hardware, an ice-industry booth, an Arthur Murray booth. Only one big Indiana industry is represented, Studebaker, reminder that Indiana's auto industry once promised to be the nation's greatest. Where are all the other manufacturers who make Indiana half an industrial state? Outside, a girl is removing her glasses to have her picture taken beside a tulip-poplar log, the state tree, and a Boy Scout is climbing the fire tower while the scoutmaster protests, and some kids are throwing pebbles at the beaver, and others are peering at the tanks of sunfish, bluegills, rock bass, black bass, and silver bass taken from Indiana's own blue lakes. At the gate a child homeward bound is crying because the balloon man is out of red balloons.

This book is about the people who came to the fair, and many more. It is about Indiana and the Hoosiers. Indiana is a various state, in a sense the U.S. in little, the U.S. with all its faults and its virtues. Here is the flowering glory of native American capitalism; here are some aspects of its decay. Here is the fire of provincial political protest; here are the false leaders who gave the people false gods. Here is the small-town mind at its best and worst. Here is the frost on the pumpkin; here is the cocktail lounge. Here are the great white manor houses on bounteous soil and the shacks that cling to eroded clay hillsides. Here are the stone castles of the financiers and manufacturers and the acres of slums in the shadows of the factories. Here are good men and wicked. Here are the dwelling places of history, some splendorous, some tawdry. Eastern fur monopolists took the region from the Indians and named it for them. What nickname except "Yankee" is better known in the United States than "Hoosier"? (It probably comes from an old word that meant at various times something large and an uncouth rustic, but the Hoosiers to whom it was first applied liked to think it came from "husher," a strong man who could "hush" his opponent in a wrestling match at a logrolling.) Is it not significant that Indiana is usually in accord with the nation politically, that it has produced so many undistinguished Vice Presidents, that the nation's population center has been within its borders since 1890, that between 1920 and 1940 its changing rural-urban balance remained closer to the nation's than did that of any other state—and so on almost endlessly, statistically? Here is Indiana, the central place, the crossroads, the mean that is sometimes golden, sometimes only mean.

Consider the boundaries—Chicago, Ohio's steel cities and neat little farms, the Kentucky hills and bluegrass below the Ohio, Illinois and the westward sweep of the great prairies. Indiana is none of these, but it includes them all. "Then there is Gary," people say. "But of course that's not really Indiana." It is, though. "Evansville and Madison—they're really Southern towns, not Hoosier. Debs isn't really a Hoosier, and neither's Theodore Dreiser, not like Riley and Tarkington." But they are, they are of this complex state, all of them, and many, many more —too many. One must choose. Perhaps it is best to choose at random without fitting to thesis.

More than most capitals of states, Indianapolis is the capital of its state. Nearly all the many elements of Indiana appear here. Whereas many capital cities are little but the homes of bureaucrats, Indianapolis is like a museum, or a fair, exhibiting samples of a culture. At its own center is the Circle. Here during the city's golden age the magnificent buildings were constructed arc-shaped to fit the curve; here in the very middle stood the Governor's house. From that spot today rises the Soldiers' and Sailors' Monument, memorial to the private soldier and the ordinary seaman, a slender spire of Indiana limestone with massive, heroic figures grouped at its base. Go now at dusk after the fair to the top of the monument in its rickety elevator and stand on the platform beneath the statue of Victory and look out at the flat darkening earth here in the interior of the United States. The streets of the city radiate from here like spokes from the hub of a wheel. The streets' names are meaningful. Straight north and south runs Meridian, straight east and west, Market. Bisecting their angles are three named for states whence came the early Hoosiers by flatboat and oxcart and Conestoga wagon —Massachusetts, Virginia, Kentucky—and the fourth is named Indiana Avenue. Squaring the Monument Circle are Pennsylvania and Illinois, Washington and Ohio. And these streets become roads, spokes of a larger wheel. Each will lead you (passing its unique section of Indianapolis) to a segment of Indiana, each different from all others.

Broad Washington Street is the National Road, in the 1850's the greatest wagon road in the world, dotted with taverns to serve the flying stages which brought Indianapolis within sixty hours of Washington, D.C. The National Road divides the state roughly into northern and southern hemispheres. The southern half is the rougher half, a region of deep-cut ravines and jagged cliffs, traversed by swift deep rivers; but this southern half was settled first, for the Ohio River was the first broad highway open to immigrants. Let us travel Indiana quickly now, hitting the high spots—the southern half first.

If you head southwest out Kentucky Avenue it will become Highway 67 and it will take you, after the White River forests and valleys and the limestone bluffs and the bleak coal fields, to Vincennes, the earliest enduring settlement in Indiana. Here on the Wabash history was made by the French Jesuits and *voyageurs*, by Lord Hamilton the hair buyer and George Rogers Clark; from here William Henry Harrison governed a vast unwieldly wilderness, Indiana Territory. Fifty air-line miles down the Wabash is New Harmony, decrepit monument to a dream of Utopia in the forest, and not far below, across the desolate grandeur of cypress swamps, the Wabash flows into the Ohio. Up the Ohio, isolated in a pocket, lies Evansville, tied by air, as once by water, to St. Louis and Louisville. North of the

Ohio stretches a dark, broken land, log-cabin and corn-liquor country, Lincoln country (here Nancy Hanks Lincoln took the "milk sick" and died, and whole towns, like Hindostan, vanished when a plague came), hill country where bear traps hang in crossroads stores and the names of the inbred hill folk are Cumberland Mountain names, yet also hill country where tourists disport themselves at French Lick Springs Hotel. The South courses strong through this region; it was no accident that the leading conspirators among the Knights of the Golden Circle came from French Lick, Salem, and Shoals, or that Morgan's raiders expected to find the citizens here eager to join the Confederacy. Here in the hills, brown in the fall with corn shocked dry and rustling up the bottomlands, is the tourists' Indiana; this was Abe Martin's home.

Head now southeast from the Circle in Indianapolis on Highway 52, black top over rolling hills. An old man clutching a corncob pipe sits on a breadbox under the shingle roof of the general store, and the fat girl at the filling station says: "Oh, *that* town. I guess it's got four names—the post office is Finley and the railroad's Reedville and on the highway it's Carrollton, and then some call it Tailholt. The railroad's been there the longest but Tailholt, that's what Raleigh called it." Raleigh—she meant James Whitcomb Riley, who was born a few miles away and wrote about the little town of Tailholt. This is Riley country. Cattle are browsing in the pasture beside a winding stream, and a man is selling watermelons at a roadside stand. Down a dusty side road walks a farm woman in bright flowered dress made from a flour sack, wearing a red straw hat and low black shoes, her shoulders stooped and her hair shingle-bobbed; she is going to catch the bus on the hard road and ride to Rushville with its stores and restaurants and massive red stone courthouse topped by a four-faced clock. Yet here where the rich plain flattens out are other things too: hybrid seed corn under scientific cultivation, enormous white farmhouses surrounded by hundreds of acres of corn. Wendell Willkie campaigned from the acreage of relatives here, but Hoosiers knew the acreage belonged to no poor farmer. This is one of the best corn and hog regions of the state, and here farming is a capitalist's enterprise, not a raggedy man's. Riley, and, even more, the lesser writers who ground out verse and prose to supply the demand he created, would lay a film over our eyes, so that we could see but a fragment of Indiana: only Aunt Mary's tiny farmhouse and not the castle of the banker down the pike, and, more largely, only the Ole Swimmin' Hole and not the factories beyond. Riley dedicated *Neghborly Poems On Friendship Grief and Farm-Life* "to the ever-faithful, whole-souled, honest-hearted Hoosier friends," but the sign on the enormous barn in the experimental cornfield is big enough to read a mile away: "No Hunting."

Eleven miles below Rushville at Andersonville the flat plain breaks, the road drops down, and you are in the Whitewater River Valley. This is hill country, rich in history as Rush County is in soil. The road soars and dips, sweeping grandly, and from it you can see the railroad, the canal, and the river running side by side in the valley. The new highway by-passes a once great town, Metamora, its canal dry, its stone-walled mill in mossy ruins, a patriarch of eighty with flowing beard sitting by himself on a smooth worn bench beneath a gnarled tree. Corn in the bottomland, tobacco on the hills, and the heart of this country is Brookville. The Whitewater Valley, which runs south from the National Road near the Ohio line, flowered early; Germans and Quakers and sturdy Southern people pushed up from Cincinnati and the Ohio and produced a glittering culture whence came most of Indiana's early great men. To this day you can see the ruins of their log cabins and stone houses perched on the steep creek banks, you can see their covered bridges and their churches. In the hills the towers of Catholicism aspire darkly to the sky, a Franciscan monastery, a Convent of the Immaculate Conception. A little farther on is Batesville. John Hillenbrand, a German from Cincinnati, halted here in the virgin hardwood forests and set up a sawmill. When the railroad came he cut its ties, sold it fuel wood, and built a furniture business and a town. He and his descendants always took care of the people who worked for the Hillenbrands and lived in their town. And that is Indiana too. On the Ohio River lies Madison, once a packing center, steamboat center, and most thriving town in the state; here James F. D. Lanier, the banker who financed Indiana during the Civil War, built his mansion. Through this southeast triangle of Indiana flow Blue River, famed for the bear stories of boyhood, and Flat Rock Creek; and embraced in it are the factories at Shelbyville and Connersville and Richmond, scenes of bloody strikes and martial law.

Go west on the National Road from Monument Circle, and after skirting the hills of Putnam County where the Methodists named a college for the circuit rider, Francis Asbury (but re-named it for the glass manufacturer who endowed it richly, Washington C. DePauw), you will reach Terre Haute at the western border, lying beside the Wabash on a broad savanna scarred by freight yards and coal piles. This was home to Paul Dresser, a song writer who wrote *On The Banks of the Wabash, Far Away;* but it was also home to his brother, Theodore Dreiser, who wrote of shanties and poverty and depravity, also Hoosier. And it was home to the men who owned the coal mines that bore and nourished and sometimes killed towns and men alike; home, too, to the Hulmans, shrewd storekeepers who built a financial empire, and to a handful of others whose descendants run the town today. Outside Terre Haute some farmers formed the state's first hopeful Grange in the angry years of protest after the Civil War. Terre Haute was a great railroad town, and near the tracks lived Gene Debs, a locomotive fireman who led the railroaders to the brotherhood of union, who loved mankind and went to prison and preached a gospel that seemed painful and alien to those who loved him as the drinking companion of Riley. In 1935 Governor Paul V. McNutt sent the guard here to quell the nation's first general strike east of the Rockies, and Powers Hapgood, the Harvard man with the rocky fists and inner fire, came down from Indianapolis to make a free-speech fight and got beaten up and put in jail. Terre Haute was always a target for uplifters, heaven for corruptionists, good road-show town. It was a sporting town, a racehorse town, a gambler's town, pleasing alike to sporting gentlemen from Chicago and St. Louis and to toil-worn miners on Saturday night.

Some fifty miles from Terre Haute, beyond the ridges and ravines of Turkey Run, is Crawfordsville, home of Wabash College and Lew Wallace. A story, probably apocryphal, says that Lew Wallace was going over to Indianapolis on the train when another Civil-War veteran, Robert Ingersoll, asked if he really believed in the divinity of Christ, and this started Wallace to thinking, with the result that he wrote *Ben Hur*. Years earlier, during the canal period before the war, Wallace had refused to prosecute Edward A. Hannegan for murder, so had Wallace's successor, Daniel Voorhees, the Tall Sycamore of the Wabash. Hannegan was their friend, a proud, fierce, quixotic man who rode the circuit as a young lawyer and outshone Webster in the U.S. Senate, and seemed headed for the Presidency when Indiana and the nation were yelling for empire.

Now let us travel the other, the newer, the northern half of Indiana. From Monument Circle, Massachusetts Avenue angles northeast along the New York Central Railroad tracks through a section of factories and gray houses; then it becomes Highway 67 to Anderson. Anderson boomed in the 1830's when the canals came, died when they failed, revived when the railroad came, and boomed mightily when gas was discovered. Here today are the vast desolate expanses of Delco Remy and Guide Lamp, subsidiary giants of General Motors. Not far away are both ancient and modern wonders—mounds left by aborigines and a large spiritualist encampment—and a little farther on is Muncie. Muncie was Middletown to the Lynds, two sociologists (actually there are four towns named Middletown in Indiana, and one is a ghost town on the stagecoach line, killed by the railroads.) Here in Indiana is the American home-town mind on exhibit. Here on a fat rich plain is a farm town that became a factory city when the gas came in, and that remained one when it failed (as others, like Elwood, did not); here dwell Court Asher, Kleagle and publisher, and, on Minnetrista Boulevard on the camping ground of the Munsee Indians, George A. Ball, glass manufacturer, financier, old man.

But this is only a small part of the northeast triangle of the state. The land is rolling, blocked off neatly by white fences and winding streams. Don't let the townsfolk hear you say so, but the towns are all alike—loafers on the curb around the shaded courthouse lawn, cars parked slantwise on the broad brick street, parking meters, the red front of Montgomery Ward's garish and glittering, the old stone or painted brick business "block" with the name of its visionary builder carved in stone under the mansard, some drugstores and hardware stores with cluttered windows, narrow staircases going up to law offices, a tavern or two. And, in recent years, something new: an upstairs hall for the CIO. This is the square, and Monument Circle in Indianapolis is only a super-square, just as Indianapolis is a super-town of Indiana. From this square, streets run out broad and shaded past a few imposing homes with turrets and twelve-foot ceilings built by the early bankers and traders, past numerous large, square houses on broad, shaded lawns owned by retired farmers, past low, neat houses with rambling porches owned by the farmers' widows, and then on out past row upon row of small new houses on tiny lots, all identical down to the paint on the door, all occupied by the men who work in the town's one, two, half-dozen factories out on the edge of town. You can tell by a town's houses whether its balance has shifted from farm to factory. The retired farmer needs plenty of room: a big, cool cellar for home-canned food, a big, dark parlor for ponderous, ungainly furniture, a big, light kitchen for Thanksgiving cooking. At night, especially on Saturday night, they all come down to Courthouse Square, workmen and farmers alike (and anyway, many a machinist was born on forty acres outside town.) One night in 1930 at Marion they came down and lynched two Negroes.

Near Marion and Gas City is Kokomo. And who was the man from Kokomo, so useful to the vaudeville comedians? Not Elwood Haynes, though he made his famous automobile here; not any of Kokomo's greats. He was never identified even vaguely; he must have been some anonymous drummer, sitting in a tilted wicker chair on the sidewalk outside the Hotel Frances on a hot summer night, his gaze following a pretty girl walking to the Isis Theater. Now, on this August night in 1946, the Isis is offering a double feature, *Shady Lady* and *Live Wires,* and a Nickel Plate freight runs right up the street beside the Frances, clanging and whistling, and some kids drive by with cutouts open, headed for the dance pavilion at Lake Manitou where a big-name band is playing one night only. Twenty-five miles north of Kokomo is Peru, the circus town on the Wabash, home to Emil Schram, president of the New York Stock Exchange, and north and east of Peru the Indiana lake country begins. Here flows the Tippecanoe River, broad and shallow and sandy-bottomed; here on any Saturday afternoon in August you can count fifty-odd boats anchored on a single lake, the fishermen in overalls and wide straw hats, their cane poles tilted to the leaden sky like ships' masts; here in town taverns or in lakeside hotels' varnished dining-rooms the talk is of bluegills longer than your hand, of whether catalpa worms are better bait than crickets. This is Hoosier fishing, and the fishermen are more likely to be paunchy storekeepers than corporation executives, and most of them have their wives and children with them. You will find the playboys shooting craps or playing roulette in the plush parlors of the Spink Wawasee Hotel on Lake Wawasee, a cavernous rococo monument to the 1920's.

On the edge of the lake country is Fort Wayne, the state's second city (in 1940), a manufacturing center bearing the name of Mad Anthony Wayne and built on the portage where a great fur post flourished in the hunting-shirt era. Not far away is Columbia City, home town to two curiously parallel Indiana politicians, Tom Marshall, the Governor who became Vice President, and Ralph F. Gates, the present Governor who wants to. On the black-top road leading out of Columbia City a grim-faced man in red sweater and brown cap is driving a jeep pulling an enormous trailer; he and his wife are headed for Winona Lake, where godly people have constructed a shaded silent community—the sign at the entrance reads "Liquor Has No Defense"; the sign in the Eskimo Inn, a large chaste ice-cream parlor, reads: *"We would appreciate if friends would refrain from Smoking,"* and this was where Billy Sunday filled the tabernacle to overflowing. Up toward the Michigan border is Goshen, and an Amish man in flat black hat and flowing beard is driving a broad flat wagon, his wife sitting beside him in a sunbonnet. The Amish settled in the northeast corner and moved westward onto rich farmland, regarded warily by their neighbors till they proved themselves good farmers and honest dealers. South Bend stands on the banks of the Saint Joseph River on a portage used by the Jesuits; today it is home to Notre Dame. And it was home to Schuyler Colfax who enthusiastically predicted in his newspaper, the coming of the railroad in the 1850's. Among his readers were

15

the Studebaker brothers who set up a blacksmith shop and then
built wagons for the Union in the Civil War. Here in Indiana
was midland capitalism on the rise, and it needed only the
thrust of the Civil War and later the thrust of the automobile to
become big business.

If you head straight south from South Bend you will enter
Indianapolis on North Meridian Street, and so you will pass the
fantastic castles the capitalists built. The outlying estates, like
that of the auto magnate Jim Allison, are still impressive. Closer
to Monument Circle some of the old stone houses have been
converted into rooming houses or funeral homes; others, on
Meridian Street once so shaded and so quiet, have been replaced
by the garish fronts of automobile row. On this north side of
Indianapolis lived Benjamin Harrison, whose home when he was
President became a center for the nation's social life, and D. M.
Parry, organized labor's implacable foe, who helped make and
break Indiana's golden age, and Booth Tarkington, who celebrated it.

If from Monument Circle you go down to the Union Station
and take a train northwest, you will pass the five hundred-mile-
race Speedway built by Carl Fisher, the promoter whose greatness spanned the years when Indiana passed from its golden age
into the new era of finance capital and advertising. North and
west of Logansport the soil becomes sandy until you reach the
Kankakee marshes, a mysterious region. On the bank of the
Tippecanoe River stands Winamac, a farming town unchanged
for many years. It is the home of Ned Gorell, a country editor
for fifty years, a fine specimen of the gentleman from Indiana,
who, though he has worked in a print shop all his life, has not
yet lost the sense of the soil, the firm belief that "even these
presses come from the soil." In Winamac you can take a lantern
before daylight and flag down the Pennsylvania, a cheering,
slightly awesome experience, and get aboard the dirty coach
and ride up to Chicago. Along the bulge of Lake Michigan the
waters and winds have made the restless dunes; here now are
twisted scrub timber and hot-dog stands and, toward the western end, the city built on sand by U.S. Steel and named for
Judge Elbert H. Gary, who said, in 1917: "Manufacturers must

16

have reasonable profits in order to do their duty." This northwest corner of Indiana is the Calumet, a grimy, sinewy, conglomerate string of cities: Gary, Hammond, East Chicago,
Whiting. Here dwell Poles and Czechs and many others who
labor in the terrible heat of the steel furnaces; here are the forests of factory smokestacks, the hummocked rows of refinery
tanks, the cracking plants, soap works, ore docks, coal piles,
cement docks, lake freighters, and endless desolate seas of
swampy wasteland; here are the political machines and gangsters with rackets and sawed-off shotguns; here are the slums.
On a clear day you can see the tower of the *Chicago Tribune*
across the corner of lake from near the Illiana Hotel; a Hoosier
says: "You wouldn't know where Indiana left off and Chicago
began if it wasn't for the soap factory." (He meant the enormous
Rinso works, almost on the state line; who but a Hoosier would
speak thus of a part of the Lever Brothers empire?) Aboard the
New York Central's sleek red and gray and chrome streamliner,
the *James Whitcomb Riley,* the murals in the diner are of
Hoosier farmland—barns and shocked corn and woods and pas-
tures; but the passengers in the glassed-in bar car are more
likely to be talking of night clubs and shows and shops in Chicago than of crops, for Chicago is less than three and one half
hours from Indianapolis. (But the traditional way to go is via
the Monon Railroad: wearing sunglasses and straw hat, you
used to sit grandly in a deck chair on the observation platform
of the last car.) From Indianapolis to Lafayette the rails cut
through small rich farms, through numerous towns where the
corn comes right down to Main Street. ("Biggest Little City In
the World" advertises one town, and a sign outside Lafayette
reads "Visiting Elks Welcome.") Not far northwest of Lafayette
begin the prairie counties where corn grows fast and purebreds
fatten on enormous farms and the farmhouses are manor houses.
Here dwelt John T. McCutcheon and George Ade and Governor
Warren T. McCray, perspicacious men all (though the Governor went to prison); it must have been this prairie and Indian
country that McCutcheon had in mind when he drew magic
into his cartoon *Injun Summer.* In recent years Chicago gangsters who longed to become gentleman farmers migrated here.
And it was from one of these great farm estates in this newest

17

corner of Indiana that the boy came, the boy with the calf that won a prize at the state fair, Jim Smoker.

That day at the fair his short smiling father took time out for lunch. As he put his elbows on the oilcloth-topped counter he was talking rapidly. He owned five hundred and eighty acres on U.S. 30 ten miles east of Valparaiso, the first sizable farm town south of the Calumet. He was raising corn and wheat and oats and feeding five hundred head of cattle. The boy Jim was feeding twelve calves this year. In the last four years Jim had had two reserve champions and one grand champion of La Porte County, and he'd been in the money in the Chicago show the last three years. This was his first entry at the Indiana State Fair. As a prize for this morning's victory he'd get fifteen dollars. He'd sell the calf for, say, three hundred dollars. "If you can bring a bull down here and win, you can double your prices on his calves right there. Fellas pay fifty thousand dollars for a bull—it's cheaper 'n buying advertisin'. The boy's cleared over two thousand dollars in the last three years. He's a farmer, likes it. I make him pay all his feed bills. He pays me five per cent interest on the money he uses to buy his calves with. And so when he makes a dollar he knows how he made it," said Smoker, stirring his coffee in its thick white mug. "He's gotta learn it like I did."

Smoker was born and raised in Indiana, up near Goshen. His ancestors were Amish—"My grandfather took the Dutch out of it, it used to be Smucker"—and he talked, smiling, about the good Amish and how they saved their money and how they made homebrew during Prohibition. Smoker left the farm where he'd been reared and started farming sixteen hundred acres in the Kankakee marshes. "I went down on that marsh ten years ago and didn't have a cent to my name. I could sell out for three hundred thousand dollars today," and he finished his hamburger and wiped his fingers on a paper napkin. All the stools at the lunch counter were in use but the counterman, hurrying back and forth in a dirty white uniform, kept yelling: "All right folks, we got 'em hot."

Smoker said: "If you ain't a gambler you don't want to be on that Kankakee marsh. I usta drown out and frost out both. But

I made her. I was growing nine hundred acres o' corn and feedin' nine hundred head a cattle and I only had four men workin' for me. I still say any young guy that's got brains enough and willin' to work can go out and do the same thing. You don't need the money. All you gotta do is show somebody you're willing to work. Of course," he added, smiling a bit, "I've had nine corn years in a row now without a miss."

With his first profits he bought five hundred acres of marshland. Two years ago the five hundred and eighty acres near Valparaiso were offered for sale. It was a show place. A Chicagoan who had made millions racketeering in the Capone days had bought it, probably intending to retire; he had erected flawless buildings and painted his name in large letters on the barn. But in 1940 gang warfare had begun again, and one of his close associates had been shotgunned to death in Chicago. The gentleman farmer hastened to take his name off the barn. Afraid this might not be precaution enough, he retired even further, to Florida, and he gave the farm to his two sons. "The sons couldn't raise nothin' on it," Smoker chuckled. "I bought it for a steal, got it for what he put into the buildings. Neighbors said it was a city man's farm and a city man's farm is too much investment. Well sure, if you have a barn that can take two hundred head of cattle and you only put ten head in it, course you can't make it. The Purdue land map shows my ground's the poorest ground in the county, too. But we got fifty bushels of wheat to the acre right now. It's just like feedin' cattle—you got to know how to do it." He stood up. "I got to get back. Got to find a place to sleep tonight." Jim was staying at the 4-H-Club dormitory, but Smoker and his wife and daughter had to find a tourist cabin. "I don't know Indianapolis so well, either. I get up to Chicago oftener."

Up the street some children were clustered around a small stand, watching a man engrave a piece of jewelry, and in the hog barn two men covered with patchwork quilts were sleeping on cots in hog stalls, and over in the Agriculture and Horticulture Building a tall spare judge was walking slowly past the melons and potatoes and tomatoes and pickles and cucumbers and pumpkins and beans and neat sheaves of grains, pinning on the ribbons. A woman in a small black hat said comfortably: "My, it was work to fix up all them bundles wasn't it?" Outside, some country boys were talking about the state basketball tournament to be held eight months later—"I'm gonna put in my order for the State just as quick as I get back." Up the sidewalk littered with sawdust crumbs and dry leaves, strolled a fat crop-haired German-American with a pipe in his mouth, his wife leaning on his arm, and a freckle-faced girl, head thrown back and mouth wide open, was staring up at big green and blue and red balloons riding high above the fair against the bright blue sky. From somewhere in the distance beyond the crowd a band played "And the monkey wrapped his tail around the flagpole."

PART TWO

Beginnings

Chapter 2

BY FLATBOAT AND WAGON

I N ORDER to understand Indiana today, we must know something of its past. Who were the early Hoosiers?

The shrewd, sharp-dealing Yankees who arrived at Vincennes not long after the Revolutionary War told a traveler that the French who already lived there "had only themselves to blame for all the hardships they complained of. We must allow [the Yankees said] that they are a kind, hospitable, sociable set, but then for idleness and ignorance, they beat the Indians themselves. They know nothing at all of civil or domestic affairs: their women neither sow, nor spin, nor make butter, but pass their time in gossiping and tattle, while all at home is dirt and disorder. The men take to nothing but hunting, fishing, roaming in the woods, and loitering in the sun. They do not lay up, as we do, for winter, or provide for a rainy day. They cannot cure pork or venison, make sour crout or spruce beer, or distil spirits from apples or rye, all needful arts to the farmer. . . . Their time is wasted too in . . . journies *to town* to see their friends. [Town was New Orleans, 1500 miles away.] . . . their indolence will never be a match for our industry."

Jesuits, fur traders, British captains, Indian intrigue, military campaigns—the American frontier drama was played in Indiana. Vincennes was settled first about 1730. There before British and Yankees came, the French lived in peace and contentment. They kept their cattle in a communal pasture and bred fine horses from Spanish strains from the Southwest. Despite their alleged laziness they raised tobacco, maize, wheat, barley, squashes, fruits, and cotton; they traded for furs and deerskins, they milled flour and butchered hogs, and when famine beset New Orleans about 1746, they shipped "upwards of eight hundred thousand weight of Flour" in addition to the regular produce: Already the river link that tied Indiana to the South was forged. Blacksmiths were few, and each farmer fashioned his own rude *calèche,* the two-wheeled cart that served as farm wagon and town carriage alike. They cultivated their gardens more assiduously than they beautified their homes. Both men and women wore clothing copied from the Indians. Weddings were celebrated for days. At Mardi Gras the wealthier citizens held open house, and the guests danced till midnight. On New Year's Day the townsmen went calling and kissed each hostess on the cheek. (The British officers' wives substituted the lips for the cheek, but puritanical Yankee settlers later put an end to the custom.)

The Jesuits brewed beer, but a red native wine, described by a traveler as "very bad," was more favored. The British replaced it with a heavy-bodied New Orleans rum called tafia; the Americans brought Monongahela whisky. St. Ange, the last French Governor, departing forever in 1764 when the British came, adjured his successors to "do away, as far as possible, with the disorder which arises from drinking." Periodically several hundred Indians came to town to barter, warriors clad in blankets and leather and ceaselessly examining their features in mirrors, the women carrying their children on their backs in sacks. A traveler, C. F. Volney, wrote in 1796: "The men and women roamed all day about the town, merely to get rum, for which they exchanged their peltry, their toys, their clothes, and at length, when they had parted with their all, they offered their prayers and entreaties, never ceasing to drink till they had lost their senses. Hence arise ridiculous scenes. They will hold the cup with both hands, like monkies, burst into unmeaning laughter, and gargle their beloved cup, to enjoy the taste of it the longer; hand about the liquor with clamorous invitations, bawl aloud at each other, though close together, seize their wives, and pour liquor down their throats, and, in short, display all the freaks of vulgar drunkenness. Sometimes tragical scenes ensue: they become mad or stupid, and falling in the dust or mud, lie a sense-

less log till next day. . . . It was rare for a day to pass without
a deadly quarrel . . . I at first conceived the design of spending
a few months among them, as I had done among the Bedwins;
but I was satisfied with this sample. . . ."

The wars that took the Northwest from France and gave it
first to England and then to the United States were little short of
disastrous to these people. Warfare meant Indian trouble. The
fur trade declined. Crops failed, a famine occurred. The stockade rotted down and government devolved upon the village
notary, who ran off with the records. Conquerors came and
went, but the French residents cared little. When American rule
began after George Rogers Clark's final victory, the first thing
they asked for was a military commandant who would relieve
them of the burden of self-government. General Arthur St. Clair
governed Northwest Territory, including Indiana, from Mari-
etta. The Indian question was paramount. After Mad Anthony
Wayne beat Little Turtle in the Battle of Fallen Timbers in 1794,
settlers poured into Ohio from New England, New York, and
the South; some spilled over into Indiana. At once they howled
that the land sharks had them by the throat, a shibboleth useful
to politicians for years to come. And indeed the system of selling
Federal lands did encourage speculation. Young William Henry
Harrison, born to wealth and politics, a hero of Fallen Timbers,
wed the daughter of a big land speculator and was appointed
first Governor of Indiana Territory. It was an unwieldy territory,
including all the Northwest Territory except Ohio; for about a
decade, pieces kept splitting off, until Indiana Territory assumed
the present boundaries of the state. Promptly Harrison engaged
in extensive land speculation. Angry citizens of the Illinois country petitioned to withdraw from Indiana Territory, and a man at
Vincennes wrote in 1809: "During the time that Governor Harrison acted as superintendant of the sales of public lands at Vincennes, he headed a land speculating company, whose object it
appears was to purchase the most valuable tracts of land, & to
extort hush money from other purchasers.—In the first case they
gave money to silence biders, & in the second they received
money for not biding themselves [and when a man protested]
the governor with an haughty air bade him begone for a damned
rascal."

The very day Harrison arrived at Vincennes, January 10, 1801, he summoned the Territory's three judges. They sat for two weeks and made some laws—six laws, three resolutions, and one act. Never had Indiana had so much government at home. Under Harrison's firm rule the French declined; in a few years their protests were silenced.

Other settlers, however, soon charged him with autocracy. Self-rule was a fiction. The power of the Governor and judges was absolute. Opposition to Harrison finally crystallized around the slavery question. When he had become Governor in 1800 the majority of the Territory's 5,641 inhabitants probably favored slavery. The French kept slaves, and many of the Americans had come from Virginia and Kentucky where slavery was established. In 1802, flaunting the anti-slavery clause of the Northwest Ordinance, Harrison and the judges, in effect, established slavery. This provoked a political uprising; already sentiment was changing; Indiana had become a border state, torn two ways, a slavery battleground long before the issue was joined nationally. Vincennes remained proslavery as Harrison had anticipated, but not the newer settlements in the southern and southeastern regions, Clark's Grant and the Whitewater Valley. A petition, adopted at a Saturday meeting at the Clark County seat, argued that many settlers had come to Indiana to get away from slavery and urged that they should be allowed to do as they wished. This was the doctrine of Squatter Sovereignty, enunciated here for the first time anywhere. Harrison had a fight on his hands. It was waged with petitions, memorials, votes, speeches, legislative chicanery, rigged elections; it was accompanied by threats and duels. The Territory was a good school of government. In it these early Hoosiers learned rebellion, something they have never forgotten.

Young Jonathan Jennings arrived in Clark County from Pennsylvania in 1806, was admitted to the bar, and was accepted by the local politicians as their candidate for Congress. He at once began a horseback canvass over the trails and traces in eastern Indiana. He found considerable support in the upper Whitewater Valley, among the peaceable antislavery Quakers. On David Reese's farm in Dearborn County, Jennings's opponent, a Harrison man, arrived during a logrolling, chatted at the farm-

house a short time, then rode away. But Jennings, arriving next
day, pitched into the logrolling and when it was done, tossed
quoits and threw the maul with the men, taking care to let them
beat him. He was a natural politician, the kind the Hoosiers
loved, almost the original model of the defender of the people
against the interests. Legends grew about him: how he seized
an ax and helped erect a log house in record time, and others.
Better still he was a wonder at organization. In one campaign
he was said to have sent a copy of his handbill to every voter,
and this paper, smeared with grease, served as window glass in
every.schoolhouse in Indiana. He managed to tie together antislavery sentiment and hatred of Harrison's officeholding clique,
and he won his seat in Congress and stayed there until 1816,
when he helped frame Indiana's state constitution and was
elected Indiana's first Governor. Later he returned to Congress,
but before his last term was ended he was hopelessly in debt and
a confirmed alcoholic. He died at fifty, in 1834, no statesman but
a wonderful politician.

By 1811 Jennings said Harrison's political career was ended,
and indeed it may have been only the War of 1812 that saved
him. Much of his time as territorial governor had been taken up
by Indian affairs. He and others had negotiated several treaties,
but alarms and murders of both whites and Indians remained
frequent. Up north at Fort Wayne the government maintained
its outpost of diplomacy, first line of defence, and fur post,
whose garrison passed its days in drinking, fighting, and gambling. Insubordinate soldiers were flogged at parade, deprived
of whisky, or confined in a dark room astride a spiked wooden
horse to cut firewood. Yet in the War of 1812 when an Indian
horde besieged the fort, this wild, bored crew held out till Harrison arrived with relief, though the buildings outside the stockade were burned and the commandant was helplessly drunk.
Since the days of the *voyageurs* the Fort Wayne portage had
been strategic. Here among the half-breeds, traders, and squatters dwelt William Wells, a mysterious figure. Kidnapped by
Indians when twelve, he was adopted by Chief Little Turtle.
He fought for the Indians against the whites at least twice; he
married Little Turtle's sister and, when she died, the daughter
of another chief. In 1793 he went over to the whites, serving as

27

interpreter and spy under Wayne at Fallen Timbers; he helped build Fort Wayne and was appointed Indian Agent. He made his peace with Little Turtle, and they visited the East together. Thereafter his movements became increasingly obscure. Living at the heart of the "villainous intrigues" among British agents and the Indians, he made many enemies, both white and red. Harrison was afraid of him. He was removed as Indian Agent, yet he warned of Tecumseh's plans.

During this period, though the settler who had murdered the most Indians was locally venerated, back East there was a great deal of soul searching about the poor red men. In the end, however, the Indians were exterminated or pushed off their lands. Harrison pursued this policy energetically, threading his way with some difficulty among cunning men like Wells, trying to enjoy life at his fine brick house, Grouseland, putting down with lessening success political rebellion, and no doubt rejoicing when events finally forced a showdown with the Indians in September 1811.

Shortly before Harrison left Vincennes to move his troops up the Wabash toward the Prophet's encampment near the mouth of the Tippecanoe, Lieutenant Josiah Bacon, a quartermaster in the Fourth Infantry Regiment, brought his wife to Vincennes from Boston. Almost at once she contracted "the dreadful fever-Ague" and caught cold "viewing the Comet, which has just made its appearance." She noted in her journal that Harrison called at her sickbed in the village's only tavern; he was "equiped for the March, he had on what they call a hunting Shirt, made of calico & trimed with fringe & the fashion of it resembled a woman Short gown . . . on his head he wore a round beaver hat ornamented with a large Ostrich feather, he is very tall & slender with sallow complexion, & dark eyes, his manners are pleasing. . . ." Vincennes she found lonely and rude: "I expect we shall stay here all Winter, which will be very disagreeable to me, for I do not like the place or people much—Dear New England I love the better then ever. . . ." Her husband left with Harrison. The troops took with them all the weapons "& left us Women & Children without even a guard, Mrs W. & myselfe had loaded Pistols at our bedside. . . ." For more than six weeks she wrote nothing in her journal. Then on November 30,

1811, she began an entry: "Still new mercies. . . ." She had
heard only garbled reports of the battle, and when the express
arrived the courier was so overwrought he could not distribute
the letters and handed them to her. "I could neither see, nor read,
and passed them into the hands of a Lady who stood by me, &
who . . . was enabled to find mine, & when I saw the writting
& held the letter in my hand I could hardly believe my own
eyes." She rejoiced that her husband's companions had "acuitted
themselves with much honor" but wondered "when will Brother
cease to lift his hand against his Brother, & learn War no more."

The Indians had attacked just before daylight while the troops
were encamped in hollow square. Young John Tipton, later a
general and Senator and already a Tennessean famed as an Indian killer, wrote in his journal: ". . . the Shawnies Breaking
into our tents a blood Combat Took Place . . . which lasted
two hours and 20 minutes of a continewel firing while many
times mixed among the Indians so that we Could not tell the
indians and our men apart. they kept up a firing on three sides
of us . . . we maid a charge and drove them out of the timber
across the prairie. . . . we then built Breastworks our men in
confusion, our flower had been too small and all our beeve lost.
Last night onley half Rations of whisky and no corn for our
horses. my horse killed . . . I had one quart of whisky."

The Battle of Tippecanoe accomplished almost nothing; indeed, it actually increased the Indian danger. But, by one of
those wonderful ironies of politics, it provided a slogan that
later would be used to elevate Harrison, scion of Virginia aris-
tocracy, master of Grouseland, autocratic territorial Governor,
to the Presidency of the United States as a champion of the common man. He did not return to Vincennes as a hero from the
battle. Indeed, it first had been reported a defeat, and Andrew
Jackson hastened to offer reinforcements. Harrison was criticized because he had lost so many men—nearly a fifth of his
force was killed or wounded, while probably less than ten per
cent of the Indians were killed—and his enemies charged him
with sacrificing one of his men to save his own life and with
being outmaneuvered, but his officers vindicated him. As Indian
forays continued and relations with Britain worsened, Harrison
urged an offensive. The settlers wanted land—they wanted all

of Canada—and he would lead them. He wanted vindication
and, anyway, his political star was sinking rapidly in Indiana.
On September 24, 1812, he was named Commander of the Army
of the Northwest; his civilian career in Indiana was ended. On
December 18 Indiana's last Indian battle was fought near Peru.
William Wells died with his third wife, a white one, in the Dearborn Massacre, and his brother-in-law, Little Turtle, died at
Fort Wayne of the gout. The British evacuated Detroit a year
later, and on October 5, 1813, Harrison beat Tecumseh and the
British in the Battle of the Thames, killing Tecumseh, who once
had called him a liar.

Now the Indian menace that had held back immigration was
gone. By flatboat and wagon the settlers came over the mountains and down the rivers. Swiftly they pressed inward from
the borders to the heart of Indiana Territory, filling it section
by section, township by township, county by county.

In the main, settlers coursed northward up the river valleys.
Some kept pressing on, but others, finding agreeable regions,
stayed and bred inward: The Longs and Ashers from the Blue
Ridge and Cumberland mountains settled the Jurdon Hills in
Morgan County before Indiana became a state and they popu-
late it largely yet. The Swiss found suitable hill slopes along the
Ohio and went no farther but cultivated their vineyards there,
founding Vevay. Brown County, cut by deep eroded valleys
and choked with knobs, was a stopping place for other families.
Some were attracted by so small a thing as a good salt spring,
which drew deer. Just as the ridge below Bean Blossom Creek
in Brown County had held back the glaciers, so it dammed the
flow of settlers, and in later years they periodically struck glacial
gold in the creek and a minor gold rush ensued. (The most valuable nugget found was worth a dollar and ten cents.) In their
snug valleys these isolated people held fast to their customs. At
their pioneer logrollings they sang old English songs, and they
sing them yet. While the rest of the state was scrambling for
progress, the residents of Georgetown, having made themselves
comfortable, settled down to build a race track and breed fine
horses, and on race day their wagers and their hill-made whisky
flowed free. The pioneers were a hard-drinking, bragging, swag-
gering lot, given to fighting for the glory of battle. But with

Hoosier shrewdness, they turned vice to profit. Fines for fighting and "profane swearing" went into the Brown County seminary fund.

A traveler on the trace from Clarksville to Vincennes in 1819 came to the falls of White River, "a broad, crystal stream . . . over a bed of sand and stone, smooth and white as a floor of marble," and found the village of Hindostan. "The baby ville is flourishing . . . and promises to become a pleasant healthy town," he wrote. Hindostan had the only store in the region. Mills were being built for grinding wheat and corn and carding wool. A ferry carried travelers across the river. The proprietors of Hindostan made it the seat of Martin County by donating land and money for the courthouse and a courthouse bell (they stipulated that the courthouse square should be used for nothing else and that ten per cent of the cash should be spent on a library). Even before work began on the courthouse and jail, the circuit-riding judge held court in the home of one of the town proprietors, and the county commissioners fixed tavernkeepers' rates—62½¢ for lodging a horse one night and 12½¢ for lodging a human, 12½¢ for feeding a horse one meal and 37½¢ for feeding a human, 12½¢ for a half pint of whisky, 62½¢ for a half pint of French brandy. They fixed tax rates too—a gold watch was taxed 50¢ and a silver watch 37½¢, an ox 25¢ and a horse 37½¢, land from 31¼¢ to 50¢ a hundred acres. The poll tax was 50¢. The town proprietors commenced selling lots. A land boom began; "people came from all parts of the east."

Other towns sprang up in this rough southwestern region of tumbling hills and deep, narrow valleys and rushing streams—Brownstown in 1815, Orleans and Paoli in 1816, Palestine in 1817, Shoals and Mt. Pleasant and especially Vallonia even earlier—but Hindostan was at the falls, and its citizens were hustlers, and soon it outstripped all others in the region except Vincennes and New Albany. But about 1826 or 1827 a pestilence struck. Mt. Pleasant, high on a near-by hill, was unscathed, but in Hindostan there were more dead than living. Some who fled were turned back from other towns; a plague, unseen and mysterious, was more feared than Indians. The town had no doctor. "The street," runs an old chronicle, "echoed to the wail of Rachel weeping for her children. The death angel stalked abroad." The cemetery on the hill grew faster than the town had ever grown. Relief was sought from the legislature; it responded by removing the county seat. The County Commissioners ordered the clerk and treasurer to take their records to Mt. Pleasant. All who stayed at Hindostan died, and today nothing remains of what promised to be a leading city.

No one knows what the pestilence was. It may have been malaria or yellow fever. The pioneers were constantly being laid low by chills, fevers, agues, and other little-understood plaints. Learned men speculated on causes and cures. President Jefferson concluded that "the scourge of Yellow fever" was probably due to America's "cloudless skies," which admitted too much of the sun's heat to earth, and so to ventilate cities he advised leaving every alternate city block vacant. Governor Harrison forthwith laid out a new Ohio River town according to the plan and named it Jeffersonville. (A few years later the plague devastated it; it was further distinguished, also to Harrison's discomfiture, as Aaron Burr's Indiana headquarters when he was conspiring to win a southwest empire.) Plague wiped out at least one other town, Palestine, and raged in Winamac, Madison, Vevay, Vincennes, Salem, Indianapolis, and Rising Sun, a steamboating town named for the glory of the sunrise over Rabbit Hash across the river.

Chapter 3

WILDERNESS YEARS

THE REPUBLIC was young, Indiana was the frontier. Numerous perils harassed the pioneer. He welcomed winter, hard as it was, for it meant the Indians would hole up; but if the sun broke warm again and the atmosphere turned hazy, fear swept the settlements, for Indian summer afforded the warriors one last chance. Everybody knew the story of Frances Slocum, the white child kidnapped and reared by Indians in northern Indiana; everybody loved Johnny Appleseed, the "teched" but noble barefoot man in rags who roamed the border, reading from Swedenborg, planting apple trees, healing the sick, warning of the Apocalypse and the coming of the Indians. Even after the Indians were gone, pioneering was a life of few comforts, rare pleasure, great drudgery, much sickness. Roads were few, impassable morasses in winter, choked with dust in summer. Ill fortune dogged the settler's every pursuit. In desperation he consulted strange oracles: he dreaded the croak of the raven, the howl of a dog, passage of birds. Peculiar visitations, like the invasion of Washington County by thousands of squirrels, beset him. At the end of the long journey from the East, over the mountains or down the rivers, across broken hills and dismal forests and prairies covered with head-high grass, lay only a forest to settle in. And after the trees were cut and the cabin built and the brush cleared and the stumps uprooted and the rails split and the rail fence built and, at long last, the earth broken with the plow and the first crop gathered, a land speculator would turn up and prove he owned the title. Small wonder that the farmer listed foremost among the enemies of man the skin-flint speculator, even ahead of the horse thief and the note shaver of the wildcat-banking days. The women worked as hard as the men. On the headstone of one grave is inscribed:

> *Thirteen years I was a virgin,*
> *Two years I was a wife.*
> *One year I was a mother,*
> *The next year took my life.*

Hardship produced a habit that persists to this day in rural areas: co-operation among neighbors. To combat loneliness in the scattered cabins, the people held quilting bees and other bees.

Into this rude wilderness, men brought dreams. George Rapp, a six-foot German with flowing beard, in 1814 transplanted his colony of religious communists, sworn to celibacy and the good life and ridiculed by Lord Byron, to the banks of the Wabash, in the southwesternmost county of Indiana. Here in the forest they constructed Harmonie, a village as neat as any along the Rhine. In 1824 they sold out to Robert Owen, a Scotch manufacturer with money and ideas who was looking for a place to set up the good society. A critic of capitalism fifty years before Marx and Engels, Owen in 1800 had taken over large mills in Scotland owned by his father-in-law, raised wages, shortened hours, corrected abuses, raised the living standard of the workmen, and yet managed to show a profit. This won him renown. Opposition by his partners, however, convinced him that attempts to reform capitalists by appeals to their better natures were useless, and so he turned to political action. He failed and made his last turn: to a fundamental reorganization of society. (We shall see the striking parallel between his experiences and those of Debs and the Hapgoods a century later.) He believed that if he could set up a society uncorrupted by the profit motive and other evils, men would become good. Unlike the Rappites' Harmonie, his New Harmony was not a religious but an economic and social experiment. To it came a conglomerate thousand, some idealists, some only misfits. Owen recruited educators and scientists, and to rough-handed settlers along the Ohio and Wabash this "Boatload of Knowledge" must have seemed a strange sight indeed. For a time New Harmony prospered, but soon dissension and thievery commenced, the workmen proved lazy and the farmers inept, and by 1827 Owen's sons admitted failure. Owen went back to England. However, the flame he had kindled did not die. Fourier was a disciple of Owenism, and Marx and Engels studied New Harmony. William Maclure revived the Workingmen's Institute and also, with Robert Owen and others, spread Pestalozzi's advanced education doctrines. New Harmony became the scientific center of America; from it David Dale Owen carried on explorations as Indiana and United States Geologist, and the leading scientists of the day studied there. Numerous Owenite communities sprang up elsewhere. Frances Wright, a disciple, became one of America's first feminists, female educators, and opponents of slavery. Robert Dale Owen, her consort, served Indiana in the Legislature and in Congress, a gentle cultured man enduring patiently the obloquy of rough-and-tumble politicians and steadfastly demanding free education, equal rights for women, and the forcible emancipation of the slaves. (It was said that his letter to President Lincoln, more than any other single document, persuaded Lincoln to issue the Emancipation Proclamation.)

New Harmony, or even Harmonie, was not the first communal experiment in Indiana. Sixteen miles up the Wabash from Vincennes, on a prairie ringed with sycamores (called buttonwoods), two dozen sectarians from Ohio planted a colony in 1808. Their sect was officially named the United Society of the Believers in Christ's Second Appearing, but other settlers called them Shakers, from their ecstatic devotional dancing, and, though esteeming them as fair dealers and skilled farmers, looked with some suspicion upon their celibacy, their abstinence from liquor and tobacco, their vegetarianism, their co-operative property holding, and their religious tenets. After the border warfare of 1813 the Shakers, two hundred strong, operated grist mills and carding machines, cultivated and fabricated indigo and cotton, raised wheat, apples, potatoes, sheep, and other crops, and maintained a self-sufficient economy, shipping their surplus by flatboat down to New Orleans. By the 1820's, however, the Methodist circuit riders had arrived in Indiana in force, and though these courageous men performed numerous good works, they devoted a great deal of energy to making war on the Shakers, already harassed by malaria, and finally drove them away.

The La Grange Phalanx, an economic experiment, was organized in 1844 by a judge and two leading farmers of Lagrange County in northern Indiana. Soon a hundred and twenty people were living in the large communal house. A Council of Industry managed all farming and manufacturing, paying the same wage to all, seventy-five cents for a ten-hour day. Other councils supervised other activities. For a time matters went well. But soon "many adventurers came in, some for want of a home, others to winter and leave in the spring," and by 1848 the Phalanx had collapsed. A newspaper commented on another such project: "What next! . . . The matter to us looks dark," and a reader wrote: "The world . . . is full of expedients for improving and ameliorating the condition of society. . . . I, for one, have no confidence in these visionary theorists. . . ."

Truly, in those early years there was a ferment in the forest, and though the forest is gone from Indiana, the ferment has not died. This quest for the better life runs like a golden thread through all Indiana's history.

These early experiments, however, were, in their own time, only curiosities lost in the crush of events. For Indiana was caught up in its first big boom. It became a state in 1816. (Promptly Jonathan Jennings, foe of officeholders, teamed up with other politicians, and for years they governed Indiana simply by rotating the offices of Governor, Senator, and Congressman among themselves, "changing hands as in a country dance.") The flatboat trade boomed on the Ohio River; in March, men brought their produce to the town landings and loaded the boats, pausing now and then for a dipperful of whisky from the barrel; they moved the boats in clusters downriver past the pirates of Cave-in-Rock; they tied up at Paducah or Natchez, and in New Orleans people jibed at their backwoods dress, their Hoosier manner, and the resentful Hoosiers licked them. Back home they were making progress of their own, native progress. Banks were chartered. Vincennes and Jeffersonville were the busiest land offices in the United States. Jennings bought from the Indians the whole middle portion of the state and to this New Purchase settlers flocked, and good times came back with the land rush. New York State was building the Erie Canal, the center of the nation's political balance was rapidly shifting westward. From the old seaboard, men streamed west. They brought a thousand heritages, and the wilderness altered these and fused them and something new arose: the Midwest, native America. Its heart was Indiana. This was the place where a man could come with nothing but his hands, could clear the forest and build a home and, with luck, build a fortune.

In Indiana, activity was leaving the southern riverboard, and moving north. Men located the center of the state, moved over a bit to the bank of White River, and platted Indianapolis. In four wagons the seat of government was moved there from Corydon in 1824. Already the Indianapolis *Gazette* was issuing from a log cabin, and Indianapolis stores were advertising Eastern broadcloth, bonnets, shoes, silver, musical instruments, and other finery; and despite the jeremiads of the Methodists, the settlers enjoyed a theatrical performance in Carter's Tavern. The farmers clearing the timber on the fertile central plains were gaining the ascendancy—criticizing Jennings's clique, demanding better roads and canals. The state was becoming a part of the nation. The election of 1824 was the first fought in Indiana on national issues—the Bank of the wicked money changers, the tariff blamed for the high cost of Eastern goods, domination of the republic by Eastern aristocrats like John Quincy Adams— and when Andrew Jackson lost the Presidency, Hoosiers cried that Adams had stolen it, and they set about forming Indiana's first effective county-by-county political organization, a machine that in 1828 swept the state for the Western hero, Jackson. Stage coaches crossed the wilderness. The farmers no longer looked only south for market; by Conestoga wagon they took their produce up to Chicago, where more worldly citizens poked fun at them. "Hoosier" still meant "an uncouth rustic," and those who bore the name began to bear it belligerently, ready to meet attack, as, indeed, they do to this day.

Brookville, the capital of the Whitewater country, still dominated the state's cultural and political life. By 1817 it possessed about eighty houses, some painted, together with five mills, a printshop, seven stores, and various artisans. In the early 1820's, Brookville merchants and lawyers prospered. James Brown Ray built a two-story house with a window so ornate that it almost lost him the election as Governor: an opposition newspaper up in Indianapolis, the raw "capital in the woods," gleefully characterized him as an aristocrat from elegant Brookville. The leading citizens of Brookville, and of the state at large, were lawyers. Indiana's early political leaders came from the bench and bar of Brookville: James and Noah Noble, Ray, Robert Hanna, Isaac Blackford and other judges, and John Test, a Congressman; Test's daughter married a man who became Governor and she bore at Brookville a son, Lew Wallace, the author of *Ben Hur.*

The Indiana woods was full of lawyers. Busy though they were in the wilderness, Indiana pioneers had time for ideas, and most of the ideas came from the lawyers and politicians. O. H. Smith was a successful lawyer and politician of the Whitewater Valley, a fine specimen of the shrewd, genial, dry-witted, horse-trading Hoosier public man of little more than ordinary ability, a type that persists to this day. He was born near Trenton, New Jersey, October 23, 1794. After the War of 1812, like so many young men, he left the aging East and rode his pony westward. At Pittsburgh he hired on as captain of a coal boat bound for Louisville. In Indiana he read law about two years, then after an examination by a circuit judge, was licensed to practice. (Not until 1935 after long litigation was the legislature empowered to prescribe qualifications for lawyers, and then it took an amendment to the constitution, which said that any voter "of good moral character" was entitled to admission to practice.) Smith soon moved to Connersville on the Whitewater. He had a sturdy body, a great mop of hair, shaggy eyebrows, and a very loud voice he loved to hear, all assets of consequence to an ambitious young lawyer. In addition, he was gregarious, God-fearing, and an opponent of liquor and card playing. Connersville had but one hotel and one lawyer; Indians and, occasionally, bears wandered in the main street. Smith paid a dollar and a quarter a week for room and board. The Third Judicial Circuit included virtually the whole eastern half of the state. Carrying with them their dog-eared copies of Espinasse's *Nisi Prius* and Peak's *Evidence,* the lawyers rode the circuit with the president judge. He was elected by the legislature to serve the entire circuit; in each county he sat with two associate judges elected locally who, though often without knowledge of the law, could outvote him. And this was the Indiana system, the American system, the stubborn refusal to yield to central authority, however capable. When the circuit judge and his bar arrived, citizens came from miles around to crowd into the log courthouse or watch the young squires strut across the courtyard, their hair done in queues three feet long and tied with an eelskin, on their heads rorum hats stiffened with glue. Once when a young lawyer began: "If the court please," the judge responded: "Yes, we do please, young man, the people have come in to hear the lawyers plead," and the lawyer launched into a three-hour oration upon the abominations that had driven his client to pull the nose of the plaintiff; at its end the judge roared: "Capital; I did not think it was in him!" and the jury forthwith cried out: "Not guilty," to the loud acclamation of the crowd.

When Squire Smith hung out his shingle who came to fee him, as the saying went? His first client in the spring of 1820 was a man who complained that a neighbor had bored one of his sugar trees without asking. ("If he had asked, he might have bored a dozen.") For this injury, after due process, Smith obtained judgment of twelve and a half cents and collected a fee of two dollars and a half. Another client was Dr. Joseph Moffitt, a respected physician of Connersville. He brought suit for slander against a newcomer whose professional shingle, "Joseph S. Burr, Root Doctor; No Calomel," hung on the hotel front above a swamp-lily root nearly as large as a man. Dr. Burr told people that Dr. Moffitt was killing his patients with calomel. Some ten of the circuit's leading attorneys were involved, and for more than a week witnesses debated whether people died "with the fever" or were killed by the "calomel doctors." In the end the jury disagreed and was discharged, Dr. Moffitt paid the costs, and the root doctor ran off to the New Purchase to set up a school for root doctors, to whom he issued diplomas after three weeks' study.

In 1824 Smith was appointed circuit prosecutor. His most celebrated prosecution was that of four robbers who in 1824 wantonly murdered nine Indians—two men, three squaws, and

four children—above the falls of Fall Creek, between Indianapolis and the village of Anderson. One of the five killers escaped but the other four were caught quickly. The settlers of
the New Purchase feared that the Indians who remained might
renew the border warfare. The U.S. Government sent agents
to persuade the tribes to rely on the white man's justice. Multitudes attended the trials. Here was an issue plain to all. The
defense recalled old outrages of the Indians. The prosecution
appealed to the jurors' respect for the law which deals equally
with all, and also to their fear of Indian revenge. The first man
to be tried was hanged, and it was said he was the first white
man executed in the United States for killing an Indian. The
other three—a youth of 18, his father, and his uncle—were sentenced to hang but a Governor's pardon was recommended for
the boy. While a Seneca chief looked down with his people
from a nearby hilltop and white pioneers thronged thick in the
valley, the uncle and then the father were hanged. Their bodies
were placed in coffins beside the scaffold. The boy mounted the
scaffold, the noose was adjusted, but lo! up rode Governor Ray
on horseback and pardoned him.

This trial was rather remarkable, for Indiana in its early days
—and later as well—was full of lynch spirit. Men carried
guns even to church, and as early as 1819 a band of Regulators
was operating over the White River country in the central part
of the state. The Regulators were partly respectable farmers unimpressed with the law's protection, partly restless young mal-
contents. One Sunday Christopher Ladd and a friend found a
man's skeleton below the bluffs of White River; their alarm
brought the Regulators, who, after brief deliberation beneath
some cottonwoods, reached the conclusion that Ladd had murdered the man. All that remained to decide was whether to hang
him forthwith or to torture him a bit first. They sought the advice
of Jacob Whetzel, who had blazed the Whetzel Trace from the
Whitewater Valley to the White River bluffs below the site of
Indianapolis. Whetzel pointed out there was no evidence against
Ladd. The mercurial Regulators freed him. He went to Brookville and sued them for false imprisonment; he won damages of
ninety-four dollars, but his lawyers' fees broke him, and the damages and fifteen hundred dollars costs broke the Regulators.

In his discursive memoirs, Smith, a witty man with a sharp eye for the curious, repeated many a tale that fits the legend of the rustic Hoosier and, indeed, helped create it. He enjoyed the yarn told by a State Senator named George Boone, a man nearly seven feet tall with enormous hands and feet, of how when about eighteen years old, he had gone sparking for the first time. On Sunday he dressed in his "best butter-nut colored suit"; though made but six months earlier, the trousers already reached only to his knees and the coat "stretched over me as tight as an eel-skin dried on a hoop-pole." Though the day was chill, it was still too early in the fall to put on shoes, so Boone waded creeks and muddy bottoms barefoot to Sally's house. At a supper of mush and milk, Sally's mother passed him a bowl, but, big and clumsy, he upset a pitcher of milk. Sally ran off, shouting with laughter, and though her parents tried to reassure Boone, he could not think of a word to say the rest of the meal. At ten o'clock Sally's mother asked: "Mr. Boone, won't you wash your feet and go to bed?" He replied meekly: "Yes, ma'am," and took the iron pot she offered as a basin. He managed to slide his feet into it side-ways, but they swelled and he could not get them out. The pain became agony. A full hour passed. Sally's mother called to ask if he was not yet finished. He asked: "What did this pot cost?" A dollar, she said; and he said: "Then bring me the ax." She did, and he smashed the pot, handed her a dollar, and fled.

Smith prospered. The second year he traveled the circuit his fees amounted to three hundred dollars, and he felt financially well off. A sharp trader, he bought a fine farm of a hundred and sixty acres, on rich land adjoining Connersville, for nine dollars an acre. He bought a two-story brick house in the heart of town for three hundred and twenty-five dollars. Inevitably he entered politics. He was elected a representative to the State Assembly, and in 1826 he was sent to Congress. Disdaining the fashionable stage, he rode his horse to Washington, reaching the Indian Queen Hotel on the seventeenth day.

Together with the courts, politics was almost the only enter-tainment of the people, and circuit-riding lawyers, replacing circuit-riding preachers, reached their greatest glory as stump speakers on the Fourth of July, muster day, and barbecue day, when farmers came out of the woods to hear them plagiarize the sentences of Henry Clay and Patrick Henry. But politics was a serious matter too. A publisher was sued for libel because he called a man "an old Federalist" in print; the jury, after hearing testimony that a Federalist was no better than a horse thief, assessed damages at a thousand dollars. It was in the caucuses of his party that Smith excelled, like so many Hoosier politicians to this day. In 1836 he was elected Senator by the General Assembly. He herded his five hundred hogs to Cincinnati, arriving there at night covered with mud. Gentlemen in the lobby inquired about the Indiana senatorial election, asking which of the two leading candidates had been chosen. "Neither," said Smith. Then who? "I am elected." "You! What is your name?" Smith told them. "You elected a United States Senator! I never heard of you before." "Very likely," said Smith, and next day sold his hogs for seven thousand dollars cash and went home to Indiana. (So Smith wrote, at least, in his memoirs; and George Ade himself never better revealed the Hoosier character, shrewd, dry, smug.)

Though Smith failed utterly to distinguish himself in the Senate, he became in later years an elder statesman in Indiana, accumulating farms, promoting railroads, writing his memoirs, practicing Federal law, traveling to Memphis and St. Louis to attend barbecues and railroad conventions, delivering orations at the State Fair, reminiscing about Clay and Calhoun and the Presidents with whom he had mingled in Washington, and attending the fashionable church of the Reverend Henry Ward Beecher on the Circle in Indianapolis.

When he sought re-election to the Senate in 1842 he was defeated by a tall young man named Edward A. Hannegan. If Smith was the party hack, Hannegan was the knight in shining armor. Indeed, more than any other, Hannegan, though nearly forgotten today, seemed to the people of his time their bright western star.

Chapter 4

SENATOR HANNEGAN,
SON OF THE WEST

S OON AFTER Ned Hannegan was born, June 25, 1807, in Hamilton County, Ohio, his parents moved to Lexington, Kentucky. Here he attended Transylvania University. A county clerk appointed him his assistant and encouraged him to study law. Although this was Henry Clay's home territory, Hannegan's father championed Andrew Jackson vigorously. In 1827 Hannegan went to Vincennes. Here two years later he married Margaret C. Duncan. But Vincennes was old and settled and full of lawyers, and Hannegan rode northward, seeking a frontier town in which to practice.

He settled in Covington in Fountain County on the Wabash. Covington was only a village, but the land office at near-by Crawfordsville had outrun Brookville's, and Indianapolis's too, as the busiest in the state; indeed, it was the busiest in the nation in 1825; and who knew?—this Wabash valley might become Indiana's new land of promise.

Ned Hannegan was admitted to the bar at Covington in 1828, when he was twenty-one. He rode the circuit for a year, gaining a reputation as a trial lawyer and a Democrat. Jackson carried Indiana, and Hannegan became enrolling clerk of the General Assembly. He went over to Indianapolis, which, Edward Eggleston wrote, was nothing but "a straggling, muddy village in a heavily wooded morass. . . . The Governor's house, remarkable for a homely bigness and a dirty color, stood in the middle, surrounded by a circular street. . . . stumps stood in the streets; the mud was navigable only to a man on a tall horse; the buildings were ugly and unpainted; the people were raw immigrants, dressed in butternut jeans, and for the most part afflicted with either the 'agur' or the 'yeller janders.' . . ."

In 1830 the legislators elected Hannegan prosecuting attorney in the First Judicial District. In 1831 he was elected to the state House of Representatives. Here he was a member of the Committee on Canals and Internal Improvements. Indiana had emerged from the hunting-shirt years a state of farmers. But the farmers had no means of getting their produce to market. They demanded canals. A bushel of corn worth twelve to twenty cents at Indianapolis was worth fifty cents on the riverboard. Impressed with the success of the Erie Canal, the new Western states were clamoring for canals of their own. In 1827 Congress had donated a million dollars' worth of land to build the Wabash and Erie Canal southwest across Indiana, uniting the Maumee near Fort Wayne with the Wabash near Terre Haute. Prospects of progress seemed boundless. An editor wrote in 1834: "Throughout our western land, the sound of the hammer and the hum of industry is everywhere heard, and the honest tradesman quickly arises to affluence. . . . who can tell what effect the west will have upon the destiny of this young republic, 'the world's best treasure and last hope.'" Ned Hannegan fought stalwartly for canals and roads and the Westerners' rights in the U.S. House of Representatives and Senate as well as in the state legislature. He battled the Bank and Nicholas Biddle and all who would deny pre-emption rights to settlers. When he spoke for a soldiers' pension bill, John Quincy Adams noted: "He went over all the old ground," but the folks back at Covington toasted him as a patriot at a Fourth of July celebration. Since the Revolutionary War the settlers who hopefully had come to Indiana had been the dispossessed. As soon as they cleared their land they began to demand a place in the sun; and Hannegan voiced their demands, he was their champion, the man who spoke for the raw West before the Civil War changed it forever.

Young Hannegan rose fast: He reached Congress when he was twenty-five years old. An Irishman below medium height but solidly made, he had a ruddy complexion, blue eyes, and light-brown hair, and he was clean shaven. He possessed both Irish wit and Irish temper, and a brooding melancholy as well. His reputation as the leading orator of Indiana, and perhaps of the nation, began almost as soon as he reached Washington. He praised the Democratic Party: "When the history of this country is written its brightest pages will be those devoted to telling what democracy has done for the growth and progress of the United States, for the prosperity of the people. Around those pages will shine a halo like that painters have given to the head of the Great Redeemer." Webster said: "Had Hannegan entered Congress before I entered it I fear I never should have been known for my eloquence." His admirers supposed that his sonorous phrases rolled forth extemporaneously; actually, an educated man, he maintained a large library and frequently wrote out his speeches in advance. He did not seek a third term in Congress in 1836, perhaps because of political expediency, perhaps because he was drinking heavily. His wife, who was extremely devoted, nursed him back to health, and he became a teetotaler. He moved to La Porte County and became register of deeds; he opened the land office at Winamac; and in this new northwest region of forests and swamps and pioneer cabins, treating with the Indians and acquiring property and practising law, he found renewed powers. He could not remain long in the woods. Elsewhere big things were happening. In 1836 Governor Noah Noble had signed the mammoth Internal Improvement Bill, appropriating thirteen million dollars, mortgaging the state's resources for half a century. Wealthy farmers had replaced log cabins with houses and now opposed free education because road- and canal-building and swamp drainage were so much more important. They worked eagerly without pay on the railroads, forgetting that a railroad belongs to a private owner and only his trains, not theirs, could use it. When the first steamboat ascended the White River to Indianapolis, the artillery company paraded in splendor on the riverbank. Indianapolis's future, her water link with the South, seemed assured, however slow the railroads might be in coming. In 1835 Indianapolis's population had been 1,683, timber stood near the Circle, and squirrels and wild turkeys abounded a few blocks away; in the next three years the canal and road program hoisted the population to 4,000. Prosperous free-swinging Hoosiers took no notice of the shameful expulsion of the last Pottawattomies—the long march from northern Indiana to Kansas which killed a fifth of the tribe and has been termed the Trail of Death.

But suddenly prosperity evaporated. The panic of 1837 struck. Money was scarce and the farmers blamed the banks. Railroad promoters fled the state, leaving useless half-finished roadbeds. The canal boom became a disaster. Indiana could not pay the interest on the internal improvement bonds. Contractors, engineers, bankers, promoters, politicians, and everybody else had been stealing. By August 1839 all canal work ceased. Unemployed canal workers turned criminal. By 1840 about five and a half million dollars had been spent to complete about 140 miles of 1,160 projected miles of canal; most of the completed work was useless.

It was no wonder, then, that the campaign of 1840 was a humdinger. And lo! who was the candidate, the people's choice, but the old war horse, William Henry Harrison, brought from the closet and dusted off and tricked out not as a Virginia aristocrat, an autocratic Territorial Governor, master of Grouseland, but, rather, as a plain-spoken old Indian fighter, a farmer now emerging like Cincinnatus to defend the common man. To honor him on the Tippecanoe battleground near Lafayette came thirty thousand men, women, and children, old soldiers and party hacks, farmers and their families on a holiday; some camped out for two days before the gigantic barbecue, and of speechmaking and hard cider, there seemed no end. Never in American history had there been a campaign like this. No nonsense, no preposterous claim, was omitted. Desperately the Democrats tried to make their platform heard but nobody listened. The people were singing "Tippecanoe and Tyler Too." They had found their hero in the log-cabin-and-hard-cider candidate. Martin Van Buren was an aristocrat, and that was that—all that the Democrats salvaged was a new party emblem, a rooster, put forward by an Indiana party faithful.

Among the Democrats submerged by the Harrison tidal wave was Ned Hannegan, making a comeback campaign for Congress. He headed the list of Democratic stump orators, but even his eloquence did not avail. Undeterred, Hannegan continued politicizing and resumed his law practice. Now thirty-three years old, rested and sober, he moved with renewed skill and assurance among his old cronies at Indianapolis and Covington, to which he had returned. In 1842 he was elected to the U.S. Senate, defeating O. H. Smith, and the story of how this came about has been used ever since to teach young politicians the value of a single vote. Several years earlier a downstate politician, Daniel Kelso, running for the General Assembly, had solicited the vote of a man whose father Hannegan had once saved from a murder charge. This man agreed to vote for Kelso if Kelso, though a Whig, would support Hannegan, a Democrat, for the U.S. Senate. Kelso won his Assembly seat by a single vote. And in the Assembly he deserted his own party's candidate, O. H. Smith, and Hannegan won the U.S. Senate seat by one vote.

Governor Willard once said: "Start Hannegan down stream at high tide, and he can gather more driftwood than any man I know, but he isn't worth a curse to row up stream." Handsome, eloquent, gallant, ebullient, charming, he was a native product of pioneer America yet he had learned the ways of the drawing-room. He understood perfectly the angry citizens of Plainfield who dumped elegant Little Van into a mudhole to demonstrate the need for improvement of the National Road, yet his conversation in Eastern salons fascinated ladies of fashion. In moving to the larger stage of the U.S. Senate, Hannegan dealt with the great issues that agitated the nation just before the Civil War. He had emerged from the wilderness onto the national scene as his state was emerging; he spoke for Indiana, for the new West. He referred to slavery as an evil but to Abolitionists as trouble-making busybodies. Calling attention to the threat of disunion, he intoned: "The same God whose pillar of fire guided our ancestors through the dark nights of the Revolution, and led them at its close, to build up this most magnificent and benign Government, will not permit his high purposes to be thwarted by the vain schemings or the mad delusions of their posterity. . . . Woe betide the man whose foot is first advanced in the unholy cause . . . Civil War. . . . There can be no peaceful dissolution of this Union. . . ."

It was as a champion of Manifest Destiny that Hannegan achieved his greatest fame. He led his party before the people in 1844: *"Polk and Annexation against The Bank and High Taxation."* Hannegan presented to the Senate a resolution by the Indiana Legislature: "Whereas the insatiate avarice and grasping spirit of the British government seems already directed to [Oregon's] subjugation. . . . [Congress should] provide for the immediate occupation, organization and defence of the Oregon Territory—peaceably if we can; forcibly if we must." The Hoosier farmers applauded vociferously; England, that old enemy, made a convenient scapegoat for their thwarted angers over the canal failure and general depression (it was not the last time England would play this role). When a banquet was tendered Hannegan in Philadelphia, he proposed this toast: "Oregon—Every foot or not an inch; 54 deg., 40 min. or *delenda est Britannia.*" In a Senate speech he said: "Oh, what a picture would the secret history of English diplomacy present! . . . Shall the mailed hand of England dictate to us. . . . The American people cannot be alarmed; they are not to be awed." He recalled 1776 when the colonies "stood for their rights in many a bloody field; and they conquered those rights from the mightiest and haughtiest power the world ever saw. . . . Now the same old enemy claims a great empire on our western coast. . . ." A visiting English lady in the gallery, Sarah Mytton Maury, was quite overcome; she threw down her glove, she later wrote, and "the chivalrous Hannegan instantly picked it up, pressed it to his lips, looked gratefully up to the gallery, bowed and placed it in his bosom." Hannegan was one of Mrs. Maury's favorites. "This is a genuine son of the West; ardent, impulsive and undaunted; thinking, acting and daring with the most perfect freedom. His spirit is youthful and buoyant. . . . The West but now begins to assert herself, to exhibit her strength . . . a political mystery. . . . The West has found a devoted lover in her Hannegan. . . . The robust character of the Western men, and their remoteness from that peculiar kind of civilization which belongs to sea board and manufacturing districts, have induced an idea that they are deficient in the proprieties and gentle moods of polished life. . . . Show me a gentler, more affectionate nature than Edward Hannegan you cannot; and, believe me, the Western men in general resemble him." She wrote: "A devoted lover of the country and of its independence, he pined at last in Washington that he was compelled to go home for a fortnight to refresh his spirits and recruit his health. I met him on the Ohio on his way. 'Come home with me,' said he to the Doctor and myself, 'come home with me, and I will show you the lovely valley of the Wabash. I can endure those hot and crowded halls no longer. I must have free air and space to roam in; I like to hunt when I please, and to shoot when I please, and to fish when I please, and to read when I please. Come home with me, and see how I live in Indiana.' But we were bound to the Mammoth Cave. . . ." Indeed, Covington then was a pleasant place. Its business prospects excelled those of dreary Indianapolis. A coterie of brilliant young men had settled there, Lew Wallace and a number of lawyers like Daniel W. Voorhees, later a Senator famed as the Tall Sycamore of the Wabash. Hannegan, Wallace, and Voorhees joined the Masonic Lodge at Covington, and Hannegan became Worshipful Master. Hannegan was the town's favorite son.

Like many men of his time he was superstitious. He refused to begin a journey or transact business on Friday or to pay bills on Monday. He sometimes brooded about the afterlife. He and two friends, Judge John R. Porter and Josephus Collett, agreed that the one who died first would visit the others in spirit. After Judge Porter died, Hannegan spent an evening with Collett; they conversed little, so ill at ease was Hannegan. Finally at bedtime Hannegan sprang up and demanded: "Joe Collett, has John Porter been back to you?" Collett said he hadn't. Hannegan said sadly: "Now I know there is no coming back after death. John Porter never broke his word."

Hannegan's hot temper and fighting prowess became legendary. In 1848 the water was let into the new Wabash and Erie Canal at Attica, a rival town a few miles north, before—reasonably enough—it was let into the canal at Covington. Hannegan rounded up some two hundred men, and led them in battle array to Attica. They seized the lock, mounted guard, and turned on the water. To protest came Ezekiel M. McDonald, a leading resident of Attica, and some fellow citizens. In the ensuing affray McDonald and other Atticans were belabored with clubs and thrown into the canal.

When Polk showed signs of appeasing the British, Hannegan attacked him violently on the Senate floor, his only apostasy:

"James K. Polk has spoken words of falsehood with the tongue of a serpent." Back home in Indianapolis the Democrats deserted Hannegan, and he lost his seat to Governor James Whitcomb (for whom the poet Riley later was named). In 1849, however, in the closing hours of Hannegan's Senate career, Polk forgave him and nominated him Minister to Prussia. He arrived in Berlin June 10. The new Envoy Extraordinary and Minister Plenipotentiary distinguished himself here chiefly, it was said, by making love to the Queen of Prussia. She was captivated, whispered Midwesterners, delighted that he outdid European fops. The jealous King, legend continues, demanded Hannegan's recall when Hannegan, defying court etiquette, publicly kissed the Queen's hand. The truth, however, seems to be that Hannegan asked to be recalled, saying: "Berlin is a dull place in the summer; how it may be in the winter God only knows, and those who have tried it; for one I do not wish to."

He returned to practice law in Covington, where Lew Wallace praised him as the town's great man. But the next year he could not even win election to the state legislature. He had become remote from local issues. A local historian writes: "As the politicians gathered in the courthouse yard in the dusk of the autumn evening and the returns came in from the out townships, Hannegan, realizing his defeat, said: 'The gloom of this night is the winding sheet of my political career.' " Forthwith, he entered the race for the nomination for President of the United States. He soon secured the pledged support of nine states. Franklin Pierce was almost unknown; Hannegan had been the only Midwest Democratic Senator who could match Webster's eloquence. His chances of nomination looked good. But he had been drinking heavily and in the spring of 1852 he came home to rest and sober up. His wife's brother, Captain John R. Duncan, was living with the Hannegans. On May 6 or 7 he and Hannegan were drinking together in the house, and Duncan told Hannegan his drinking would lose him the Presidency. The two men quarreled. Mrs. Hannegan, knowing her husband's ugly temper, sought to intervene, but the quarrel grew more violent. Duncan called Hannegan a coward and slapped his face. Hannegan seized a Spanish dagger and drove it to the hilt into Duncan's body. Duncan, near death, absolved Hannegan. Hannegan threw his arms about him and, sobbing, kissed him repeatedly. Duncan died next day. Newspaper editors saw in this a temperance lesson. Hannegan was charged with manslaughter. His friend, young Lew Wallace, was the prosecuting attorney, and he presented so weak a case to the Grand Jury that it refused to indict, with the result that Wallace was forced to resign and move to Crawfordsville. To replace him Daniel Voorhees was appointed; he refused to have the Grand Jury review the case, and, severely criticized, he left town and went to Terre Haute.

Hannegan tried to resume his political career, but though he had escaped prosecution, his party shunned him. Embittered, he wrote to a friend: "I have closed all connections with parties, for it is all in vain. They will absolutely falsify what I say right before my face. . . . The dirty puddle of politics . . . I want to follow my profession and to amass, as I believe I can, a competency for old age." In a postscript he added: "I spoke at Crawfordsville, and sent you a paper with a brief notice of it. They failed to report the heads of my speech as they promised. . . ." His old fire flashed briefly when John C. Fremont was a candidate in 1856: "He rests his whole claim to the suffrages of the people on the one fact that he found a pathway across the Rocky mountains. This he did through the aid of some Indian guides. . . . So is a mountain goat a pathfinder, but the goat, for that reason, does not aspire to be a buffalo."

Then his wife died, and he found he could no longer remain in Covington. Probably early in 1857 he set out to find a place to start over. He had in mind New Orleans or Memphis, but in St. Louis he was persuaded to stay. He opened a law office, and for two years he prospered. His old eloquence before juries returned. But he continued to drink, and soon it was said he was using morphine as well. Nevertheless, encouraged by success, he determined to re-enter politics. His friends of the St. Louis bar arranged a great mass meeting for February 24, 1859, to launch his comeback. He was to be the principal speaker. The presidential nominations for 1860 were at issue. He was to advance the cause of Stephen A. Douglas. An enormous crowd gathered to hear him. His friends congratulated him; the stage was set for a triumph. But to brace himself, he had taken whisky and perhaps morphine as well; and the man who introduced him

51

eulogized him too long. By the time Hannegan arose to begin his address, the liquor had worn off, he had passed from exaltation to stupefaction, and little but incoherent mumblings fell from his lips. Heartbroken, he stumbled to his room. The next morning he was found on his bed, dead from an overdose of morphine that, some said, he had taken deliberately. In life he had represented the pioneer Midwest; it had vanished by the time he died.

PART THREE

Growth

Chapter 5

IN CIVIL WAR

H ANNEGAN's fight at Attica was quixotic; the canal aque-
ducts were already rotting. A year earlier the Madison Railroad
had reached Indianapolis. The farmers had preferred canals to
railroads because they could use their own boats, not some East-
erner's cars. But the canals failed, and the railroads hitched Indiana irrevocably to the industrial East just as the rivers had
tied it to the South in the past.

The new Constitution of 1851, written to meet a Jacksonian
demand for more power for the people, was only a symptom of
deep change. The Irish canal workers settled in Indianapolis and
the Germans came, and both resisted the temperance forces,
though they called their saloons "groceries." To uphold native
Americanism the Know-Nothings organized, thirty thousand to
fifty thousand strong in Indiana, with ritual and secrets; politicians denounced them as "ill-omened birds of the night."
Learned lecturers and gifted mediums roved the countryside,
working their miracles in farmhouses and schoolhouses, and
on their heels came debunkers, stirring bitter controversy. William Miller prophesied that Christ would come again between
March 21, 1843, and March 21, 1844, and for a whole year peni-
tents hastened to revival meetings. Unemployed canal workers
became counterfeiters and horse thieves and blacklegs, infesting
the northern swamps; the legislature in 1852 empowered societies of vigilantes to arrest horse thieves, and in Lagrange County,
following an awesome parade at an old settlers' reunion, the

55

Regulators lynched at least one man and filled the jails. Bigoted Bible searching replaced camp-meeting fellowship. A preacher bragged that "it was the amen corner of the Methodist Church that defeated Governor Bigger." Settlements on the rivers and canals were reborn along the railroads. The village store became a whittler's club, a forum, a news center. Newspapers sprouted: the muster-day orator was doomed. Farmers began raising crops for cash, not for their tables alone; stock and grain, corn and hogs, became the base. A few farmers even built two-story brick houses and kept fine driving horses. By 1860 Indiana had nearly as many farmers as today (though the total population has trebled). The first State Fair was held at Indianapolis in 1852. (It lost $320.21.) Up at Crown Point, Solon Robinson, defender of the squatters, turned to writing on agricultural science. Young Clem Studebaker stood in the throng that cheered the first train to reach South Bend and with his brother Henry, having saved about sixty-eight dollars, bought a blacksmith shop. Soon James Oliver arrived and began making plows. Native midland capitalism was planted. Over on the Wabash a German immigrant, Herman Hulman, arrived at Terre Haute and began his career as businessman and financier; Terre Haute, spurred by Chauncey Rose's coal-hauling railroad, promised to become the state's first railroad and manufacturing city, and to another immigrant family a son was born, Eugene Victor Debs. And four years later the first Pullman car was constructed.

Down on the river the old order was approaching decadence. Wealthy Hoosiers took the cars from Indianapolis to Madison, which was clinging precariously to its rank as the state's largest city. Here Jenny Lind sang in a packing house, and Captain Charles Lewis Shrewsbury, who had made a fortune in river shipping, and James Franklin Doughty Lanier, who had made an even greater fortune in banking and railroad finance, had spent some fifty thousand dollars apiece to build two of the finest homes west of the Alleghenies. The steamboat *Eclipse*, most magnificent on the Western waters, and a score of others ploughed the river from various points between Cincinnati and New Orleans, and in their saloons couples danced and men gambled for high stakes, gentlemen from the Kentucky bluegrass and from Indiana's landed estates and countinghouses.

Everywhere towns but recently fur posts became manufacturing centers. The city incorporation law was passed. Manufacturing was leaving the pioneer home and moving to the rail center; it was hiring outlanders as factory hands. By 1860 Indiana had 5,323 factories employing 20,755 persons and producing nearly forty-three million dollars worth of goods. In 1853 the Wabash and Erie Canal at last was finished; but in the same week the Indianapolis Union Station was completed. The Indianapolis & Bellefontaine Railroad linked Indianapolis directly by rail to the East.

And in the maze of railroads Indianapolis was the hub. This was the place, the coming place. True, in wet weather only Washington Street could be used by heavy wagons, but the city was building fast. Successful men earned a thousand dollars a year, and some even "kept a girl" for housework and drove a two-horse carriage or barouche. A plumber arrived in 1853; he had come to work on the Bates House. Business was good. Stores opened at 6 a.m., closed at 9 p.m. E. C. Atkins began manufacturing saws. By 1860 Marion County had about a hundred manufacturing establishments, which produced a million dollars' worth of goods. Men wore tall silk hats daily, and, in cold weather, shawls. Boys of twelve addressed girls as "Miss" and were called "Mister." The clergy proscribed theatergoing, dancing, and card playing. Though a menagerie was considered educational, circuses were abominations against God. On Sundays good people read nothing but religious literature and frowned even on walking. Theatricals grew in popularity, however. The *Journal* in 1851 accepted its first theatrical ad. Henry Ward Beecher united in wedlock a state legislator and a touring actress. A stock company opened the Metropolitan Theater in 1858. Indefatigable "Old Subscriber" charged in a letter to the *Journal* that in Cincinnati the same company had attempted a blasphemous representation of God. The theater kept getting into trouble. In desperation the manager offered the orphanage a substantial donation in 1859, but a terrible row ensued and the tainted money was spurned. The manager left town in disgust.

As early as 1843 a wandering dancing master had opened a school in Indianapolis; he announced himself as Professor Follansbee but the Hoosiers characteristically called him "Do-se-do." Young people defied taboos and learned the waltz, cotillion, and polka in his classes at Browning's Hotel. During the Civil War some great man invented a pack of cards divided not into spades, hearts, diamonds, and clubs but into swords, drums, flags, and cannon and the face cards bore images of generals, captains, and goddesses of liberty. Soon imitators were producing card games like "Authors," and before moralists could sound the alarm the bars were down completely. The social set played kissing games like "Sister Phoebe" and "Threading the Needle," it attended grand balls and sang *Ben Bolt* and *Old Dan Tucker* and *Rocked in the Cradle of the Deep.* Governor Whitcomb had entertained only a small select group; but Governor Wright, a nearly overpoweringly democratic champion of the farmers, threw wide the doors to all.

The politicians felt the spirit of change. In the middle 1840's Robert Dale Owen had sought to give the people new ideals—the rights of man and civil liberties—but the practical issue of slavery crowded them out. Questions asked of Hannegan and other senatorial candidates anticipated by ten years the propositions which Lincoln put to Douglas. Indeed, as we have seen, in Territorial days antislavery opponents of Governor Harrison had anticipated Squatter Sovereignty. The issue kept rising. Indiana was a border state. In the Legislature Hannegan said: "The gentleman from La Porte . . . even . . . tells us that in the State from whence he came 'beyond the mountains,' the statute presumes that truth may be told by a black man as *well* as by a white! Carry on the presumption of negro virtue, and where, sir, will it end? . . ." In 1845 a Negro was beaten to death by a mob in downtown Indianapolis. The Constitution of 1851 barred free Negroes from entering Indiana; those already there had to register with the county clerk. A law of 1853 prohibited Negroes from testifying in a case involving a white. Indiana politicians relaxed gratefully when Congress settled the slavery question with the Compromise of 1850. An Indiana Methodist conference in 1853 denounced slavery, however; the Reverend Mr. Beecher termed it an "utter abomination," and the antislavery Quakers on the upper Whitewater goaded public opinion just as they had supported Jonathan Jennings. They were led by Levi Coffin, whose home near Richmond became a main-line station on the Underground Railroad. Southern slave-holders hated Coffin as the "President" of the Underground Railroad. He was said to have succored Eliza, the heroine of Harriet Beecher Stowe's book. Though the railroad carried relatively few slaves it turned public opinion against the armed Southern horsemen who hunted down runaways like foxhunters, and a jingle ran:

> *Ho! the car Emancipation*
> *Moves majestic thro' our Nation*
> *Bearing on its train the story*
> *Liberty! a nation's glory*

Indiana wanted to compromise but events snowballed. Citizens with relatives in bleeding Kansas met anxiously. One of John Brown's raiders was Governor Willard's brother-in-law, and the Governor requested Daniel Voorhees to defend him. Government machinery broke down completely twice. Once the Democrats refused to help choose a U.S. Senator, and Indiana had but one; again the deadlocked Assembly failed to pass appropriation bills, and the state asylums were closed and the blind and insane sent home. The old parties splintered. A hodge-podge People's Party was formed to oppose the Democrats; Columbus Stebbens, a newspaperman, led it away from Know Nothingism and gave it a platform that would guide it when it became the Republican Party. Henry S. Lane and Oliver Perry Morton led the new Republican Party in Indiana, and Lane presided at its first national convention. The state's population had almost doubled in the last twenty years, the state was throwing its weight around. Morton was the new leader. A cold, forceful young man, logical rather than eloquent in stump debate, he was beaten for Governor in 1856 by an old-style spellbinder, but it was the last victory for a man like Hannegan or O. H. Smith. In 1860 Brown County hill folk might chant at torchlit processions:

> *Republicans may bite their nails,*
> *May rave about their Lincoln rails,*
> *But can't come up to Steve's coat tails,*
> *Then ho, for Douglas, ho!*

but at Indianapolis, Lane and Morton quietly made a deal. They carried Indiana; Lane took office as Governor January 14, 1861, told the Legislature: "The doctrine of secession . . . is a dangerous heresy," was sent two days later to the U.S. Senate, and Morton moved up from Lieutenant Governor, all according to plan. Matters were in terrible shape. The state was divided. Clement L. Vallandigham, insisting that the West-South alliance be preserved, found supporters south of the National Road, a section linked yet economically to the South. The Democrats wanted conciliation, the Republicans were uncertain. From the balcony of the Bates House, Lincoln spoke innocuously; Hoosiers considered him an impractical dreamer, and Morton tried in vain to get out of him a statement of policy. The state was broke; thieving politicians were completing the ruin begun by the canal failure. The Assembly wasted an entire session debating some five hundred resolutions on national policy which actually were already obsolete and soon were proved so.

Morton knew he had but a few months to get ready for war. He was only thirty-six; he was big and hard and determined. While Lincoln still vacillated and the debate over coercion raged, Morton said bluntly: "If it was worth a bloody struggle to establish this nation, it is worth one to preserve it." Befuddled by months of oratorical compromise, Hoosiers were not prepared for Sumter. A contemporary wrote: "The whole earth itself seemed to reel under the blow. . . . Through the long Saturday that followed . . . business houses were closed, and men with clenched fists and high beating hearts stood on the street corners and at the doors of the telegraph office. That night . . . the streets of Indiana were black with breathless multitudes. . . . When the banner appeared . . . hats were taken off, as in the presence of something sacred; and shouts beginning, it might be, brokenly and in tears, rose and swelled, and made walls and skies resound. At ten o'clock a dispatch was announced: 'Sumter has fallen.'" Next day every minister offered prayer for Lincoln and the Union. A mass meeting at Indianapolis overflowed the Courthouse, moved to the Metropolitan Theater, and spilled over into the Masonic Hall. Lincoln called for seventy-five thousand volunteers. Morton wired him: "On behalf of the State of Indiana, I tender to you for the defense of the nation, and to

uphold the authority of the government, ten thousand men."
Morton's call was posted in every village square. Indiana's quota
was 4,683; a week later twelve thousand volunteers had assembled at the fairgrounds, hastily renamed Camp Morton, at
Indianapolis. Lew Wallace greeted them as Morton's adjutant
but soon he was off to command troops in the field. Morton
called a special session of the Legislature and demanded reorganization of the militia, a law punishing treason, and a million-dollar appropriation. He got two million dollars plus everything else he asked for. Sumter had pulled the state into line
behind him. He pressed his advantage. He not only raised
troops; he armed and equipped them. He induced society ladies
to collect and knit warm garments. He deluged Lincoln and
Stanton with messages demanding more vigorous prosecution
of the war and the appointment of aggressive generals, suggest-
ing campaign plans and offering to take the field himself. He
lashed the state and nation remorselessly; he was a national
figure.

During the fall enlistments held up well; at a Winamac meeting "fiery speeches were made, patriotic airs were sung, and
beautiful ladies with bewitching smiles passed round the fatal
enlistment roll." But people began to receive the impression
that the soldiers were not enjoying their glory. Camp Morton
became a dreary prison camp. In two years 1,187 Southern
prisoners died there, including 315 of diarrhea or dysentery and
495 of pneumonia or pleurisy. A Southern girl wrote to an im-
prisoned beloved: "I will be for Jeffdavise til the tenisee river
freazes over, and then be for him, and scrach on the ice:

> *Jeffdavise rides a white horse,*
> *Lincoln rides a mule,*
> *Jeffdavise is a gentleman,*
> *Lincoln is a fule."*

The South was stubborn, casualty lists lengthened. In the fall of
1862 doubts beset the Hoosiers, old loyalties were resurrected.
Men denounced the "unjust" war. The draft was announced,
postponed, announced again. County commissioners began appropriating bonuses for volunteers, but with little result. The
Democrats, complaining that Morton was trampling on civil

liberties, carried the election, and Morton had a hostile legislature on his hands.

And now he rose to his greatest power. Now as never before, the lightning of high drama played around the Statehouse dome. He was the type of man whom Indiana has produced best—the man with the bludgeon who knew what he wanted and knew how to get it. The Assembly refused to receive his message, sought to prove he was an embezzler and to strip him of military control, and, wrangling, adjourned without appropriating any money. Forthwith Morton borrowed from county boards and banks. But not enough; and so he went to Washington and began running Indiana right out of the national treasury. He borrowed a million dollars on his personal unsecured notes from James Lanier the Madison banker who had moved to New York. All this was illegal. Did Democratic editors criticize? Morton had them jailed. Did reluctant farmers resist the draft? They were impressed. Morton's detectives and Federal marshals were everywhere. Morton, who never before had held public office, set up a military autocracy. He found justification: Southern sympathizers organized the Knights of the Golden Circle, a ritualistic secret society with a hideout near Shoals, and soon came into the open. The Knights' meeting on the Statehouse lawn in May 1863, with speeches by Vallandigham and Voorhees and Thomas Hendricks, was broken up by the cavalry, a comic-opera battle, but the invasion by Morgan's raiders a month later appeared more serious. When Morgan crossed the Ohio, Morton called on loyal people to rise, for it appeared that Morgan expected to be greeted by fifty thousand disloyal Knights. Few rose to either support or fight him as he swept across southern Indiana. Morton claimed the Knights had plotted to murder him, and a military court tried the leaders throughout his successful campaign for re-election, sentencing some to death and others to imprisonment. (Later Morton, having used them to achieve his purpose, worked hard to obtain pardons for them, and the U.S. Supreme Court, in upsetting the conviction of one, Lambdin P. Milligan, ex parte Milligan, established an important principle of American justice: the Constitution rules even in emergencies.)

As Booth gathered his conspirators on North Seventh Street

in Washington, Lincoln visited Booth's hotel near by and addressed a crowd that had assembled to watch Morton receive a rebel garrison flag captured by the 140th Indiana. Six weeks later Lincoln's body lay in state at Indianapolis. The Negroes convened to petition for suffrage. George W. Julian, a politician of national stature from Irvington, an Indianapolis suburb, demanded full suffrage; many opposed him violently; Morton tried an uneasy straddle. Julian and Schuyler Colfax pushed him hard, and in 1866 he capitulated and waved the bloody shirt. He went to the Senate in 1867, along with other of the new Republicans who had won the war. After he suffered a paralytic stroke, he delivered his vitriolic speeches seated, a crabbed, bitter man, one of the most vindictive of the radical reconstructionists. Colfax, a South Bend publisher, was elected Grant's Vice President. The Democratic majority in the Indiana Assembly balked at ratifying the Fifteenth Amendment (suffrage for former slaves); Morton locked the doors and shoved the amendment through. Morton was honest, ambitious, forceful, irreligious, primitive. By 1869 he, more than any other man, was speaking for the national administration. He had put Indiana deep into the war—he sent to war 196,363 men, that is, 74.3 per cent of Indiana's total population capable of bearing arms, more, broadly speaking, than any other Northern state. Over thirteen per cent of these died. And Morton was determined that to the victors—that is, to Indiana and the Republican Party—should belong the spoils. And they did. For thirty-five years the boys in blue got preferments, handouts, and favors—cash and political power that contributed mightily to Indiana's coming of age. Indianapolis emerged from the war a city. In 1865 two Indianapolis bankers paid income taxes on more than thirty thousand dollars each, downtown Washington Street property sold for eight hundred dollars a foot, baseball began, "the quiet town with its simple life was gone forever," and more than half the populace was new. And Indiana emerged a rising manufacturing state. The warmakers had needed big business, all they could get. The war put Indiana into business. Studebaker wagons had hauled troops and supplies. The census of 1860 showed 20,755 persons employed in Indiana manufacturing; in 1870, 133,221. Morton teamed up with the Northeastern radicals; it is entirely appropriate that today his statue on the Statehouse steps faces East, whence came railroad magnates and financiers. The middle states were no longer West, they were Midwest. Indiana was set to go. It no longer was frontier wilderness; it was a civilized state that carried weight in the Union. The forests were cleared, and on the plains capitalism took root and grew. Let us trace this rise of midland capitalism.

But before the mighty cities appeared, before the manufacturers and merchants and financiers obtained full control, the farmers cried out once more in protest. Already during the war they had complained of the speculators' monopoly in flour and pork. And as the nutcracker of railroad monopoly and postwar farm depression squeezed tighter and tighter, they rose in revolt.

Chapter 6

REVOLT ON THE FARM

Today, when the Indiana farmer enjoys a radio, an automobile, electricity, and free daily mail delivery, it is almost impossible to realize just how dreary his life was at the close of the Civil War. (Even today dirt farming is hard work, and sometimes after working for months in fair weather and wet, farmers lose a crop to frost, hail, flood, drought, or speculators.) Eighty years ago it seemed to each, and with some reason, that everyone in the world was his enemy—the storekeeper who charged him exorbitant prices, the commission man who paid him little for his produce, the railroad magnate who hoisted the freight rate high. He lived in abysmal darkness and isolation. His roads were impassable most of the year, and when he did go to the capital, or even to the county seats, people hooted at him or cheated him. He was the butt of unnumbered jokes, a despised grubber of the earth, an oaf. His wife toiled without respite. He possessed almost nothing but his farm, and usually that was mortgaged; of comforts or aids to the spirit he had almost none. Machinery performed labor in the cities but not on the farm. The farmer's methods were those of his grandfather, and if land eroded or wore out or if a bug got into the corn, well, it must be God's will.

And after the Civil War, prices fell but freight rates stayed high and so did interest rates. Restless veterans went West and raised crops that competed with their fathers' crops; prices skidded lower. Meanwhile in town the farmer beheld a boom—

bankers and railroaders, manufacturers and merchants, were bound for glory. And the farmer stood in the mud and waited for the sheriff. It was all very well for city men to write enraptured of Indiana's unrivaled agricultural resources. O. H. Smith had advised a State Fair audience: "If you are a farmer, fix your standard high. . . . Very much of the value of a farm depends upon the care you take of it. . . . See that you have good fences . . . plow deep . . . plow straight. . . . Keep the rows free from weeds and grass. . . . Treat your work animals kindly. . . ." And he had warned against liquor, cards, absence from church, and indolence. Well, they had worked hard and behaved themselves, and what had happened?

On Christmas Eve 1869 John Weir called together twenty-eight farm men and women in Honey Creek Township outside Terre Haute and told them about the National Grange of the Patrons of Husbandry, organized two years earlier by O. H. Kelly. Kelly had patterned it after the Masonic order, invented an elaborate ritual of moral lessons and various degrees (Laborer, Cultivator, Harvester, Husbandman), invited farm women to seek corresponding degrees (Maid, Shepherdess, Gleaner, Matron), and contacted local farm leaders, including Weir. But the Grange, at first nothing but a secret club designed to elevate the spirit, grew slowly. Kelly had laid the powder train; a spark was needed. The depression after 1870 provided it. Delegates to the 1874 National Grange represented a half million farmers. On March 1, 1872, Weir set up the Indiana State Grange and launched an organizing campaign. He scarcely needed to. The suffering farmers flocked to join, mobilizing for battle. This was the first revolt in the new age. All over the state they met by lamplight in farmhouses and schoolhouses and churches; their wagons churned the mud of the backroads as, emboldened, they moved into county seats and met in the courthouse. Up in northwestern Indiana a handful of rich men had drained vast swamps that the original settlers, lacking capital, could not till; here fifty-four granges sprang up in a single year. By 1873 more than four hundred local granges had been formed throughout the state. Their original objectives might have been social and educational, but one would not have guessed it if he had heard the Grangers, standing in some lonely building on a windswept hill, peering in flickering light at a songbook held rigidly before them, singing:

> A Ty-rant stalks o'er this fair land,
> And marks for his un-just op-pres-sion
> Each son of toil, whose stur-dy hand
> Creates the wealth in his pos-ses-sion:
> That Tyrant, with the mighty power
> Of gold and bonds as his do-minion,
> Bribes courts, and dic-tates laws of trade,
> And scorns to yield to just o-pin-ion.
>
> A-wake! to arms! let free-men strike
> For Jus-tice now, for Free-dom ev-er:
> Let mon-ey-kings and railway-lords
> Know *that our* will *their* rings *can sev-er.* . . .

Some of their songs pledged union with rising urban labor, but others mingled moral lessons with suspicion of the cities:

> You may drive your fast horse if you please,
> You may live in the ver-y best style;
> Smoke the choic-est ci-gars, at your ease,
> And may rev-el in pleas-ure a-while;
> Play billiards, from morning till night,
> Or loaf in the bar-room all day,
> But just see if my words are not right:
> You will find, in the end, it don't pay. . . .

In the grim mid-seventies a mortgage was no joke, although later a song like this would have delighted vaudeville comedians:

> Mary, let's kill the fatted calf and celebrate the day,
> For the last dreadful mortgage on the farm is wiped a-way.
> I've got the papers with me, they are right as right can be—
> Let's laugh and sing to-geth-er, for the dear old farm is free.
>
> I've riz up many mornin's an hour before the sun,
> And night has overtaken me before my work was done.
> When weary with my labor 'twas this tho't nerved my arm—
> Each day of toil will help to pay the mortgage on the farm.

And, Mary, you have done your part in rowin' to the shore;
By takin' eggs and butter to the little vil-lage store;
You did not spend the money in dressing up for show,
But sang from morn to even-ing in your fa-ded cal-i-co.

And Bessie, our sweet daughter—God bless her little heart,
The lad that gets her for a wife, must be, by natur', smart—
She's gone without piano, her lonely hours to charm;
To have a hand in payin' off the mortgage on the farm.

I'll build a little cottage soon to make your heart re-joice;
I'll buy a good piano to go with Bessie's voice;
You shall not make your butter with that old use up concern,
I'll go this very day and buy the finest patent churn.

Lay by your faded calico and go with me to town,
And get yourself and Bessie a new and shining gown;
Low prices for our produce need not give us now alarm,
Spruce up a little, Mary, there's no mortgage on the farm.

While our hearts are now so joyful, let us, Mary, not for-get,
To thank the God of Heaven for being out of debt;
For He gave rain and sunshine and strength in-to my arm,
And lengthened out our days to see no mortgage on the farm.

These were angry men singing. They had no great leader. Their crusade was not manipulated. These men organized themselves, spontaneously, out of toil and trouble. They were disgusted with the corrupt politicians who offered them nothing. The Crédit Mobilier scandal, enmeshing Schuyler Colfax, only justified their wrath. Casting about for a single enemy they fastened on the railroads. They protested bitterly at Vanderbilt's secret maneuvers to gain control of the key Bee Line. And then came the panic of 1873. Young people left the depressed farms and went to the city, where they walked the streets with the other jobless. Even in Indianapolis the postwar boom collapsed. Disorganized strikes occurred, and rioting. Fighting monopolistic farm-machinery manufacturers, the Indiana Grange began co-operative purchasing. "Hold your hogs," cried the farmers. Their American Cheap Transportation Society met at New York; frightened

Congressmen met at St. Louis. Jay Cooke failed; the banks called their paper; farmers lost their homes. Henry Ward Beecher denounced the farmers, saying that in the Legislature they were less honest than the rich. Money grew tighter. Grangers met at Indianapolis in the fall and came up with the "Indiana plan," which became the Greenback platform. In 1874 the Grange reached zenith in Indiana: three thousand locals, sixty thousand members. It seemed headed for enduring strength. All over the nation it was experimenting with co-operatives, even co-operative manufacture. But economic planning was ineffective or absent. (A cream co-op was set up in a section of Indiana ill adapted to dairying.) Farmers who kept books on the barn door made poor businessmen. The Grange's harvester factory in Iowa failed. Lawsuits followed. All over the country Grange members resigned, fearful they would be held personally liable. They already had begun to grumble at the national leaders. By 1878 in Indiana there were but 521 local Granges with about sixteen thousand members.

But though the Grange subsided, the ferment did not. In April 1874 President Grant vetoed the inflation bill; in June the first convention of the Greenback Party met at Indianapolis. James Buchanan, an Indianapolis lawyer and editor, called for a National Greenback Party. It was founded at Indianapolis, another heterodoxy that had its beginning in Indiana. Greenback clubs sprang up all over the state, the largest, probably, at Terre Haute. But they only confused the gubernatorial campaign, and the regular Democrats elected "Blue Jeans" Williams, an ugly, well-to-do, six-foot-four-inch farmer who said: "I just grew up between two corn rows." He was a plain man with mud on his boots and, surprisingly enough, probably the only dirt farmer ever elected Governor of Indiana. The regular politicians had discovered that the farmers' protest, which had seemed so unmanageable when voiced spontaneously by the unbossed Grange, could be dealt with after all. The pattern had been repeated, the pattern of protest swallowed by professional politicians that was cut when Jennings made shrewd use of the people's anger at Harrison's autocracy.

But the farmers' protest was voiced effectively again in the late eighties by the Farmers' Alliance and the Farmers' Mutual Bene-

69

fit Association. Ignored by the major parties, these groups sought
to make common cause. As the delegates gathered in June 1890,
a newspaper spoke of them as wayward groping children. Groping they were: they haggled longer over the liquor question than
over whether to form a third party of their own. They were
reluctant to leave the established parties. During that summer
and early fall they were in turmoil. In Daviess County the
F.M.B.A. and Knights of Labor nominated a joint county ticket.
Men at a secret meeting in Martinsville determined to organize
a co-op store. At the Rockville Fairgrounds the F.M.B.A. held a
"monster picnic"; parading farmers, led by a brass band, bore
banners reading: "United We Stand," "Equal Rights for All and
Special Favors for None," and took a half hour to pass the courthouse. The Indianapolis *Journal* might speak contemptuously of
"calamity orators," and urge earnestly that the Republican Party
"is the best farmers' party, as it is the best party for all other
classes," but these people had endured twenty years of farm depression, and the Republican Party, and the Democratic too, was
doing nothing for them, and the years of hardship showed in
their faces as they came in their wagons and on the hated railroad cars to Indianapolis in the September heat of 1890. They
gathered on the 24th in the Criminal Court room, about a hundred men determined "to hold a State convention and inaugurate
a new party." There were delegates from the Greenback and the
Union Labor parties, from the Alliance and the Grange and the
F.M.B.A.; they were nearly all farmers. The *Journal* wrote: "It
was a good-looking body of elderly people, not altogether busi-
ness-like in the conduct of deliberation." The one-legged chairman began at once: "There is something rotten in Denmark, and
the American people are becoming aware of the fact that there
is a class of legislation going on that is producing wealth on one
hand and poverty on the other." He had a powerful voice and
he cried: "When my country called me, in 1862, I left my plow
and went forth to fight her battles. I lost one leg to free four
millions of black slaves, and I have another leg I am willing to
lose to free fifty millions of white slaves." It was hot in the courtroom, and crowded. What should the name of the new party be?
The delegates all tried to talk at once—People's Industrial Party,
Farmers' and Laborers' Industrial Party, Independent Union

Party, People's Party. The chairman settled it: The People's Party. Its emblem? They voted down the rake and the hoe, they adopted the plow and the hammer, for they wanted the votes of the city masses. The platform condemned child labor, high taxes and public debts, and gifts of public money to railroads and factories by towns that wanted them. All the while Democratic politicians stood hopefully in the corridors, but the delegates nominated a state ticket of farmers, voted to take up a collection to finance the campaign (one delegate was reported, probably maliciously, to have suggested borrowing the money from the government), and adjourned. The new party polled only seventeen thousand votes that November.

But it held more dogged meetings through 1891, and Indiana sent large delegations to meetings all over the Midwest. The two major parties, balanced evenly, had become nothing but ends in themselves; only the splinter parties of protest raised the issues of the new society and they seemed about to rendezvous. The national convention of the Farmers' Alliance met at Indianapolis in November 1891 amid uncertainty. The advance guard installed itself in the Bates House and the new, turreted English Hotel. The newspapers devoted whole pages to interviews with the leaders. Rumors flew fast. A large, powerful leader said that representatives of the Rochdale co-operative in England had been invited. Would the Alliance join the new third party, the People's, that seemed to be forming? "The Alliance is much older than the third party, and elections come and go. . . . It so happened that the Cincinnati convention indorsed the Ocala demands. . . ." The Farmers' Mutual Benefit Association was meeting here at the same time across the Circle; would the two organizations join? Possibly. The national president of the Alliance arrived with his private secretary and installed himself in a comfortable suite on the second floor of the English overlooking the Circle. The Alliance leaders were "dead against Cleveland." In hotel rooms the leaders caucused, and the ornate lobbies buzzed with talk. The suave railroads had granted a one-fare rate from all points west of the Mississippi. For a week each train brought new delegates, six thousand of them, men in five-button jackets and wide-brimmed hats and beards and boots, men with small valises and drooping mustaches and slicked-down hair and round, high-crowned hats and bow ties and pleated coats, men who had been busy selling binder twine at half the monopolists' price, men from the Kansas and Texas plains, from the broad rich valleys of California and Washington State, men from all over the nation, earnest, determined men with dreams.

On November 18 the Supreme Council was called to order; it wasted a morning wrangling: Many delegates had relied on the Alliance to pay their fare home, but was the treasury not too low? The F.M.B.A. had the same problem. Delegates fingered fiat money resembling greenbacks, inscribed "certificate of production," "money in its true sense." The speakers failed to show up for a morning mass meeting at huge Tomlinson Hall but that night a hundred and fifty F.M.B.A. men massed in front of English's and marched in a body to Tomlinson Hall, and nearly eight hundred Alliance men joined them, and as they took their seats and the president of the Indiana Alliance appeared, the glee club sang: "Yes, the farmer is forgotten who supplies the wealth of all," and back at the hotel great, curious Ignatius Donnelly, a stocky man with a round young face, arrived from the Northwest and caucused with the Alliance and F.M.B.A. leaders, and by the time they went to bed the decision had been made. There would be a third party ticket in the field next year.

Next May, People's Party delegates from seventy-two Indiana counties met at Indianapolis and nominated a state ticket, declaring: "The land . . . is the heritage of the people." In July thousands of men and women streamed into Omaha, Nebraska, and held the first national convention of the Populist Party. Donnelly wrote their platform: "We meet in the midst of a Nation brought to the verge of moral, political, and material ruin. Corruption dominates . . . the people are demoralized. . . . The newspapers are largely subsidized or muzzled; public opinion silenced; business prostrated; our homes covered with mortgages; labor impoverished and the land concentrating in the hands of the capitalists. The urban workmen are denied the right of organization for self-protection; imported pauperized labor beats down their wages; a hireling standing army, unrecognized by our laws, is established to shoot them down, and they are rapidly degenerating into European conditions. . . . From the same prolific womb of governmental injustice we breed two great classes—tramps and millionaires." The Populist leaders scared the old parties mightily by announcing that their presidential candidate would be Judge Walter Q. Gresham of Indiana. He was born near Corydon, a Civil War major general, a lawyer and Federal judge who had been converted by reading Donnelly's novel *Caesar's Column.* If the Populists could steal a Republican judge, who was safe? But the Judge declined unless the nomination could be unanimous, which it could not, and the Populists nominated General James B. Weaver of Iowa, a conservative whose name already had lost its magic. The Democrats and Republicans breathed easier; here was a man who would meet them on their own ground, the ground they knew so well. General Weaver opened his campaign at Vincennes on July 20, 1892; the hostile *Journal* reported he arrived the night before "from the West" and was met by no one, that the Populists lacked a county organization at Vincennes, that the state party lacked funds. The jubilee had been advertised "by small handbills less than ten by twelve inches in size," jeered the *Journal;* the railroads had not even advertised excursion rates. Nevertheless, the next day nearly three thousand people gathered in the oppressive heat at the fairgrounds. The *Journal* said: "There are a good many who do not understand the meaning of the People's party, and the jubilee to-day was the cause of a large number of conservative people turning out to hear and see what was going on. . . . Not a sign of the stars and stripes could be seen on the entire grounds." Above the crowd mottoes hung from shade trees: "Lord Carnegie Will Not Vote For Weaver." General Weaver spoke earnestly for three hours. They passed a bushel basket, gathering, the *Journal* estimated, seventy-five dollars. Then a thunderstorm broke up the meeting, and that night General Weaver addressed a fairgrounds that was almost empty. In November the Democrats carried Indiana and the nation for Cleveland; Weaver polled twenty-two thousand in Indiana, a slight percentage gain over 1890 but less than four per cent of the total vote. The Hoosiers would not follow him; no more would the nation. The farmers' revolt was finished: It reached an orthodox dead end with Bryan in 1896, and an old Granger was elected Governor on the Republican ticket that McKinley headed.

But who cared? In the eighties the state at large had begun to cash in on the prosperity that Civil War victory had promised. Though poverty plagued the farms, the cities were rising, the factories were swelling, and the boom was on. It had begun with a roar from deep in the earth, the roar of natural gas.

Chapter 7

THE GAS BOOM

I N 1876 men boring for coal at Eaton, near Muncie, sank their diamond drill six hundred feet into the earth, and foul fumes issued forth amid awesome noises. Word spread that their drill had bitten into the roof of the devil's cave, and in dread they plugged the well. But in 1884 gas was discovered at Findlay, Ohio; immediately manufacturers flocked there and the town prospered. Hoosiers remembered the old devil's cavern, unplugged the bore, drilled 322 feet deeper, and struck gas so strong that when they channeled it through four pipes and lit it, a ten-foot flame, visible twelve miles away in Muncie, burst from each pipe. Thousands of townsfolk hurried out by buggy and wagon. They could feel the heat sixty feet from the well. They crept close to sniff the gas and announced with pleasure that its odor was not noisome.

Gas fever swept the state. Overnight, wagon salesmen and apothecaries and even farmers became wildcatters. Developments were discussed round every courthouse square. Wells were sunk everywhere without regard to geology. When gas came in, the drillers did the obvious thing: lit it. As a result towering flames burned night and day in town and country alike. Special Sunday excursion trains carried excited citizens, burdened with basket lunches and children, to the gas field. Probably nothing else ever so captured the imagination of the people of Indiana. And no wonder—here beneath their feet all these years had slumbered a giant, and now they had wakened him.

When the spectacular flambeaux blazed on the darkened countryside beside farmhouses theretofore lit only by pioneers' candles and coal-oil lamps, it was as though Indiana had suddenly burst out of her night.

And in a very real sense she had. About this same time the gas failed abruptly in Ohio, and stranded manufacturers hurried across the state line. The Indiana field lay roughly northeast of Indianapolis, with Muncie and Anderson near its center. In 1886 this was a farming section. Gas brought industry.

Signs of the new age already had appeared. Chauncey Rose, the railroader, struck oil in front of the Terre Haute House. Although iron ore was soon exhausted at Terre Haute, the ironmasters remained. The first coal mine was opened at Shelburn in 1868; geologists said coal deposits covered 6,500 square miles around Terre Haute. The Knights of Labor arose. During the great railroad strikes of 1877 (which Eugene Debs opposed), Lew Wallace laid aside his pen and once more led a company of militiamen. Robert Dale Owen died that year and so did Oliver P. Morton. The Erie Nickel Plate reached Hammond, and at South Bend James Oliver invented the chilled-steel plow. German-language newspapers were founded at Indianapolis. John Purdue and others donated two hundred thousand dollars for a university at Lafayette. Indianapolis put down its first pavements, of wood block, in 1870. Moralists across the nation denounced the Indiana divorce laws. The price of a vote in Indianapolis in 1876 was ten dollars. In 1880 Lew Wallace published *Ben Hur,* and William H. English built English's Opera House, where nearly every great actor and actress after Sarah Bernhardt appeared.

Before 1897 some 5,400 gas wells had been drilled in Indiana. Indiana's five-thousand-square-mile gas field was the nation's largest. Moreover, the flow was dependable. People thought it would last forever. At Anderson, a farming village living on memories of the canal days, citizens met in the courthouse January 25, 1887; gas had been struck at Kokomo, Marion, Noblesville, Muncie; should Anderson sit by idle? The citizens subscribed twenty thousand dollars, drilled near the Midland Railway station, and struck gas on March 31. "The people went wild with excitement" and sightseers and capitalists from all over the United States flocked to Anderson. When they dismounted from the trains at the Panhandle depot or the Big Four depot, they were confronted by a huge pine arch that spanned the street and was ornamented by flambeaux. The flame from the first well at Anderson towered a hundred feet into the night with a roar "like the running of a heavy railroad train," and for a month the people did little but gape. Finally on May 24 at another courthouse meeting, citizens organized a board of trade to deal with an inquiry from a Connecticut manufacturer as to "what inducements" Anderson was offering manufacturers to locate there. Trading in leases became brisk. Sidewalk superintendents watched the laying of mains angrily: rumors had arisen that Standard Oil was secretly behind the enterprise, and a newspaper prophesied darkly that Anderson would end in the hands of "the Octopus." A rival Citizens' Company was formed and, presumably, the secret agents of the Octopus withdrew in the night.

Even well-laid pipe lines leaked in cold weather, and explosions resulted. In 1888 a store proprietor on North Main Street smelled gas, went to the cellar, lit a match, and the gas exploded. Frequently citizens were wakened by dull booming explosions and, rising to follow after the horse-drawn fire trucks, gazed disconsolately upon a clutter of gingerbread and bric-a-brac. The When Block, symbol of Anderson's growth, was wrecked. An explosion in a house was heard two miles away, but marvelous to the pious, the Baptist church directly across the street was undamaged.

In a shower of rocks big as hens' eggs, workmen fought to control a gusher at Hartford City; fifty million feet of gas were escaping daily and "There are grave doubts about the workmen's ability to 'pack' the monster." On December 14, 1890, the Indianapolis *Journal* reported that Elwood was "the gem city of the natural-gas belt" and said capitalists were expected that week from Cincinnati, Indianapolis, Logansport, and Columbus and Coshocton, Ohio. Elwood gave a tin-plate company fourteen acres on the Kidwell farm beside the well "Vesuvius"; the company sent its lawyer out to Elwood, and soon his son, Wendell Willkie, was born there, February 18, 1892.

By 1893 some three hundred million dollars had been invested in factories in Indiana; about three hundred factories had been built directly because of gas. A historian wrote: "The efforts of the genii of old have been fairly eclipsed."

When in 1886 the well at Eaton was rebored, Muncie, a farm town, was changed forever. A few months later a syndicate of capitalists bought real estate worth $150,000, and soon people were talking of Muncie as the "Birmingham of the North"; nobody resisted the change or doubted its value. The *News* rhapsodized:

> *Tell me not in mournful numbers*
> *That the town is full of gloom,*
> *For the man's a crank who slumbers*
> *In the bursting days of boom.*

Houses were scarce, rents rising fast. One evening in the lobby of the Kirby House a newcomer complained he couldn't find a ground-floor office. Up spoke James Boyce and asked how much rent he'd pay. He said sixty dollars. Boyce pointed to a good vacant lot across the street and said: "Gentlemen, if you will rent the rooms I will have a brick building there in a week's time." He worked his men all day and by gas light all night and within the week he had erected a brick building with a ninety-six-foot front and six rooms for stores, each with a handsome plate-glass window. The Indianapolis *Journal* described Muncie as a "thriving city of eight thousand people. Though small, it is metropolitan. Here are the essential conveniences of the largest American cities, without their dust, disease and foul air. The Muncie citizen orders his groceries by telephone, his residence is lighted by artificial gas, his place of business by electric light, having choice of both systems, the Brush and Edison incandescent, his meals are cooked by natural gas; there is a good fire department and the Gamewell fire alarm system; he has three railroads, and will soon have an electric line of cable street railway; there is a first-class system of water works . . . sewerage and clean macadamized streets . . . public schools that have no superior in the state . . . a free public library. . . ." And all this in a few months. Home town pride swelled mightily. The Muncie *News* of April 12, 1887, said: "Speculators expected to find in Muncie an Indiana village like Portland, Anderson or

New Castle, with a sickly natural gas flame as a curiosity," and reported that one astonished visitor said: "Why this is not a Hoosier village, but an Indiana city."

Inevitably Muncie attracted criminals and prostitutes. By 1890 Muncie had at least a score of whorehouses, and in each from four to eight girls practiced. Moralists complained that respectable men fathered bastards by loose women. In 1900 a drummer reported that a High Street theater surpassed the Bowery in New York "for downright lewdness and immorality." A local historian noted: "The 'quart shops,' low dives and other haunts of vice flourished without check . . . deemed . . . a necessary part of industrial prosperity . . . moral forces . . . had not increased apace with the material expansion. . . ."

Of all the factories that came to Muncie the most important, by any standard, was the glass factory of the Ball brothers. Their career—and it is paralleled by many others in Indiana though usually on a lesser scale—is the story of the rise of midland American capitalism, not transplanted, but a native growth. The Ball brothers were descended from an Englishman who came to the American colonies about a hundred and forty years before the War for Independence. Their father was a restless inventive farmer and trader, not notably successful. Their mother, a strong God-fearing woman, taught them to help each other, a doctrine they never forgot. They were born between 1850 and 1862 in this order: Lucius Lorenzo, William Charles, Edmund B., Frank C., and George A.

When their father died in 1878, Edmund and Frank C. began manufacturing at Buffalo, New York, small wooden tubs for fish packers. The other brothers joined them. The factory burned. They started anew, making metal kerosene cans. They began making the cans out of glass encased in metal. Soon they were also manufacturing fruit jars. Natural gas was discovered in Indiana. Fuel was a major factor in glassmaking. Moreover, the Midwest market for glass jars was growing. The Balls visited perhaps a dozen communities. Each had a newly formed and useful board of trade (later many of them became little but employers' associations designed to hold down wages). It is said that Muncie gave the Balls free fuel, $5,000 cash, and some land to locate there. George A. Ball has said that Muncie's gas

promised to last and "perhaps Muncie had a better selling
crowd." The Ball brothers built a plant on a seven-acre cornfield
on the edge of Muncie and got into production in 1888. F. C.
Ball was president, Edmund vice-president and general manager, William secretary, George A. treasurer, and Lucius director
(but Lucius devoted most of his time to medicine). They stacked
the jars in the field like cordwood to await summer shipment.
The only other sizable factory in Muncie made bentwood products; it folded up when the wood was gone and carriages became outmoded. The Balls gobbled up one tract of property
after another until they owned seventy acres. News of their
success spread. Soon almost every town had its factory making
hand-blown glass. Windfall, Ingalls, Yorktown, Upland, had
visions of rivalling Muncie, Anderson, and Marion. But, as
George Ball has said: "When the time came that they had to put
in enough money to buy some machinery, they just closed up
their doors and went back to farming. They hadn't bought anything but some moulds."

The Balls were among the first to foresee the failure of gas.
While prodigals still burned flambeaux, they installed control
valves. Before long they employed more people than anybody
in Muncie.

After the gas grew weak at Muncie they built factories at new
gas fields in Kansas and in Texas; they established plants in
Illinois and Oklahoma; they built or bought a paper mill and a
corrugating plant and a zinc mill and a short railroad. They
diversified—banks, real estate, a retail store, newspapers, a
brewery, oil in Texas, oil pipe in Pennsylvania. Frank C. became
a director of the Federal Reserve Bank of Ohio and of the Borg-
Warner Corporation of Chicago. George A. became chairman of
the Merchants National Bank of Muncie and a director of the
Merchants Trust Company, Banner-Whitehill Furniture Company, Kuhner Packing Company, Borg-Warner; he invested
heavily in the Great Lakes Portland Cement Company, the In-
tertype Corporation, the Dictaphone Corporation, and others.
Edmund became a director of some traction companies, Warner
Gear Company, Durham Manufacturing Company, Merchants
Bank and Trust. And so on—the list grew longer and longer.
Theirs was a family enterprise. Their leader seems to have been

"Mr. F. C.," a rather impressive man, with high forehead and soft curling mustache. After two of the brothers died in the 1920's, he and George A. were the active ones. Their activities engaged the attention of Congressional committees investigating patents, holding companies, and other aspects of the concentration of economic power. One brother became a Republican national committeeman, another was mentioned as a possible candidate for Governor or Senator, at least one contributed to the Liberty League that opposed Roosevelt's New Deal.

But although they expanded beyond Muncie they retained their weighty influence there. It was a pervasive influence, extending almost everywhere. They employed Muncie's best legal talent. They bought the largest department store in town. They held controlling or large interests in many of the city's manufacturing plants, sometimes through their banks, and businessmen trembled at their displeasure. They built large homes on Minnetrista Boulevard overlooking White River, and ambitious matrons persuaded their husbands to move to that end of town. They owned the preferred stock of the town's largest newspaper. Did a new member of the Chamber of Commerce have a project in mind? The secretary would have to see what Mr. F. C. had to say. Did the mayor propose a major project? Of course the Balls would be consulted. And in latter years their children, their sons-in-law, and other relatives gained money and influence.

Their word carried weight if only because they were enormously successful. They set the pace, the example; perhaps if one acted like them one might actually become like them. Their influence increased most during the 1930's. Were old idols crumbling? On the eve of the bank holiday the newspaper announced: "Ball Brothers Guarantee Sufficient Cash to Meet Needs of 3 Muncie Banks." Not only that, but the Balls kept old employees on the payroll and in other ways aided the townspeople. Their fruit-jar business prospered, for housewives everywhere turned to home canning: It was cheaper, it occupied their jobless husbands. Of course, this was not immediately apparent, and the Balls' prosperity in the midst of ruin seemed little short of miraculous. And it was a dramatization of this success which gave George A. Ball national prominence. For one day in 1935

Ball, with a Cleveland man, stepped up and bid three million dollars cash for control of the vast railroad empire of the Van Sweringen brothers, who had mortgaged it to Morgan bankers. Wall Street was amazed at a man from Muncie—or from anywhere else—who in those troubled times could come up with three million dollars cash, and on the streets of Muncie Hoosiers chuckled that old George A. had outfoxed the Morgans. And a Senator subsequently remarked that Ball and his associate had got control of twenty-three thousand miles of railroad for "about the price of two first-class locomotives." Moreover, Ball had obtained a key position in American holding-company finance. He probably had intended for the Van Sweringens to resume control. But they died, and he was left with the Chesapeake & Ohio, Nickel Plate, Erie, Missouri Pacific, and lesser railroads as well as terminals, warehouses, bus lines, coal companies, and other enterprises. To control them Ball had formed a super-holding company, Midamerica Corporation. Senators Burton K. Wheeler and Harry S. Truman later described Midamerica as "a mere portable convenience which could be taken along by a businessman on a trip, as one takes a traveling bag." Its first directors' meeting was held in a New York hotel room, its second in the same room, and its final meetings in another room. In testifying about this before the Senate subcommittee, Frank B. Bernard, a flinty, dogged Muncie banker and Ball's financial adviser, proved a difficult witness. Senators Wheeler and Truman concluded that Federal legislation was needed to regulate or abolish railroad holding companies. They also investigated Ball's disposal of the railroads. Bernard was anxious that Ball, who was then about seventy-five, should sell. But the Federal income tax on his profit would be enormous. (Subsequently, the profit proved to be about five million dollars, though this was reduced after litigation.) And the residue would be subject to high inheritance taxes. "For the solution of these tax problems," reported the Senators, "another holding company was formed by Mr. Ball." This was the George and Frances Ball Foundation; its purposes were stated as "religious, educational, and charitable." To it Ball donated his Midamerica common, stipulating that if future Indiana tax laws should be unsatisfactory, the Foundation might flee. The Senators reported: "A large profit has been realized, but no income tax will be paid on it. No inheritance tax will be paid. . . . These losses to the Government result from the creation of a charitable, educational, and religious corporation. That corporation is completely dominated by [Ball]. The corporation is not obligated to distribute very much of its funds. . . . In consequence, the man who controls it may still be able to exercise the power which control of these nontaxable millions of dollars confers. . . . While the charitable . . . purposes were not being served, the public charitable . . . purposes the tax would have furthered are . . . also not being served; or other taxpayers are obliged to pay more. . . ." By 1946 the Foundation had made no large gift. However, to most people in Muncie it appeared just another Ball charity, cast on a grand scale. Earlier the Balls had bought the moribund Eastern Indiana Normal University at Muncie, endowed it richly, and presented it to the state of Indiana; today it is named Ball State Teachers College. They gave a million to Indiana University, two million to a general hospital for Muncie, a half million to the Riley Memorial Hospital for Children at Indianapolis, other large sums to the Masonic Temple Building Association, the Y.M.C.A. and the Y.W.C.A., the American Legion, all at Muncie, to colleges elsewhere and to other good works. They became college trustees, they received honorary degrees (but "Dr. F. C." never replaced "Mr. F. C.") and honors from the Knights Templar and Scottish Rite; a memorial statuary group, "Beneficence," was erected in their honor (although unseemly rumors about its instigation were printed). Unquestionably their philanthropies are among the most extensive of any family in Indiana.

It is certainly not possible now to render final judgment on whether the Balls' influence on Muncie has been beneficial or baleful, and it may never be possible, at least not until archeologists investigate American capitalism. About all one can do is report the opinions of some Muncie people.

Most Muncie people are eager to attest the Balls' "democracy." The Lynds located a man who repeated fondly how one of the Balls borrowed an overcoat for a party in 1889 because he didn't want to buy a new one when he was just starting in business. Another man recalls: "E. B. Ball was the most democratic of them all, he'd be walking through the plant and see a fellow trying to tighten something with a wrench and he'd stop and help him." Muncie people are fond of pointing out that "G. A. and his wife and daughter go to the early show at the Rivoli just like anybody else," of telling how G. A., though past eighty, comes to work every day and uses a plain office with an old-fashioned roll-top desk and works in his shirt sleeves and has been known to take an upper berth in a Pullman car. "They were just like us when they started out," young businessmen will tell you, for the Balls represent the American dream come true.

Although at one time or another wild tales have circulated concerning members of the younger generation, the original brothers lived lives above reproach, and almost no malicious gossip has touched them, a remarkable thing when one considers their conspicuous wealth. They are described only as honest Christian gentlemen who believe without hypocrisy that unrestricted free enterprise for manufacturers, great profits, low wages, and large munificence constitute the best possible social system.

There can be no doubt, however, that many people in Muncie resent the Balls. One man said: "I doubt if there's a man cashes a paycheck in this town that they don't take a cut of it one way or another." People seem to resent the Balls simply "because they are tired of hearing about them." A newcomer to Muncie is quickly struck by a monument on the bridge, a plaque on the Legion home, and other testaments to their munificence. Indeed, newcomers appear to resent them more than older residents, who have become inured. People will tell you: "They run the town," "They may not come out in the open but if they're against something they can kill it," and so on. George A. Ball is inclined to ascribe this to jealousy of the Balls' success, which he professes to find difficult to understand. Reminded that some people resent his family, he has said: "Sure—some people in Muncie are crazy too."

A widespread tale says that the Balls once used their influence to discourage other manufacturers from locating in Muncie, for fear they might compete for control or might raise wages. Muncie union leaders long considered the Ball company their greatest antagonist. It was the last major Muncie concern to sign a contract with the CIO. A reporter who interviewed George A. Ball on business conditions at the time of the Van Sweringen deal quoted him as saying: "Business recovery is solid. . . . It will absorb a large part of the present unemployed. But there will always be some unemployed and some discontented people. There always have been and always will be." Union leaders believe this controverts the evidence (his benevolence) that he possesses a sensitive social conscience. Other persons believe, however, that any Muncie citizen in need can always get a job at Balls'.

Few American small manufacturing cities have been locally controlled so late as Muncie. A widely held Muncie view is: "I don't see what General Motors does for the town—they just take money out. The Balls take it too, but at least they give it back." By 1946 their strength seemed to be waning. Subsidiaries of General Motors and other factories had come (bringing labor unions with them) and the Ball glass works was no longer the largest employer in town, though it did a thirty-million-dollar business annually. Muncie had grown larger, too large, perhaps, for single-handed control. Moreover, George A. Ball was the only one of the original brothers still alive, and, grown old, he had abandoned many of his former activities. One man, perhaps the most promising member of the younger generation, had been killed suddenly. The future of the Ball interests appeared somewhat uncertain. One effect of their control—or was it due to general conditions of American capitalism?—was the absence of rising young entrepreneurs: The bright young men of Muncie, like the imported managers, were working not for themselves, but for somebody else, either Ball or another. In 1946 George A. Ball still ran his glass factory. The offices had been modernized with teletype machines and soundproofed ceiling, but the floor was tile, the outside walls were high and red, and George Ball's office was unpretentious and on its walls hung ancient pictures of his family. He was a tall, thin, erect man with bushy white eyebrows and a white brush of a mustache; he moved vigorously, his voice was resonant, his eyes could flash in sudden anger and he had the manner of one unaccustomed to having his wishes disregarded. (Nevertheless, even when his temper flared he might unexpectedly appear amused.) He collected books and belonged to a number of clubs; he had flown and traveled and sent his daughter to Vassar. He remembered clearly the details of old business deals, but he most enjoyed talking about his early years in Muncie. He talked about them with a trace of regret, for he thought: "The town hasn't changed so much, in a way, but the people have changed. Their ideas of living have changed. There's more carelessness, people aren't as serious as they used to be, they're more happy-go-lucky. There's less recognition—" frowning quickly, ominously "—of other people's rights than there used to be." He was eighty-three years old. "I don't know. When it was a town of five thousand I felt I knew everybody in town. Now I don't know anybody. There are so many new faces."

A few scoffers had said the gas wouldn't last ten years, and in truth it didn't last twenty. The 1891 legislature forbade the burning of flambeaux; during the winter of 1905 gas heat failed even at Muncie, and shortly thereafter gas gave out almost everywhere. Alexandria and Elwood declined; Matthews, a gas-lit boom town between Muncie and Marion, today is nothing but a brick street. None the less, few major factories left the state. No new gas field was discovered immediately elsewhere, and, moreover, new cities were rising, the Midwest was booming, and Indiana was the heart of the Midwest. The gas failure didn't matter; by then nothing could stop Indiana.

PART FOUR

The Golden Age

Chapter 8

THE BEST YEARS, THE BEST
PLACE

MANY FARMERS were moving to the hamlets, and hamlet dwellers were moving to the towns, and townsfolk were moving to the cities. Every town felt a great yearning to be called a city. Between 1890 and 1910 Madison and New Albany were replaced as leading cities by new manufacturing towns like Terre Haute, Brazil, Muncie, Anderson, Indianapolis, Evansville, Fort Wayne, South Bend, Gary, by new coal towns like Clinton and Linton, by the new stone-quarry centers, Bedford and Bloomington. Here was the new market hungry for manufactures. Up at Whiting, a tiny hamlet in the Calumet district, Standard Oil built the world's largest refinery, the first step in transforming desolate dunes and swamps into Indiana's greatest industrial region, and one of the nation's greatest. Inland Steel came to East Chicago. Oil, ignored by the gas seekers, started a fresh boom. Electric interurban lines crisscrossed Indiana, competing with steam railroads before the automobile arrived. An 1885 law provided for good highways, needed so long. On March 31, 1880, a journalist reported, Wabash, Indiana, became the first electrically lighted city in the world. Many cities commenced to pave their streets, and arc lights sputtered bravely where flambeaux had blazed. The Indianapolis *Journal* published two or three columns daily on "Affairs of the Railroads." A historian had written in 1876: "In regard to population, wealth, progress, enterprise, commerce, manufactures, agricul-

ture, intelligence, the State of Indiana . . . is in all senses, a
First Rate State." And indeed so it seemed, now in the late
1880's and the 1890's: Indiana's golden age was at hand.

At bottom, the golden age was the age of capitalism. New
industry brought prosperity. Where men had found forests they
had built factories that made them rich, and everybody thought
the wealth was going to flow out to the rest of the people. No
wonder they were proud. But the golden age was much more
than a matter of manufacturing statistics. It was an era of good
feeling, of good living. The golden age meant a way of life, a
cast of mind. It meant a Hoosier who was proud of his own
success and his neighbor's success and his town's success, a man
who was confident of the future, a man who sometimes shrewdly
wore the cloak of rusticity the better to conceal his schemes.
The rude backwoodsman had come to greatness, just as he had
known he would; he had confounded those who jibed at him.
And all this is the Indiana idea, the idea that people elsewhere
hold of Indiana and the Indiana character; it arose during these
golden years.

Pioneer hardships were ended, enlightenment and culture
were suddenly ready to hand. Delighted with invention and
prosperity, the people indulged huge appetites; they dined well
and drank well, and every man had many friends and time for
pleasure. Even material decline did not dismay them. Down at
Brookville the mill whose abandonment had seemed disastrous
became a picturesque subject for painters. The canal's commercial failure had seemed catastrophic; but now young men
rented boats at the old mill and rowed their sweethearts a mile
upstream to the locks at Boundary Hill, and in the winter they
went ice skating on the turning basin below the town. True,
dreary abandoned stone houses up the creek banks told the
stories of discouraged sons, but at Christmas time the dance in
the Brookville Town Hall was the greatest ever. True, the wild
pigeons no longer roosted up at Yellowbank so thick they broke
the tree limbs, but there still were plenty of squirrels and quail,
and any farmer could put a net across a stream and get a wagonload of fish.

Those were wonderful times for children. Full of thoughts of
ghosts, they would climb through the basement window of the

Waltz mansion, an enormous white house built by a distiller; they would pull themselves upstairs on the dumb-waiter and wander through the vast, gloomy ballroom, through dusty bedrooms and drawing-rooms. In those days a boy's mother would say: "Come on, we're going visiting," and they'd spend all day at a neighbor's house, the mother chatting while her son played: People were neighborly. One man recalls: "Why I remember when I was a kid, an old lady lived here in town, her husband worked at the mill and he was always going off on a spree, and mother'd send me down to help her out, she was like Old Aunt Mary that Riley wrote about, she was a grand old lady, she had cookies and everything, they tasted so good I never did find any cookies like that anywhere. And I suppose Riley got into something like that when he was a kid."

Old John Hillenbrand, a German from Cincinnati, had settled over at Batesville and cut the hardwood and run a sawmill; when the railroad came he cut ties and supplied wood for fuel. He went into the hardware business and the furniture business until soon the Hillenbrands and Romwebers owned just about everything worth owning at Batesville, as they do to this day. They own the bank and the newspaper and Batesville real estate, farms and timber and the only hotel; they gave the town a country club, park, library, high school, gymnasium, swimming pool, sewage system, electric lights; they took care of employees who got sick or grew old; they made little fuss or show, and everyone was a bit surprised when one died and left an estate of forty million dollars. And yet was not that proof once more that any poor boy could get rich? There was such proof aplenty in Indiana. The story of pioneer enterprise, huge profits, tight control, and large benevolence, all coming to flowering in this golden age, could be told many times.

People pulled for the old home town, boosterism was meaningful. When the gas failed, Marion seemed certain to become again nothing but a crossroads trading center. A glass factory folded up; so did others. Jobless men who had flocked to town sat silent on the courthouse curbing; a third of the boom-time population departed; the new brick street, wide enough for a city of a hundred thousand, mocked bright dreams. Storekeepers, bankers, lawyers, and others had invested in the town's future. Now grimly they met. Well, cash inducements and advertising had lured industries here once. Dubiously they raised about a hundred thousand dollars. And their cash brought new industry; and before long Marion was, as it is today, among the state's busiest industrial cities.

In these hopeful years where two new roads crossed at a hamlet or a road met the railroad, a town arose. Optimistic businessmen built "business blocks," the pride of the home folks, with shining mansards and glistening lightning rods. A whole new layer of architecture was superimposed on the layer of squat buildings with grinning gargoyles built after the Civil War, so that today, strolling slowly down Main Street, past yet a third layer (of shiny glass brick), one feels like an archeologist stripping a civilization layer by layer. Up on the bank of the Tippecanoe River, Winamac, a farm town, boasted in 1883 five dry-goods stores, sixteen groceries, five hardware stores, three furniture stores, eight milliners, two merchant tailors, two photographers, seven restaurants, together with ten lawyers and eleven dentists and doctors. The only industries were a lumber-yard, a planing mill, and a grain elevator, but who needed industry?—the soil was rich. As befitted a town of dignity the town trustees in 1881 passed a resolution extending Winamac's sympathy to President Garfield's "stricken family." A plan was afoot to raise eight thousand dollars to aid the projected Fort Wayne & Pacific Railroad—the name alone reared dreams of grandeur.

These years, the late eighties and the nineties and the early years of the new century, were the best years, and Indianapolis the best place. Here were the fine restaurants, the celebrated bars; here were the brawl and bustle of commerce and industry; here were the magnificent buildings constructed with little regard to cost; here ready to hand were the inventors' marvels; here were fashionable ladies and gentlemen, some of them famous everywhere, riding around the Circle in handsome carriages; here were literature, music, and art, and here sin beckoned from a narrow doorway; here, in short, was a farm boy's new and shining dream world. Yes indeed.

The city's appearance alone was pleasing. English's Hotel was only the first building to accommodate itself to the arc of the Circle; others soon followed, massive stone piles, until almost any segment vaguely evoked schoolbook pictures of the Colosseum, curved and graceful. Early cobblestone pavements had been rough and sloppy, wood block had rotted, a material called "Vulcanite" had turned so sticky in the summer that people called it the "Yucatan pavement." In January 1890, twenty-seven business and professional men formed the Commercial Club, held a paving exposition at Tomlinson Hall, badgered the mayor and City Council, and agitated for a new city charter to enable the city to deal better with its paving and other problems. Through the summer the citizens met nightly in a hot little office on Market Street to draw the charter, repairing afterwards to the drug store in the Halcyon Block to refresh themselves "with soft drinks only." The Legislature granted the new charter, and soon workmen were laying brick, wood block, and asphaltum pavements in profusion; almost as rapidly other workmen were tearing them up to lay water mains, gas mains, streetcar rails, sewers. A forest of telephone and electric light poles sprang up, and in the Mile Square around the Circle the wires were so thick they resembled an awning. Agitation for a new waterworks was constant. Mayor Denny in 1888 denounced the use of mule-drawn streetcars as "cruel and disgraceful." Horses once hitched in front of stores were stabled in livery barns. Sunlight invaded gloomy parlors, shiny horsehair upholstery gave way to bright fabrics, metal bedsteads appeared, base burners became more resplendent than ever. Parades were almost everyday occurrences on Washington Street, which was a hundred and twenty feet from curb to curb. Meridian Street south of Washington to the tracks was uproarious with the clatter of freight wagons and the cries of teamsters; farther south dwelt the working people. North Meridian Street was a peaceful thoroughfare lined with mansions surrounded by spacious lawns and approached by carriage drives, and here, and on Delaware and other streets, dwelt the rising business class that ran the city.

The idea for the Commercial Club was William Fortune's, a *News* writer; the leadership was Colonel Eli Lilly's, a Civil War veteran whose chemist's shop was becoming a pharmaceutical laboratory of national renown. A newspaperman and a businessman—how often that combination has operated in Indiana. The

93

club published influential brochures on civic projects and on the great G.A.R. encampment of 1893, when the bepennoned S.S. *Kearsarge* was drawn up on the Statehouse lawn. The Commercial Club raised $50,000, borrowed $125,000 more, and erected an eight-story clubhouse on Meridian Street, and here at noontime dined three hundred business leaders and men who expected to become business leaders.

Indianapolis drew fewer Europeans than many Midwest cities, but she had a large German colony, and the history of the Indianapolis Maennerchor went back to 1854 and that of the Turngemeinde even farther; in 1898 the $175,000 Das Deutsche Haus was completed, one of the finest German clubhouses in America. The first Germans who came as a result of the 1848 revolution were cultured intellectuals; later came aggressive storekeepers. Clemens Vonnegut's hardware store prospered greatly, and so did Henry Schnull's grocery business.

The stores on Washington Street contained marvels of all sorts—custom-made shirts at Paul H. Krauss's, custom-made suits at Kahn Tailoring ("Makers of the Kind of Clothes Gentlemen Wear"), imported toys and china and cut glass and sterling silver and cutlery at Charles Mayer's, high-priced clocks and bronzes and diamonds and pottery at Julius C. Walk & Son's. George J. Marott's shoe store was one of the largest and handsomest in the nation. The merchants were full of "git up and go." They paid the railway fare of customers from a hundred miles away. For weeks in 1875 the newspapers carried a half-page ad: "*When?*", and then for more weeks: "*When* Will It Open?" When it finally did open, it was the When clothing store; John T. Brush, its proprietor, was an early practitioner of public relations. If a boy bought a suit, John Brush gave him a baseball and a bat, and John Brush hired some musicians and decked them out in resplendent uniforms, and on Saturday nights they played on the portico of the When Building, and nearly everybody in town came down to stand in Pennsylvania Street and listen. Brush became interested in Indianapolis's baseball team, then a member of the National League, and developed several renowned players; he bought control of the Cincinnati Reds and, finally, of the New York Giants.

Large crowds attended the baseball games in the park on

Capitol Avenue. Any sporting event drew crowds. To be sure, only men attended the bare-knuckle fights in the smoky clubs, and mainly sporting men at that; but ladies took up tennis and archery and, a little later, bicycling. Old residents say that Indianapolis "went bicycle crazy" in the nineties. Bicycle manufacturing was a million-dollar industry in Indianapolis by 1900. On holidays cyclists swarmed everywhere, many wearing knickerbockers or the brilliant uniforms of the Zig Zag Club or other cycle clubs. They cycled to Cincinnati, and a "century run," a hundred-mile trip, was a good Sunday's outing.

There was always plenty to do. You could cycle along the shaded canal towpath; you could sit on the lawn and listen to music at the boulder bandstands in the parks, drink beer or wine in the German gardens, visit the zoo at Riverside Park, take a ride on the steamer *Sunshine* on White River at Broad Ripple Park or on one of the launches on the canal at Fairview Park. The interurban company that owned Broad Ripple Park installed dance pavilions, box ball and bowling alleys, a cafe, a bandshell. On a hot Sunday afternoon, the rowboats on the river were little more than oar's length apart, the young men in suspenders and straw hats dawdling at the oars, their ladies in shirt-waist dresses and flowered hats holding parasols against the summertime sun. On Memorial Day you took a boat from the waterworks boathouse on the canal at the Yellow Bridge up to Golden Hill and then walked through the fields to Crown Hill Cemetery; in this peaceful domain slept Oliver P. Morton, a great force spent.

Indianapolis was a good road-show town. The *Journal* reported on September 12, 1890: "No sort of weather can prevent Julia Marlowe from having audiences in Indianapolis." The leading theaters were English's and the Grand but a man could find anything he wanted—melodrama at the Park, once the Metropolitan where Joe Jefferson had played but in the nineties a "10–20–30 house"; pretentious burlesque at the Empire at Wabash and Delaware streets where Weber & Fields and, later, Sophie Tucker appeared. Indianapolis became a main-line stop on the Keith-Orpheum circuit. And it had its own Dramatic Club, too: When it opened its 1890 season with *Engaged* at the residence of J. H. Baldwin, its well-to-do young cast included

95

Booth Tarkington. In 1891 William Forsyth and Theodore C. Steele, who with other artists had painted the leading men and the most picturesque scenes of Indiana and had been dubbed the "Hoosier Group" by Hamlin Garland, opened the Indiana School of Art in the old Beecher Church on the Circle.

For years, despite the farmers' market on the first floor and the truck gardeners' stands in surrounding streets, cavernous Tomlinson Hall was the great musical showplace. The G.A.R. sponsored the first May Music Festival there in 1886 to help raise the monument fund, and thereafter to Tomlinson came the Metropolitan Opera orchestra, Sousa's Band, and great singers. Later the Mystic Shrine of Masonry erected the Murat Temple, faced with brick and terra cotta, its minaret topped by an astonishing scimitar, crescent, and star. Masonry's Grand Lodge of Indiana had been organized in 1818, and by the nineties its pageantry sometimes seemed to dominate the Indianapolis scene. Masons, Odd Fellows, Red Men, Knights of Pythias, Royal Arcanum, Knights and Ladies of Honor, Elks, Woodmen, Harugari, Ancient Order of Druids, Ancient Order of Hibernians, Knights of Columbus, B'nai B'rith—almost everybody belonged to something—Hoosiers are joiners. The ritual of the Tribe of Ben Hur was based on Wallace's book. The old General, full of honors, helped organize it, and it managed to get his statue placed alongside Oliver P. Morton's in the national statuary hall at Washington. When Scottish Rite degrees were conferred in 1891, the *Journal* reported that costumes and paraphernalia had cost four thousand dollars. On November 10, 1891, more than a hundred church ladies met at the Propylaeum to form a council of women: "At the appointed hour," the *Journal* reported gallantly, the chairman "entered and called the ladies to order. A mere formality, as the ladies were in the most beautiful order." There was much interest in "hypnotism or mesmerism" and spiritualism. The *Journal* of December 15, 1890, described a trance into which one Ruth Hughes entered: "She said she was in heaven, and talked with the Savior. . . . She also saw former acquaintances burning in the fiery furnaces of hell, but would give no names. . . . The audience could not be gotten out of the church tonight until the lights were darkened, compelling thousands to look for their wives and children with matches. A whisky-flask was thrown through a window, badly injuring Mrs. George Lamb, a lady in the audience, who was hit in the face. Miss Hughes will finish her vision when she regains consciousness."

At a gospel temperance meeting in Y.M.C.A. Hall, a speaker said: "If prohibition confines itself to trying to close the [saloon] door what is to become of the poor fellow who cannot go by it?" and the state's Lieutenant Governor said: "My heart is deeply stirred. . . . On my way here to-night I saw a poor woman, much too thinly clad for this cold weather, watching near a saloon door for her husband to coax him home. And this made me more determined than ever to hear Francis Murphy." Francis Murphy the evangelist said: "This is a beautiful school-house and Christ is to give us some lessons. He is a kind schoolmaster. The schoolmaster I went to was not that kind. His name was Savage, and he was one. We don't want any more savages; we want civilized people." Another speaker recited:

> *At the punch-bowl's brink*
> *Let the man stop and think;*
> *As they say in Japan,*
> *First the man takes a drink,*
> *Then the drink takes a drink,*
> *Then the drink takes the man.*

The evangelist "closed with an exhortation for signers, and quite a number put on the blue ribbon."

However, the scattered German beer gardens and working-men's saloons enjoyed brisk patronage, and so did the downtown wine rooms. The Levee was a gaudy free-wheeling center of sporting life. It extended north on Illinois Street from the Union Station and across Washington a couple of blocks, with gambling houses trickling off into Market and Ohio. At Washington and Illinois stood the Bates House, its cuisine for a time famed nationally. Shaffer's restaurant was termed the Delmonico's of the West, and Richard Stegemeier arrived to open a restaurant. Perhaps the most elegant cafe was the Circle Park, with massive mahogany columns and ornate, gold-leafed ceiling. North of the Bates House in the Windsor Block was Chapin & Gore's saloon, dispenser of fine whiskies and cigars. In the same Block the

Marceau & Power photographic gallery made wonderful portraits of actresses and Presidents, and if they displayed a society girl's picture in their window, her fame as a reigning beauty of the town was assured. Across the street was Billy Tron's saloon and a gambling house and a row of lesser saloons. South of Washington Street on Illinois, Pop June, a white-bearded patriarch descended from seafaring Yankees, ran the Shell Oyster Bay and Marine Inn. Customers heard many times the tales of how earlier Junes kept famous inns down East, of how one June had been selected to row Lafayette ashore, of how another had imported the first elephant to the United States and taken him on tour, traveling by night and exhibiting him in the tavern barns by day. The Levee was thronged nightly with men in hard hats and gaudy vests and large diamonds, gambling men from St. Louis and Chicago. Levee legends abounded. One midnight a traveler wakened in his room in a little hotel near the Union Station and saw by moonlight a black-bearded man with a red bandanna wound round his head asleep in the other bed. A new arrival, apparently; the hotel was crowded. The traveler went back to sleep. By daylight he saw that what he had supposed was a red bandanna actually was a white handkerchief soaked in blood, which also had stained the pillow and the stranger's beard. The traveler hurried to the door. It was locked. How had the stranger entered? The traveler turned to waken him. But he had disappeared. So had the bloodstain on the pillow. The traveler hastened to the landlord. He fearfully admitted that a bearded man had been killed a week earlier in a brawl in the hotel barroom over a woman or a gambling debt and that for the sake of silence the landlord had permitted the brawlers to bury the body in the yard behind the hotel. And Anton Scherrer who tells the legend maintains that years later excavators found a skeleton in the yard.

Indianapolis's first hack stand had been down at the south end of the Levee near the station. The saloons, restaurants, hotels, and resorts of pleasure there trapped most of the tired drummers who hit town, until the fancier Bates and Occidental hotels sent runners to meet the trains. The most elegant bawdy-house in town was Queen Mab's, where the girls were said to possess seminary educations and where champagne, not beer, was the standard drink. Beer, however, pleased the girls in the small, discreet cottages scattered over town, each with its red light glowing cozily in the transom, in the cribhouses on West Maryland and West Market beyond the Statehouse, and on Court Street, a downtown alleylike thoroughfare where a saloon had provided a burlesque and variety show since the Civil War. Church elders might cry ruin, but sin increased. Incredibly, the census takers reported in 1890 that Indianapolis had nearly as many brothels as New York. The Levee mourned the passing of the Bates House, torn down in 1901 to make way for the Claypool, finest in the West. Waiters and bartenders then were singing *The Pardon Came Too Late, Just Tell Them That You Saw Me,* and *On The Banks of the Wabash, Far Away,* by Paul Dresser, a Terre Haute boy who became a Broadway *bon vivant.* On a fine summer Sunday morning Paul was fooling around at the piano, and he asked his brother Theodore Dreiser what would make a good song. Theodore said: "Why don't you write something about a State or a river? Look at 'My Old Kentucky Home,' 'Dixie,' 'Old Black Joe'. . . . Take Indiana—what's the matter with it—the Wabash River? It's as good as any other river, and you were 'raised' beside it?" and so Paul wrote the music and Theodore wrote the first verse and chorus.[1] The legislators, celebrating Washington's birthday in 1913 with a musical program, liked it and made it the state song.

Indeed, Hoosiers were confident, were in their prime. The When Store took five columns of the front page on November 23, 1890, to advertise: "American Energy is irresistible. . . . Having demonstrated more ways of getting rich than were ever known before, Americans now are learning with all their might how to enjoy themselves"—men who had once relaxed at home in boots and business clothes now needed slippers and a lounge jacket. Advertising was heavy as the holidays approached. The Bowen-Merrill Company, 9 & 11 West Washington Street, booksellers, stationers, and publishers, advertised Meredith Nicholson's new book *Short Flights,* "a dainty book of poems for the

[1] Though the lyrics of this song appear in Burns's *Annotated Indiana Statutes,* Vol. XI, Title 60, ed. of 1943, as part of the Act adopting the song as the state song, the lyrics are not printed here because the copyright holder, Paull-Pioneer Music Corporation, has withheld permission.

Holidays." D. H. Baldwin & Company offered a wonderful assortment of pianos, L. S. Ayres & Company had almost everything. This Christmas of 1890 was the biggest ever. The day before Christmas business streets were thronged with people carrying rocking chairs, hobbyhorses, bicycles; and more toys and candy were sold than ever before "this year of grace." Santa Clauses sat in show windows; one gave up early in the afternoon, probably hastening back to a saloon, for he left behind a sign reading, "Gone until next year, 1892" (the next year was 1891). Residential mail carriers were overburdened despite the aid of delivery wagons and streetcars. The express office was piled hopelessly high; in the preceding week a single train had brought seven carloads of express matter. The Atlas Engine Works, one of the new industrial giants, presented four hundred and fifty turkeys to its employees. Street corners were piled high with holly wreaths. On Christmas Eve, Sunday schools all over town presented children's choirs, Santas, recitations, and trees laden with gifts for the children. After distributing a quarter of a ton of candy, a Meridian Street church charged a potato, apple, or loaf of bread "for the poor" as admission to "a literary and musical programme of much excellence"; another congregation offered a cantata, "the singers appearing in costumes which probably followed the minds of the children deep into their dreams."

Chapter 9

JAMES WHITCOMB RILEY
AND COMPANY

L AWYERS and politicians and writers—Indiana produced them in profusion in this golden age. By 1886 Indiana was a doubtful pivotal state in national politics; every means was used to win or steal it. Only twice between the Civil War and 1920 did a defeated presidential candidate carry Indiana, and only once was there no candidate for President or Vice President from New York or Indiana. In 1886 Sim Coy was the Democratic boss of Marion County (Indianapolis), a shrewd, rough saloonkeeper, reputed the illegitimate son of a prominent man. He became a member of the Democratic county committee at twenty-one and was repeatedly re-elected to the city council, and no ward in the city possessed finer streets and sewers than his eighteenth, for Sim Coy always looked after his constituents. He wrote: "The political field is no place for a timid man. . . ." Faithful party workers boasted they had risked the penitentiary for their party but few were as frank as Coy. Only a chump, he said, was honest. Nevertheless, he was a man of principle. If somebody gave him money "to buy a crowd," he bought it or returned the money, and he had only contempt for the man "who wouldn't stay bought when he was bought." In 1886 Coy and the boys, counting the ballots, forged the tally sheets to steal the office of criminal judge, and Coy and an election judge were sent to prison by a Federal court. After he had served his term, however, his friends on the Levee re-elected him to the council by a bigger majority than ever.

The gathering places for the Indianapolis Democratic politicians were the Grand Hotel and the bepennoned new Denison, both operated by Tom Taggart. Of him a biographer wrote: "It has fallen to the lot of very few, if any, men, to exercise as much influence over Indianapolis as Thomas Taggart. . . ." Born in Ireland, Taggart went to work in the Indianapolis Union Station restaurant in 1877. He soon bought it. He made many friends among the railroaders, and they elected him county auditor in 1885. He rose rapidly. In 1892 when he was Democratic state chairman his party carried the state by twenty thousand. He was three times mayor of Indianapolis. He became a member of the Democratic national committee. An election fraud indictment against him was dismissed, and he, the amiable "easy boss," retained control of the Democratic machine, nearly securing the presidential nomination for Senator Sam M. Ralston in 1924. He and other Indianapolis men brought in a Mexican copper bonanza. He made the French Lick Springs Hotel in the southern Indiana hills a retreat for weary Democrats, millionaires, and moneyed sports of all kinds.

Though the Republicans controlled Indianapolis, they probably never had a plurality of the white votes. They won by voting bought or deluded Negroes, floaters, and dead men. In 1888 their perfidy shocked not only Indianapolis, but the nation. Benjamin Harrison, Indianapolis's own, was their presidential candidate; for weeks torchlight paraders carried bell lamps almost nightly, singing:

> *The train is coming around the bend;*
> *Good-bye, old Grover, good-bye.*
> *It's loaded down with Harrison men;*
> *Good-bye, old Grover, good-bye.*

Harrison and Cleveland debated the tariff loftily and promised reform, a word of which the third parties had made them uneasily aware, but the work that counted was being done on the Levee, in the alleys and the dives. On October 24, W. W. Dudley, national Republican treasurer, wrote to an Indiana county chairman: "Your committee will certainly receive from Chairman Huston the assistance necessary to hold our floaters and doubtful voters. . . . Divide the floaters into blocks of fives, and put a trusted man with necessary funds in charge of these five, and make him responsible that none get away and that all vote our ticket. . . . Make a personal appeal to your best business men to pledge themselves to devote the entire day. . . ." The Indianapolis *Sentinel* published the letter, and a national scandal ensued; Dudley howled that "somebody has been robbing the mails," which was true enough, but he did not disown the letter. Following a rather peculiar charge by a Federal judge, a grand jury refused to indict him, however, and Harrison was elected anyway, presumably with the aid of floaters and vigilant "best business men." A journalist agitating for the Australian ballot said he could find no one in Indianapolis except a labor leader who knew enough about it to write intelligently on the subject. Harrison in the White House put Federal District Judge William Allen Woods on the circuit bench. Woods had succeeded Judge Walter Q. Gresham, Populist hero, Postmaster General, Secretary of the Treasury, Secretary of State. Indianapolis's leading law firms were Hendricks, Hord and Hendricks; McDonald and Butler; and Harrison, Hines and Miller, and from them came an Attorney General, a Vice President, and a President. In addition, Charles W. Fairbanks, a younger lawyer, became vice president. In 1896 Albert J. Beveridge, Fairbanks, Jim Watson, and other young Republican orators stumped Indiana to stem the Bryan tide. These young men from Indiana made national news and history too.

Lew Wallace built Indianapolis's first apartment building with the proceeds from *The Prince of India*. School teachers met in a reading circle "for professional reading and general culture study," using "not school text-books, but gems of literature, in elegant form, suitable for the library or center table." Lay readers too formed clubs; as many as forty flourished at a single time, and the Indianapolis Literary Club, founded in 1877, included "nearly every man of any real prominence in the city." It is doubtful, however, if the clubs influenced what came to be called, misleadingly, the Hoosier school of writers. In the early 1830's John Finley had written *The Hoosier's Nest*, probably the first printed use of "Hoosier." But James Whitcomb Riley, a thin, puckish man, became Indiana's poet laureate, almost surely more beloved of the Hoosiers than any other man.

When he began publishing, many of his readers, though only recently moved to town, already regarded country life with nostalgia when they read:

> *O its then's the times a feller is a-feelin' at his best,*
> *With the risin' sun to greet him from a night of peaceful rest,*
> *As he leaves the house, bare-headed, and goes out to feed the stock,*
> *When the frost is on the punkin and the fodder's in the shock.*

Riley was a city boy or at least a town boy. He was born in Greenfield, about 20 miles from Indianapolis, in 1854, and his father was a prosecuting attorney and state legislator. Riley wrote:

> *Wasn't it pleasant, O brother mine,*
> *In those old days of the lost sunshine*
> *Of youth—when the Saturday's chores were through,*
> *And the "Sunday's wood" in the kitchen, too,*
> *And we went visiting, "me and you,"*
>   *Out to Old Aunt Mary's?*

He knew the pleasures, not the hardships, of country life. He liked to remember the brilliant Christmas Day when he and a couple of other boys skated down Brandywine Creek, broad and bordered with hackberries, with fish darting beneath the gleaming ice; they caught a train at New Palestine and the engineer stopped to let them off at Sugar Creek and they skated back to the National Road and then walked the four miles home to Greenfield. Riley left Greenfield, not far from Tailholt which he later made famous, when he was a young man, and he lived most of his life in Indianapolis. This migration was duplicated by many others, who enjoyed:

> *You kin boast about yer cities, and their stiddy growth and size*
> *And brag about yer county-seats, and business enterprise,*
> *And railroads, and factories, and all sich foolery—*
> *But the little Town o' Tailholt is big enough fer me!*

He studied law but soon gave it up to join a traveling "patent-medicine and concert wagon," and he wandered about, earning his living by painting advertising signs on fences and barns. He got jobs on the *Dispatch* at Kokomo and on the *Democrat* at

Anderson, where he perpetrated a Poe hoax that brought nothing but notoriety; he moved to Indianapolis, and in 1877 the *Journal* began to publish the poems that made him famous. Many were full of sentimentality and bathos:

> *When Bessie died—*
> *We writhed in prayer unsatisfied;*
> *We begged of God, and He did smile*
> *In silence on us all the while;*
> *And we did see Him, through our tears,*
> *Enfolding that fair form of hers,*
> *She laughing back against His love*
> *The kisses we had nothing of—*
> *And death to us he still denied,*
> *When Bessie died—*
> > *When Bessie died.*

He preceded "My Ruthers" with this parenthetical note: "(Writ durin' State Fair at Indianapolis, whilse visitin' a Soninlaw then residin' thare, who has sence got back to the country whare he says a man that's raised thare ort to a-stayed in the first place.)"

> *I tell you what I'd ruther do—*
> *Ef I only had my ruthers,—*
> *I'd ruther work when I wanted to*
> *Than be bossed round by others. . . .*

Hoosiers enjoyed his use of dialect, which at once praised and poked gentle fun at Hoosier rusticity, and they liked his praise of the homely, the everyday, but they loved him most because he caught a spirit of neighborliness that somehow from a distance seems the *Zeitgeist* of the nineties.

> *Granny's come to our house,*
> > *And ho! my lawzy-daisy!*
> *All the childern round the place*
> > *Is ist a-runin' crazy!*
> *Fetched a cake fer little Jake,*
> > *And fetched a pie fer Nanny,*
> *And fetched a pear fer all the pack*
> > *That runs to kiss ther Granny!*

Sometimes he made even poverty seem attractive:

> *Pap's got his patent-right, and rich as all creation;*
> *But where's the peace and comfort that we all had before?*
> *Le's go a-visitin' back to Griggsby's Station—*
> *Back where we ust to be so happy and so pore!*
>
> *The likes of us a-livin' here! It's jest a mortal pity*
> *To see us in this great big house, with cyarpets on the stairs,*
> *And the pump right in the kitchen! And the city! city! city!—*
> *And nothin' but the city all around us ever'wheres!*
>
> *Climb clean above the roof and look from the steeple,*
> *And never see a robin, nor a beech or ellum tree!*
> *And right here in ear-shot of at least a thousan' people,*
> *And none that neighbors with us, or we want to go and see!*

The veneration of Riley began only after Bill Nye, an established wit, introduced him to an assemblage of authors at New York which included Lowell, Twain, Howells, and Cable. When Riley had read "When The Frost Is On The Punkin," James Russell Lowell leaned over to William Dean Howells and asked: "Who is that wonderful young man?" Mrs. Grover Cleveland invited Riley to the White House. A booking agent named Amos J. Walker—Riley said he was responsible for the joke, usually attributed to Riley, about the dinner guest who declined to carve because he "never could make the gravy match the wall paper" —signed Riley up for a joint tour with Nye. They gave readings and skits, attracting huge crowds everywhere. Those years with Nye, Riley thought, were his happiest. Lockerbie Street in Indianapolis, where he made his bachelor home, was world renowned. He visited London, and Sir Henry Irving entertained him, and Coquelin thought he was doing naturally what Coquelin had been striving all his life to learn. Wherever Riley went children crowded about him. Yale and Pennsylvania conferred honorary degrees. Indiana fell all over itself in praising him. He gave a reading before the Indianapolis Press Club, and so did Lew Wallace and a new writer, Meredith Nicholson. (Eggleston was in New York.) When he appeared at Winona Lake to give an entertainment, the crowd interrupted a preacher's address to cheer him. When he gave his first public reading at Greenfield in fifteen years, the town band serenaded him, and so many people went to Masonic Hall that one man warned that the ancient building might collapse if they stamped their feet.

Despite all honors, despite even his own almost ostentatious love for the homely, Riley did remain a people's poet, for they understood him and they framed his poems in their parlors. And he dwelt among them rather than in a poet's tower, performing his act and reading his verses and telling jokes like any carnival clown, drinking with Gene Debs and other railroaders at Terre Haute or with newspapermen in saloons on the Levee, enjoying good food at Indianapolis's best restaurants. About him legends grew, and in some of them his own character appeared as it did not in his verse, and it is the Hoosier character, it is what links him with the best Indiana has produced. As a man of letters he was obliged to read papers before the Indianapolis Literary Club, but once at the John Herron Art Institute, enduring a dull, lengthy discourse upon the definition of art, he whispered to a neighbor: "Speakin' o' art—I know a fellow over 't Terry Haute 'at kin spit clean over a box car." Again, he and Nye, waiting for a train at the crowded Union Station, set down their grips, took out their watches, and, pointing at the dummy sheet-iron clock dials that announced train arrivals and of course differed, argued heatedly about which clock was right. Rural travelers who believed them honestly befuddled gathered, amused, and when Riley and Nye began a bitter denunciation of the depot management, a man from the crowd told them the clocks were fake, and Nye withdrew in shame. Just so, Riley, by no means an unlettered or untraveled man, had accompanied his dialect poems with letters to the *Journal* signed "Benj. F. Johnson of Boone." Once, standing on the curb in front of the Denison, he told a friend: "I was just thinking what an awful humiliation it must be to an Almighty God to create a universe, and then have to submit it to Ambrose Bierce and Bob Ingersoll for criticism." (Bierce spent his boyhood in Elkhart.) In 1916 newspapers devoted whole pages to Riley's obituary, and the worship of things he and his poems had touched approached idolatry, and William Herschell of the Indianapolis *News* wrote:

> *Children, tread softly in Lockerbie Street*
> *Some one you loved now lies slumbering there;*

> *Someone who loved you in comradeship sweet*
> *Rests at the foot of Eternity's Stair.*
>
> *Voices kept calling him out of The Past,*
> *Voices all fondly familiar to him;*
> *Then came the one—he must answer at last—*
> *Dear Old Aunt Mary was calling her Jim!*

Riley's work created an enormous demand for poems in praise of the homely, the simple, the rustic, the Hoosier. Herschell was the most successful of many writers who labored to supply the demand. A drinking newspaper poet like Riley, red-nosed, successful, beloved, and sometimes crochety, Herschell wrote: "Goodbye, Ma, goodbye, Pa, goodbye, mule, with your old heehaw" but in Indiana he is best remembered—he died in 1939 —for his poem, "Ain't God Good to Indiana?" and its first stanza reveals how synthetic was this post-Riley verse:

> *Ain't God good to Indiana?*
> *Folks, a feller never knows*
> *Just how close he is to Eden*
> *Till, sometime, he ups an' goes*
> *Seekin' fairer, greener pastures*
> *Than he has right here at home*
> *Where there's sunshine in th' clover*
> *An' there's honey in th' comb;*
> *Where th' ripples on th' river*
> *Kind o' chuckles as they flow;*
> *Ain't God good to Indiana?*
> *Ain't He, fellers? Ain't He, though?*

He seemed to be talking about something that was no longer there, something that had died with Riley before the 1917–18 war.

The best of Riley, the dry, phlegmatic Hoosier unimpressed by pretense, was carried on by George Ade and Kin Hubbard. In one of Ade's plays we have the county chairman saying to his bright, young candidate in effect: "All right boy, you get along out there with your Galahad speech while I put on the gum shoes and go get the votes." The famous line, "You're a hell of a Baptist," is from *The College Widow*. Ade's *Fables in*

Slang demonstrated his inventive way with vernacular, and some of them had an edge. Kin Hubbard had an even sharper edge, as he showed in his "sayings" of Abe Martin first published in the *News*:

It's th' good loser that finally loses out.
We're all purty much alike when we git out o' town.
Mr. Lemmie Peters, whose graduation essay, "This Is Th' Age o' Opportunity," caused so much favorable comment a year ago, almost took th' agency fer th' Eclipse Fly Swatter yisterday.
Stew Nugent has decided t' go t' work till he kin find somethin' better.
Now an' then an innocent man is sent t' th' legislature.
Carpenter Joe Moots dropped a hatchet on his toe when th' whistle blew t'day.
It's no disgrace t' be poor, but it might as well be.
Miss Fawn Lippincut says she wouldn' marry th' best man on earth, but we supposed she wuz much younger.

Clifton Fadiman, an anthologist, considers Kin Hubbard ". . . the best of the crackerbarrel philosophers. . . . He is a Hoosier Rochefoucauld." Though Hubbard cast his sentences in rustic idiom, he was a newspaperman and blackface comedian, and though George Ade made his home in the rich farming country near Kentland, he disliked farming. Both men, like Riley and John T. McCutcheon, a cartoonist, really were city men, men whose only pretense was to simplicity and whose stock in trade was derision of pretense. (To Ade was attributed, perhaps inaccurately, the line: "Many good men come from Indiana; the better they are the quicker they come.") In all their work, as George Leighton, a journalist, has said: "The idea is always the same: The semi-acid tongued, horse-trading, prosperous, rather generous character." Probably at some time or other everybody from Indiana has protested that he is a rustic unused to city ways, but he probably never met a city slicker he did not secretly believe he could outdo. Ring Lardner should have been a Hoosier. Even in Booth Tarkington, as Leighton has said, "beneath the goo, you see the fabled character of Indiana in his impregnable middle class prime." You see him in Tarkington's *The Man from Home* "in the character of Daniel Voorhees Pike of Kokomo who was turned loose among the corrupt Europeans on the Riviera (about 1908) and with his wisecracks and homespun virtues confounded continental evil. . . . The same hard-to-beat Hoosier."

Charles Major was publishing *When Knighthood Was in Flower;* Meredith Nicholson, *The Main Chance* and *The House of a Thousand Candles;* Maurice Thompson, *Alice of Old Vincennes;* George Barr McCutcheon, *Graustark* and *Brewster's Millions;* Tarkington, *Monsieur Beaucaire;* best-seller romances that made the home folks proud. (Most of these authors wrote books commenting pungently on Indiana, and the home folks ignored them.) Tarkington stood out. If, as some believe, books read by succeeding generations of children have the best chance of survival, it may be that Tarkington will be remembered mainly for the Penrod books, but while he lived his critical fame rested on *The Gentleman from Indiana, Alice Adams,* and the trilogy of Midwest city life: *The Turmoil, The Magnificent Ambersons,* and *The Midlander.* He once wrote sadly: "This writer was born in a quiet, lovely little city, Indianapolis, Ind. . . . That small city . . . exists no more than Carthage had existed after the Romans had driven plows over the ground where it stood." He saw heroes as valiant, heroines as virtuous; more important, as Alexander Woollcott wrote: "The fabric of American life as Tarkington saw it contained the hum of lawn mowers, the swish of garden hose playing at sundown on the phlox and petunia and heliotrope; the sound of neighbor calling neighbor; the fragrance of new-made bread sifting from summer kitchens."

The son of an attorney, Tarkington was born in 1869 in the 500 block of North Meridian Street in Indianapolis; his family soon moved to 11th and Pennsylvania Streets. He was educated at Exeter, Purdue, and Princeton, where he played the banjo, wrote songs for the glee club, went drinking, and discussed suicide and sex. A rich uncle carried him through lean years of unsuccessful writing and cartooning and amateur theatricals at Indianapolis before he wrote *The Gentleman from Indiana.* The year *Beaucaire* was published, 1900, he earned twenty-seven thousand dollars, and he never again earned less. He dressed elegantly, traveled, lived high, moved in fashionable circles. He joined the Players' Club in New York. Celebrating the Chicago opening of a play of his, Tarkington bought the entire stock of a Loop fruit stand and sent it to the producer's hotel room. After spending the night in a New York bar or club, he liked to waken a bum at dawn in Central Park and present him with a grapefruit. He seemed an eternal sophomore. Once, driving to Lafayette to attend the opening of a George Ade play, he paused at each village to announce that Senator Beveridge and Vice President Fairbanks were following in another car. When the second car arrived, Harry Leon Wilson and a companion accepted the plaudits of the crowd. In a Lafayette saloon after the play, Tarkington decided that another customer, a stranger, resembled Edgar Allan Poe. This man, a road-show press agent, returned with them to Indianapolis, where they installed him at a country club and introduced him as Poe.

Riding high, Tarkington was elected to the Legislature, though stage fright struck him dumb when he rose to speak at Engine House No. 4. (William Jennings Bryan thought it a pity he hadn't remained mute in his only other campaign appearance.) The Governor vetoed the only bill he introduced, one to establish a broom factory for the blind. Tarkington quit politics. With Harry Leon Wilson and Julian Street, Tarkington traveled to Capri. There an Indiana politician introduced him to an English drinking companion, and from their conversation Tarkington and Wilson wrote *The Man from Home,* which made Kokomo famous.

Tarkington quit drinking in 1912. He was married twice. He established a summer home at Kennebunkport, Maine. Though nearly blind in his later years, he dictated popular novels. He worked hard. He collected antiques and paintings. In his expensively furnished home he entertained most of the notables who visited Indianapolis, for he was one of its most honored citizens. He resisted change, voted the straight Republican ticket, strenuously opposed Franklin D. Roosevelt, and wrote: "To my oldfashioned mind, the liberty we lose when the government plans our future security is worth more than the benefit this security could possibly give us. Hardship, it seems to me, is a part of life, a test and builder of character." He died in 1946, the year in which Theodore Dreiser, whose first major works also were published around 1900, died. Though Dreiser too grew up in Indiana during its golden age, he beheld it from a different vantage point in Terre Haute, as we shall see.

When in 1919 Meredith Nicholson published *The Valley of Democracy,* a summing up of life in the Midwest toward the close of the golden age—though he could scarcely have known he was standing at one of the peaks of history—a reviewer in the *Indiana Magazine of History* wrote: "The author flits with grace from parlor car, summer resort and city club to the serious conclusions of the western historians. One is- left with the suspicion that somewhere in the background are the busy millions of whose busy life and thought these clubs, societies and activities are merely surface indications. . . . I quote 'Mr. George Ade's Indiana farm is one of the State's showplaces. [Ade] says that its best feature is a good nine-hole golf course and a swimming pool.' Again, 'One night, a few years ago, on the breezy terrace of one of the handsomest villas in the lake region, I talked with the head of a great industry whose products are known round the world.' It is hardly necessary to point out that conclusions drawn from such sources are liable to be over colored. . . . Chicago does not live on the boulevards nor sit in the music halls nor picture galleries. It lives in the smoke, grime and sweat of the factories and counting houses. . . . It is better perhaps to write of the more pleasant things even at the expense of fact, of the social settlement rather than of the slum, of George Ade's golf course and swimming pool than of the distressing tenements that still disfigure too many of our western farms."

It certainly had seemed better, for golf courses and swimming pools were the fruits of new wealth, new invention, new capitalism. True, farms were distressed, factory workmen were discontented. But there was so much more wonder than struggle in this first new capitalism. Who would not rather marvel at the horseless carriage than debate the wages its maker paid his employees? Every clerk, watching the top-hatted gentlemen drive round the Circle, was more hopeful than envious, for who knew where the lightning of riches might strike next?

Chapter 10

LEADERS FOR THE NEW AGE

A curious thing kept happening. True, the social leaders were old families of bankers and lawyers and manufacturers, people like the Atkinses and Fletchers and, of course, Benjamin Harrison, the astute, aloof President who was a grandson of William Henry Harrison and belonged to the blue bloods and to the high-toned First Presbyterian Church. But new manufacturers, new lawyers, even some new bankers kept rising; men kept starting up alley machine shops that in a few years became giant enterprises. They kept enlarging what was then solemnly called the four hundred; indeed, perhaps the most striking thing about this golden age was the constant renewal. By the time Riley had reached zenith, Kin Hubbard was on the way up; by the time D. M. Parry's buggy works had become big business, Carl Fisher and Jim Allison were starting. Invention reinvigorated old establishments. Ellis Nordyke, a millwright with a tiny shop, joined Daniel W. Marmon and manufactured automobiles. The economy was expanding and the Indianapolis capitalists expanded with it; their factories made engines, pumps, hardware, woodenware, carriages, machinery, bags, bedding, furniture, electrical equipment, plows, caskets. They made almost everything that a gentleman in Indiana could want, they supplied the national market, their products were world renowned, and they made enormous profits.

Indianapolis was central, labor was cheap, railroads were good, the population was growing. Invested capital trebled from

1870 to 1900, banks expanded mightily. Outside capitalists began to arrive. The New York Central built a whole new suburb, Beech Grove, southeast of the city and invested five million dollars in "the greatest locomotive hospital in the world." But the native capitalists kept control; they built castles, toured Europe, sent their sons East or abroad to school, dined at Delmonico's in New York without trepidation, visited the Union League Club in Chicago, built fortunes. Benjamin Harrison's mansion at 1230 North Delaware Street was something of a national social center. Harrison had built it in 1872, a brick home with fourteen high-ceilinged rooms on the first two floors and a ballroom on the third reached by a spiral staircase; the front door, engraved "BH," faced east. On New Year's Eve in 1900 the rich opened the new home of the Columbia Club with a ball in the gold-ceilinged ballroom. The club had been organized as the Harrison Marching Club in 1888, and the great bays of its new five-story clubhouse on the Circle overlooked, appropriately, the new monument built to honor the men who had won the Civil War for the Republicans. The club's membership included almost everyone who mattered in Indiana, so far as money or power went.

The crowning glory to these golden years was the automobile. When it arrived citizens were not yet quite accustomed to natural gas heat, electric lights, indoor plumbing, and the telephone, or to riding to work over paved streets on mechanical streetcars, or to seeing Indianapolis blanketed with factory smoke. One day a great crate arrived at Sam Pearson's cigar store near Pennsylvania and Maryland Streets; it held a shiny new Benz automobile from Germany. Charles Black came over from his near-by carriage factory, bringing his helper, and they climbed boldly aboard and started off. At Maryland and Illinois they ran into the Grand Hotel and smashed a buggy; they turned north and at Washington Street crashed into a show window; they turned back east and at Meridian and Washington, "the crossroads of the nation," smashed another show window. None the less, they had driven the first automobile on Indianapolis streets. Black, fascinated, copied the Benz, using parts lying about his carriage factory and adding a new touch, a whip socket. And not many miles away, at Kokomo, Elwood Haynes invented the American automobile.

Haynes, born at Portland, Indiana, October 14, 1857, early displayed the inventive bent that enabled so many young Hoosiers to find their natural home in machine shops. Educated at Worcester Polytechnic Institute and at Johns Hopkins, he became, during the gas boom of 1890, field representative for the Indiana Gas and Oil Company, which proposed to build a pipe line to Chicago. He had a lot of driving to do and "it occurred to me," he later recalled, "that some better means of locomotion over the highway than the horse and buggy might be procured." After discarding steam and electricity as the propelling power, he turned to a gasoline engine.

Work on the pipe line languished and his own dream grew. In the fall of 1892 he moved to Kokomo and ordered an upright one-horse marine engine from Grand Rapids. He set it up in the kitchen and cranked it, and it tore loose from its moorings; luckily one of the battery wires became disconnected. One by one he solved his problems. Once, studying the tractive resistance of rubber tires, he pulled a bicycle behind a buckboard, scribbling rapidly to record the pull registered on a scale. At last on the Fourth of July, 1894, he hauled the 820-pound machine to the street. There neighbors clustered about it so thickly he dared not start it. So, amid jeers, he hauled it ignominiously with a horse-drawn carriage three miles out on a turnpike. On the way he met what he described as "a bevy of girls" on bicycles who "wheeled aside, separated like a flock of swans and stared wonder-eyed at the uncouth and utterly unexpected little machine." He started it. "It moved off at once at a speed of nearly seven miles an hour and was driven about one and one-half miles into the country. It was then turned about, and ran all the way into the city without making a single stop. I was convinced, upon this return trip, that there was a future for the 'horseless carriage.'"

The strange contraption aroused wonder and anger. Once an old man with a wagonload of tomatoes became so engrossed that when his horse shied he dropped one of the lines and with the other pulled the team down an embankment. Haynes paid for

115

the damage. Again, when a gentleman and his lady in a buggy would not let Haynes pass, he opened the cutout; the buggy dashed off, pursued silently by Haynes, who, when he got close, again blasted with the cutout; and only after a three-mile flight at eight miles per hour, during which the buggy was overtaken several times, did it turn aside. Once when the one-cylinder motor snorted and died on the Punkin Vine Pike near Kokomo, Haynes greased it with butter from a near-by farmhouse. When irate citizens declared his contraption had no right on the highways, attorneys proved the contrary. He drove to New York in 1899, leaving a trail of shying horses and wrecked buggies. Along the Hudson River he met "a party of summer girls on vacation" in a spring wagon, and their "sober, staid looking old horse" jumped a stone wall; Haynes helped the girls retrieve it.

Haynes made notable contributions to metallurgy. Technical societies, the Hoosier Automobile Club, and the Chicago Auto Club honored him. He became president of the Kokomo Y.M.C.A., a director of the Citizens National Bank in Kokomo, and an elder in the Presbyterian Church; he was the honor guest of an Indianapolis-to-Los Angeles auto caravan in 1913, and he died April 13, 1925, having lived to see the auto industry forsake Indiana for Detroit.

In the early years, however, Indiana was indeed the capital of the auto industry. South Bend had the Studebakers, Anderson and Kokomo and Logansport had other manufacturers. Indianapolis was, as usual, the leader. Here carriage makers, bicycle makers, millwrights, and others as well became auto makers. The Marmon, the National, the Waverly, the Overland, the Cole, the Empire, the Premier, the Chevrolet, the Parry, the Pathfinder, the Marion, the American, the Duesenberg, the Stutz, the Frontenac, the Lafayette—at one time or another nearly a score of automobiles was built at Indianapolis. Indianapolis was crowded with promoters and inventors, young men with big ideas. Schebler improved the carburetor and made a single-cylinder, chain-drive car. Willys was making the Overland. Stutz and Newby and Fisher and Allison and Dixon and Duesenberg—great names all in auto history—they, and many more too, flocked to Indianapolis. It was said that even Henry Ford wanted to come and took Detroit only as a second choice.

From the outset Hoosiers loved the automobile as they had loved the bicycle. Waverly had been making good bicycles here for years; now it made an electric auto. Fred S. Duesenberg, born in Germany, took up bicycle racing in 1898, set two world records that stood for more than a decade, built a racing motorcycle in order to have a machine to pace him, and so became an auto engineer of world renown. And Carl Fisher too was a bicycle racer. More than anyone else Carl Fisher symbolized the glorification of the automobile in Indiana, and more than anyone else's his career bridged the gap between the manufacturer and the promoter in Indiana.

Fisher was born at Greensburg January 12, 1874. Working as a news butcher, he saw the rising Indiana towns through soot-grimed windows of railroad cars. He got a job fixing bicycle punctures at a curbside station for twenty-five cents each. The Fishers were poor. Carl went to Indianapolis and started a bicycle shop on Pennsylvania Street. It became a hangout for cycling enthusiasts, including young Jim Allison. Allison and Fisher rode together. Soon Fisher expanded his shop, and when the automobile came along he opened a garage on the Levee and then another a few blocks farther north on Illinois Street; he and his mother lived over it on the second floor. Fisher, a sport, was gaining a reputation as a bike racer, but he was becoming more interested in the auto. He sold so many makes of cars that his garage resembled a motor show. At it newspapermen interviewed tourists who dared cross the continent from New York. Fisher, a restless good-looking young man with an oval, soft, almost womanish face, kept wanting to expand. An old friend has said: "He never had a thousand dollars in those days but he had a place to spend twenty." Once he advertised that he would throw a bicycle off the highest building in town and that the person who retrieved it would get a new one. When the police warned they would arrest him, he threw it off and went to the station to surrender, followed by a crowd. He was shrewd, agile, full of schemes and promotion stunts. More than most young men of Indianapolis he was in tune with the twentieth century. When a man came along with an idea for illuminating the headlights and tail lights of autos with gas from a running-board tank, Fisher and Allison borrowed a thousand dollars each, organized the Prest-O-Lite Storage Battery Company in 1904, and built a little shanty up at 28th and Pennsylvania Streets where Fisher had a couple of cheap lots he'd acquired in one of his trades.

Jim Allison was a serious, rugged, intelligent man, a year and a half older than Fisher. He had been a poor boy who sold lead pencils and newspapers on the downtown streets, and he learned frugality well. He ran Prest-O-Lite, though Carl Fisher was its president and got the publicity. Fisher traveled in a fast crowd. They drove to Dayton for week-end parties, they raced their cars along dusty country roads. He dressed well, dined well, drank well; and often beside him in his runabout sat a pretty girl in choker collar and hat with wide swooping brim. One day Fisher and a friend put on their dusters and took a ride to Greenfield, twenty miles away, to try out a new car. It broke down on the way back, not once, but many times, and to hoist it up and wire it together, they tore down half the fences between Indianapolis and Greenfield. And once when Fisher was out and under, he said: "There ought to be a track to test these cars out before the public gets 'em." By that time Fisher, his cap turned backwards, was piloting bucket-seat race cars around treacherous dirt tracks; in 1904 he set a world record at the Harlem track— two miles in 2:02 minutes—and a year later he was a member of the American team defeated in Europe. He and Allison, together with Frank Wheeler of Wheeler-Schebler carburetor, and Arthur Newby of Diamond Chain and National auto, built the Indianapolis Motor Speedway beside the Crawfordsville Road, where they already had constructed a large new Prest-O-Lite plant.

After the first race in the summer of 1909 on crushed rock and tar, a brick pavement was laid. The Speedway cost seven hundred thousand dollars, Fisher said, and for several years it lost money. On Labor Day 1910, in a five-mile event for small stock cars, "Emmons won, coming in holding down his hood over the engine." In 1911 the proprietors decided to hold but one race a year, and that of five hundred miles. This has been done every year since but for wartime interruptions. A Marmon won that first five hundred. Soon the Indianapolis bricks were world famous, synonymous with "the roaring road." To them came Barney Oldfield and Dario Resta and Howdy Wilcox and Ralph De Palma and Ray Harroun and all the other great drivers. Fisher hired Steve Hannegan, a local newspaperman, to publicize the five hundred, and he stayed with Fisher many years before leaving to become a free-lance press agent. Publicizing Fisher in 1925, Hannegan wrote that Fisher "has the agile mind of a press agent."

Indeed he had. He made balloon ascensions abroad and in Indiana. In 1909 he piloted the balloon *Indiana* in the Aero Club of America's national race and described his "thrilling aerial ride" in long newspaper articles. With one companion he made his ascent on June 5 from the Speedway, while forty thousand spectators (his estimate) gaped and the military band played *The Star-Spangled Banner*. The wind carried them south over the hills of Brown County, where squatters shot at them. At times they were becalmed. Their timid carrier pigeons refused to leave the basket at eight thousand feet, so they dropped a message in a paper bag. Once winds carried them upward at a rate (Fisher wrote) of eight hundred feet per minute; at ten thousand feet they got out the blankets; at twelve thousand they tried to deflate but could not; only at fourteen thousand did the winds relent. They landed in Tennessee, having been in the air nearly forty-nine hours.

Fisher married an Indianapolis girl and bought an old homestead near Riverside Park on the northwest side of town and remodeled it. The sixty-foot living-room had Oriental rugs, huge logs burned all day long in a fireplace, and numerous loving cups adorned the mantle. A billiard table and a piano stood in opposite ends of the room. There was a glass-enclosed porch with stone fireplace and swings and couches and writing desks and a Victrola; there were gardens, a greenhouse, a garage, and a tennis court. Fisher enclosed the tennis court with glass to permit play in the rain, and he built a platform on the sideline so James Whitcomb Riley could watch. Later Fisher built two other courts on his Florida and Long Island estates; the three cost about half a million dollars. He was living high. In 1912 a lovely brown-haired singer sued him for half a million dollars, charging breach of promise. She recited how he had asked for a velvet slipper she had worn when they met in 1902; how, "a poor man, selling automobiles," he brought prospective customers to her home, where she sang to them; how he promised her a winter home in the South and a summer home in the North; ". . . then we will build us a castle up in the mountains, and we will have our ponies, our saddle horses, our automobiles, our boats, our dogs and guns, a grand piano, and you can sing and I will lie before the fireplace and listen . . . and thus we will go down into old age, happy, joyful, loving each other until the grave." But he summoned her to his office, called her "dear," told her he had married another, and gave her some money. Seeking more, she estimated his fortune at two million dollars, his annual income at eight hundred thousand dollars.

Where did all this money come from? From Prest-O-Lite and real estate and other ventures. Fisher and Allison promoted the town of Speedway City (barring Negroes from it). Sometimes Allison despaired of Fisher. Once Allison managed to arrange a bank credit of forty thousand dollars for Prest-O-Lite; soon, startled to learn he was overdrawn, he discovered that Fisher had spent a fourth of the money for a boat. Though Allison established the Allison Engineering Company in Indianapolis to do war work—just as it did twenty-five years later—he was no engineer. Rather, he hired engineers to develop his ideas (asked where he went to college, he replied: "God damn it, I can hire all the college boys I need for fifteen dollars a week"). When Prest-O-Lite was consolidated with Union Carbide, Allison retained his interest. His banking and his real-estate holdings expanded. His estate on Cold Springs Road probably cost more than two million dollars—he spent ten thousand dollars for the silver and bronze chandelier in the main lobby, brought stonemasons from Philadelphia to carve the fireplace, installed mahogany woodwork and inlaid oak flooring and an eighteen-thousand-dollar pipe organ and furniture of French design fashioned on the spot, hired sculptors to construct an aviary of Italian marble and artists to adorn the walls of the study with sporting murals. The grounds comprised a bluff overlooking five artificial lakes; he built a swimming pool and kept game and birds and employed thirty-five servants. He built a Florida home on Star Island in Biscayne Bay; he contributed to charities and churches and when he died on August 3, 1928, he was reputedly worth about four million dollars. He had married a girl from an old Indianapolis family; he was divorced and he married his former secretary only a few weeks before he died. His former wife sued his bride for alienation of affections, claiming she had used on him "the fine arts of lovemaking, at which she was a skillful expert." The suit was withdrawn, and the courts awarded Allison's mother the bulk of his estate.

About a year before Allison died, he and Fisher had sold the Speedway to a syndicate of Detroit men. By then the auto industry had forsaken Indianapolis for Detroit. By that time too Fisher had gone elsewhere. As early as 1914 on a yachting expedition to Florida he had leased a key south of Miami from the Government and built a twenty-five-thousand-dollar retreat. Another man bid the key in at auction and offered Fisher three thousand dollars for his house. Fisher, enraged, set it afire, went ashore, and in a wilderness of swamp and saw grass developed Miami Beach. Will Rogers said of Fisher: "He's the man that took Miami Beach away from the alligators and gave it to the Indianians." Reputedly worth thirty million dollars, divorced in Paris, remarried, master of three estates, hero of the 1920's, he took his speculative profits north and put ten million dollars into Montauk Point, Long Island. But a Florida hurricane knocked him flat. His creditors took over. His Montauk Beach Development Company went into receivership in 1932. That year Fred Duesenberg, who always had complained because the highways wouldn't accommodate the speed of his cars, was killed in an auto wreck. When Fisher died in 1939 he reportedly was worth less than a non-liquid million dollars; all he owned at Indianapolis was a cemetery lot. His funeral was held at Miami Beach, on an open flagged terrace amid oleander bushes and palm trees; three thousand dollars worth of flowers, especially his favorites, tuberoses, lay on his casket. The city hall was closed and flags flew at half mast. In 1943 Fisher's ashes were interred in Crown Hill cemetery at Indianapolis.

Long before that the glory had departed Indianapolis. The Levee had grown shabby, the authors were warming over old themes, eternal promise had evaporated, the inhabitants of the Columbia Club had grown crochety, the auto industry and many others that grew up before the 1917–18 war had moved away.

By the next war, Studebaker in South Bend was all that remained of the great Indiana auto industry, except for some colonial outposts of the Detroit emperors. True, during the 1920's Indianapolis enjoyed a boom (though farmers went broke), and to many people today those years, not the nineties, are the good old days. But that boom was one of promotion stunts (Carl Fisher abandoned manufacturing for promotion). It was a very different boom than that of the nineties, which had been broadly based on expanding industry and commerce. In 1900 perhaps no other place on earth displayed more native charm or held out greater promise than Indiana. It did not fulfill this promise, it lost much of its charm. What happened? We shall examine this decline in detail.

To understand what went wrong we must begin about 1900, for as early as that, although it was not then apparent, Indiana was getting hardening of the arteries. David Maclean Parry was a manufacturer of buggies at that time. He knew trouble when he saw it and he cried alarm at once. Other Indianapolis men shared his views, but he was the most foresighted, or at least the most vocal. Mr. Parry was a manufacturer, financier, and, above all, a "practical sociologist." A contemporary estimate of him ran: "As a large employer of labor, Mr. Parry has been deeply interested in the vital issues between capital and labor that have characterized recent popular movements, and he was the first man to make a stand against unjust demands and unlawful methods adopted by some of the organized-labor bodies, which he considered a direct violation of American principles. . . . He is well known in Indianapolis as an enthusiastic student of sociology and its problems. . . ." Mr. Parry was a small man, five feet six inches tall and weighing 125 pounds; he had pale eyes, thin lips, an oblong face, a squared jaw, and a long nose. Contemporary portraits usually showed him as "A Man of Business," seated at a roll-top desk in double-breasted striped vest, striped pants, black coat, wing collar, black bow tie. Is it not significant that in those bright, early days Indiana historians of standing wrote dismal works hymning the praises of the capitalists? Truly capitalism flowered and was beloved in Indiana, and hardly anyone suspected that all was not well. Jacob Piatt Dunn, an Indiana historian of real eminence, began his biographical sketch of Mr. Parry: "The glory of our great American republic is in the perpetuation of individuality and in the according of the utmost scope for individual accomplishment. . . . David M. Parry . . . may well be designated as one of the valiant and resourceful 'captains of industry' [of] Greater Indianapolis. . . . Not in an ephemeral way is his name associated with the word progress. . . . distinctly a man of ideas and ideals. . . ."

David M. Parry was born to Welsh, Republican, and Presbyterian parents in Pennsylvania on March 26, 1852; about nine months later they moved to a farm in the Whitewater Valley. At sixteen, David clerked in a general store at Laurel for ten dollars a month. With money earned as a traveling hardware salesman, he bought a hardware store in Rushville; he sold it in 1882 and bought a carriage shop in Rushville. He convinced farmers they needed a two-wheeled cart of general utility. Expanding in 1886, he rented part of an old wheel works in Indianapolis. Three of his brothers joined him. They began by turning out one hundred carts daily with forty employees; soon they were producing one thousand carts a day and employing 2,400. About 1890 they began making four-wheeled surreys, piano-box buggies, phaetons, road and spring wagons. Parry carriages soon were famous, the Parry Manufacturing Company on Parry Avenue at the Vandalia tracks was bigger than the next five biggest carriage factories in the world put together. In 1909 Mr. Parry incorporated the Parry Auto Company, with capital of a million dollars. At one time or another he was a leader in construction of the Indianapolis & Southern Railroad and the Newcastle & Toledo traction line, chairman of the South Dakota Central Railroad, president of the Overland Automobile Company, of the American Manufacturers' Mutual Fire Insurance Company, and of the Automobile Insurance Company of America. He had had two children by his first wife, who died at twenty-four; he remarried and begat seven more children. He established a hundred-acre estate in Golden Hills near Fisher's and Allison's estates. He was a member of the First Baptist Church, a thirty-second degree Mason, an Odd Fellow, an Elk, and "a lifelong Republican, but democratic in his instincts." He was a founder of the Columbia, Country, and Marion clubs, and president and director of the Indianapolis Board of Trade and the Commercial

Club (later the Chamber of Commerce). He also became president of the Carriage Builders' National Association, of the National Civic Association, and, finally, of the National Association of Manufacturers of the United States.

Mr. Parry had enough money, presumably. Now he turned to good works, to instructing the multitudes, giving them the benefit of his accumulated wisdom, leading them on the right road to progress. In a phrase, he turned to "practical sociology." Here he was, a self-made man, the end product of native American capitalism—and a Hoosier product. One might expect of him the benignity which Riley ascribed to Hoosiers. He had made his money in the gay, warm, friendly Indianapolis of the nineties. Now what did this elder statesman of enterprise have to say?

He said: "It is the business of every man to honestly get all he can."

He said: ". . . mankind . . . is bound by certain fixed laws . . . it is right and just that one man should obtain more of this world's goods than another. . . . That is what causes progress and the evolution of the race. . . . The law of supply and demand is the great law. . . ."

He said: "There is that old battle cry of unionism that labor produces all. If labor had to produce all, mankind would today be next door to starvation and nakedness. . . ."

He said: "Labor gets more and more and capital less and less every year."

He said: "[The trades union movement is] a standing mob engaged in acts of open rebellion against the government. . . . insurrections . . . they have blustered, threatened, assaulted, and murdered. They even threaten helpless women and children. I know the leaders . . . will disclaim responsibility . . . but they are nevertheless the accomplices of the brutal and ignorant men whom they have incited to commit such outrages. . . . I am a friend of the workingman. . . ."

He said: "The creation of classes in this country is to be severely condemned. . . ."

He said: "I believe many of the labor leaders would guillotine us if they could."

And all this about 1900. There can be no doubt that Mr. Parry was the most outspoken foe of organized labor of his time and perhaps of any time. He achieved this distinction soon after being elected president of the National Association of Manufacturers in 1902, and he gloried in it. His friends said that "he was not opposed to labor and that the laboring man was always helped and encouraged by Mr. Parry. He was known to be kind to his own employees. . . ." He once indicated that his battle with labor unions began with a petty quarrel. The painters' walking delegate complained that the steps of Parry's mansion had been painted below scale. "I told him," said Mr. Parry, "that I knew nothing about his union scale and cared less, and showed him out of my office." According to Mr. Parry, Samuel Gompers, then head of the American Federation of Labor, came out to inspect Mr. Parry's porch steps, made a speech, and announced a national boycott of Parry products. This, said Mr. Parry, only advertised his business. "The boycott [is] . . . immoral and un-American."

He carried great weight. He "was generally credited with being one of the leading forces which, during the administration of President McKinley restored an equilibrium between capital and labor in this country." President Theodore Roosevelt slapped him on the back and said: "Parry, how would you like to go on the national ticket with me in 1904?" and Mr. Parry replied decorously: "Mr. President, I am only here to invite you to attend the national convention of American manufacturers, which meets at Indianapolis in the coming May." Mr. Parry became an evangelist; he made speeches, gave out interviews, wrote letters. At his instigation the N.A.M. was reportedly raising a fund of a million and a half to fight labor. He announced he had received threats and had stationed an armed guard at his home to protect his family. Sam Gompers commented mildly: "Why, we all get such letters." Gompers came to Indianapolis for Labor Day in 1903. The parade started at 9:44 a.m. Behind the lead carriage marched 5,708 men, and women too, and it took them an hour and a half to cross Illinois Street on Washington. The cigarmakers came first, three-deep and carrying umbrellas; the horseshoers wore black shirts and leather aprons; the bakers were in white. The structural ironworkers were accompanied by a billy goat, symbolizing unionism, and a kid bearing a sign

125

"Parry's model union." Some of the electrical workers were in electric automobiles, and the young ladies of the United Garment Workers rode in buggies. There were no floats, few furbelows, for this was a demonstration of massed strength. Gompers, who had spent Sunday at the Claypool visiting his old Hoosier friends—he had lived on Ohio Street for a couple of years—addressed the crowd at the fairgrounds. The crowd was disappointed that Parry had declined an invitation to debate with Gompers, but it enjoyed running races, boxing and wrestling matches, dancing, and "a big baby show." Parry, interviewed by the *News*, said: "So Labor Day is over. Well, I'm glad the boys had a good time." Citizens were cowed, public officials afraid of labor strength, he said, though he did not comment directly on the fact that the mayor had paraded with the workingmen. He said: "If labor will eliminate its execrable program of law defiance, I prophesy industrial peace once more. . . . We move fast in this country. . . . Let the union incorporate, take full responsibility such as rests upon employers and I prophesy we shall soon see the passing of the walking delegate and the professional troublemaker."

He didn't believe in the law of arbitration: "The Constitution of the United States is good enough for me. Either a man has a right to run his own business or he has not. . . . The idea of arbitrating the question whether an employer can employ a man who does not belong to a union is absurd. It is revolutionary. It means that individual liberty is destroyed. . . ." He thought workmen should have the right to strike, ". . . but they have no right to interfere with the business of their employers or with the men hired to take their places." He didn't think that labor's "economic ideas will make much headway unless they can be inflicted upon the country by force," nor did he think the United States could be run on an eight-hour day, for: "The majority of men work ten hours, and that is an indication that it requires a ten-hour day to produce enough to satisfy the needs of humanity." He didn't believe in giving the worker a share in the business: "He will never believe that he is fairly treated, and if money is lost he will not be willing to take his share of the losses . . . a bad thing all around."

To many worried manufacturers Mr. Parry must have seemed

a brave knight indeed. When he addressed the first national convention of the Citizens' Industrial Association of America in the Claypool Hotel, the four hundred delegates rose and cheered, and from among them burst such cries as "that's good" and "that's the stuff" and "say that over again." (Mr. Parry obliged.) The *News* headline was *"EMPLOYERS ATTACK ORGANIZED LABOR."* The convention telegraphed Congress, packed a lobbyist off to oppose the anti-injunction bill ("an attempt . . . to begin a reign of terror"), and approved Mr. Parry's suggestion that a well-financed "bureau of information" be established to influence "political parties and . . . public officers."

Mr. Parry was a tireless bantam. His book, *The Scarlet Empire*, after appearing in the official organ of the N.A.M., was published by Bobbs-Merrill, whose predecessor had been Indianapolis's great publishing house during the days of Riley. It was a fanciful satire on Atlantis, which had fallen prey to socialists. Individualism was dead, initiative stifled, personality, temperament, heart, and love all atrophied; and Mr. Parry proved that all this was impractical and bad. A journalist wrote to Mr. Parry: "Smash 'em, Mr. Parry, smash 'em!" His book and Upton Sinclair's *The Jungle* were published almost simultaneously. Mr. Parry attacked the muckrakers, who were then busy denouncing corruption, inflated corporate profits, and trusts as producers of slums, child labor, poverty.

The Central Labor Union of Indianapolis catechized him on his views. It asked what he considered "legitimate purposes" of trades unions, and he replied: "Legitimate purposes are such as are lawful, and illegitimate purposes are such as are unlawful. This answer ought to be sufficiently explicit even for the most obtuse intellect, but many labor leaders appear to be constitutionally defective of comprehension when the subject of law is broached. . . . It is unlawful to use opprobrious and insulting language such as 'scab' to a non-member of your organization. It is unlawful to hurl brickbats at him or frighten in brutal fashion the women and children of his family. . . . Force methods are un-American. The great majority of the men in the unions are unquestionably law-abiding citizens at heart. But. . . . A great many unionists boast of their belief in socialism.

. . . a man who really believes in socialism is a traitor at heart to his country." The union asked Mr. Parry if his motives were patriotic or selfish, and he replied: ". . . Patriotism is enlightened self-interest." It asked whether he favored "natural" or "artificial" regulation of industry, and he wrote at length of beneficent capitalism, "horde of officials," slavery to bureaucracy, socialist dictators, freedom of individual action. It asked if he thought existing institutions fostered special privilege or restricted opportunity, and he said he didn't know but if labor thought so, it ought to seek redress at the ballot box. He maintained that labor unions had lowered wages, and when the union asked: "Would the working people belonging to the unions be any better off if your ideas were to prevail?" Mr. Parry replied: "Yes, unquestionably."

Past sixty, he began to dispose of his holdings. With other leaders of the N.A.M., he started on a trip around the world "to study the forms of government of other countries and inquire into the commercial relations that the United States had with them," but he was stopped as he was about to sail from San Francisco: The Senate committee investigating lobbying wanted him. Later he got as far as China when war prevented him from visiting Russia. En route home he fell ill—"it was believed that the poor food he received while in foreign lands brought about the illness"—and he died May 12, 1915, at his Golden Hills estate, and he was buried in Crown Hill.

David M. Parry had not been mistaken when he thought he detected a ferment at work. It had begun in the eighties though it lagged behind the rise of manufacturing, just as wages axiomatically lag behind prices. Scarcely had legislators dealt with the Grange demands (largely after the Grange was done for) than they were besieged by labor: Nearly every Indiana legislature after 1890 considered labor legislation. A State Board of Charities, a Workmen's Compensation Act, factory-inspection labor laws, and a law forbidding discharge of an employee for union activity were produced by pressure from the Socialists, the unions, and the remnants of the Populists. Young Senator Beveridge, addressing a wealthy audience in New York in 1898, tried a straddle: he denounced abusive big business as well as fomenters of discontent. He, like the state and nation, welcomed the coming of the Spanish-American War: Imperialism was safe. Beveridge became its foremost apostle, and one can hear the confidence of the triumphant gentleman from Indiana ringing in his speeches. He told the Union League Club in Philadelphia: "The Philippines are ours forever. . . . The Republic never re- treats. Its flag is the only flag that has never known defeat. Where the flag leads, we follow, for we know that the hand that bears it onward is the unseen hand of God," and in his maiden Senate speech in 1900 he said: "And just beyond the Philippines are China's illimitable markets. We will not retreat from either. We will not repudiate our duty in the archipelago. We will not abandon our opportunity in the Orient. We will not renounce our part in the mission of our race, trustees under God, of the civilization of the world. And we will move forward to our work, not howling out regrets like slaves whipped to their burdens, but with gratitude for a task worthy of our strength and thanksgiv- ing to Almighty God that He has marked us as his chosen peo- ple, henceforth to lead in the regeneration of the world. . . . God has not been preparing the English-speaking and Teutonic peoples for a thousand years for nothing but vain and idle self- contemplation and self-admiration. No! He has made us the master organizers of the world to establish system where chaos reigns. . . . He has made us adepts in government that we may administer government among savages and senile peoples. Pray God the time may never come when Mammon and the love of ease shall so debase our blood that we will fear to shed it for the flag and its imperial destiny. . . . And so, Senators, with rever- ent hearts, where dwells the fear of God, the American people move forward to the future of their hope and the doing of His work." Hoar of Massachusetts might complain that "the words Right, Duty, Freedom, were absent," but the Senate galleries went wild. Beveridge was young, he was fiery, he knew what he was talking about (had he not just returned from the Philip- pines?), and back in Indiana he was a hero in the Hoosier ora- torical tradition. When he had been elected the Columbia Club had entertained him at the Denison, and when the grand march ended at the Marion Club Ball, his portrait was suddenly illu- minated with electric lights. On New Year's Eve 1900 he was a distinguished guest at the opening of the new Columbia Club, together with Harrison and Fairbanks and others, and Riley read a poem. He differed politely with the venerable Harrison, and the club members were titillated.

But they were not amused when in 1912, new issues having overshadowed the march of the flag, Beveridge joined the Progressive revolt. How, the clubmen grumbled, did a nice young man like that ever get mixed up with anything so disreputable as the eight-hour day? They removed his picture from the calm walls of both the Marion and the Columbia clubs. Beaten and embittered, he sailed for Europe. In 1915 some newspapermen caught Theodore Roosevelt visiting Elbert Gary's mansion, and the year after that Beveridge followed Roosevelt back to Hughes Republicanism, and the Marion and the Columbia clubs restored his portrait. Thereafter, except for a pronouncement upon the League of Nations ("America first! Not only America first, but America only!") and an unsuccessful campaign in 1922 for the Senate, he devoted his time to writing biographies of Lincoln and Chief Justice John Marshall. His revolt, like Roosevelt's, always had seemed like a phony revolt, the revolt of the outs against the ins, the revolt against the wicked committee chairman by the committee member who wants to become chairman himself. There was unrest in Indiana all right, as Mr. Parry had noted, but its leader was not Albert J. Beveridge, its leaders were half-forgotten labor men, its hero was Eugene V. Debs of Terre Haute.

PART FIVE

Voices of Protest

Chapter 11

EUGENE V. DEBS

I

F YOU take the Pennsylvania west from Indianapolis about fifty miles, you pass from flat farmland into a rough, broken region, scraggly trees on the hills, a little corn in the creek bottoms, here and there weed-grown wagon roads once used for hauling coal, a round black patch on the hillside and a cluster of gray, windowless houses and the spoil piles of old coal workings, everywhere sunlight bright on the mottled bark of the sycamores. At seventy miles the train will break over the rim of wooded hills and cross a savanna beside the Wabash, a gray savanna overhung by smoke, plaited with rails, pocked by gravel pits and coal piles, half-mile strings of coal cars parked on the tracks, squat gray shacks on the gray-brown flats, stunted trees; man's only towers the smoking brick stacks, the only splashes of color the lonely little red cabooses. And the train will halt, just like the Vandalia did years ago, at the Terre Haute depot, a grimy grotesque red structure with turreted tower and roof of many slopes and "Union Depot" carved proudly in sandstone up where the pigeons roost. From the station you can cross a little park and you will find a single-storied brick building offering sleeping rooms, all that remains of the St. Nicholas Hotel, and across the alley behind it stands Gene Debs's home, a gray, two-and-a-half-story frame house with a slate roof and two chimneys and a broad, shady L-shaped porch, a home fit for a capitalist when he built it in 1889. Eighth Street is lined by trees and by gray houses with porch railings made of cement blocks in geometric patterns. If you walk a few blocks south you will reach the long, thin business district of Terre Haute, strung, bars and banks alike, upon a single thread—Wabash Avenue. Many of the stores at street level present chromium and glass-brick fronts; but if you step back to the curb and glance up you see that these buildings were erected in the great years, the eighties and nineties, for they have flat, ugly faces, narrow, peaked roofs, old dates and old names under the eaves. Here are the *Tribune* and the *Star,* owned by the Fairbanks estate. Crawford Fairbanks accumulated forty million dollars distilling liquor and brewing beer, trading in Wabash Avenue real estate and engaging in so many other enterprises that today the unseen ramifications of his estate reach all over town. Here at the main crossroads on the site of the old Prairie House is the Terre Haute House, in the lobby a painting of "Nancy Hanks," a racehorse that set a world's record here. Behind the Terre Haute House stands the Grand Opera House. Terre Haute was a good road-show town. Catercorner from the Opera House stands the great, gray Rose Clinic endowed by Chauncey Rose, railroader, oil wildcatter, financier, builder of Terre Haute and Indianapolis, founder of Rose Polytechnic Institute. He ran the Vandalia in Debs's day before it became a part of the Pennsylvania system. William Riley McKeen was a banker and builder of the Pennsylvania— James Whitcomb Riley wrote:

> . . . *And where's as clean*
> *A fi-nan-seer as Rile' McKeen.* . . .

—and his son Ben became an operating vice president of the Pennsylvania, and the McKeen name is carved on the Fairbanks Block on Wabash Avenue. Not far from the Opera House is a part, but only a small part, of the Hulman enterprises. Francis Hulman, a German immigrant, in 1850 established a wholesale grocery firm with $2,100; under his brother Herman it became one of the largest west of the Alleghenies. Herman bought a distillery, sold it to Crawford Fairbanks, bought another, traded it, promoted railroads and new industries, taught his sons the business, endowed a hospital. In 1945 his grandson, Anton Hulman, Jr., one of the most powerful men in Terre Haute, paid about $750,000 for the Indianapolis Motor Speedway. And there once more is the pattern—a man who came from across the sea or over the mountains to start a store or shop and became a financier, the grandson who controls the fortune, runs the town, and rides a hobby.

Out Wabash Avenue toward the river stands the Vigo County Courthouse, its bell bequeathed by Francis Vigo, who financed George Rogers Clark. Across from the courthouse a sign in the window of a dingy little saloon says: "Eat here and keep your wife for a pet. Meals 25¢," and the massive bar is of mahogany and so are the pillars flanking the mirror. There is a piano in one corner. In one of the last booths sits a white-faced, thin woman with bright, hollow eyes, black dress, scrawny chest, bright-red lipstick, hair cut in bangs. She is all alone, watching the workingmen at the bar. Back of this saloon, north on Second and Third Streets and on side streets, lies the District, the old tenderloin, gaudiest in Indiana in its heyday in the nineties and early 1900's. When the girls hit town they had to register at the police station; if they wanted to leave the District, even to go shopping, they had to get permission from the Sergeant. They had to display health certificates, renewed weekly by approved physicians, over the headboards of their beds. The Terre Haute whore became famous. The fanciest establishment was Madame Brown's, a brick abode with a glass canopy, patronized by businessmen who could afford the ten- or fifteen-dollar fee. The living-room—one wall was mirrored—was cluttered with expensive bric-a-brac, antiques, a grand piano, and Oriental rugs, and when you walked in through the front door, you came face to face with a life-size reproduction of Watts's picture of Sir Galahad leading a horse. Madame Brown ran an orderly establishment, and the District was scandalized when a drunk somehow got in and vomited in the water fountain. Through the week the madames could count on the custom of discreet married men and eminent pillars of church and civic affairs, and nearly every Saturday was a payday. The coal mines paid on the tenth and twenty-fifth of the month ("No use takin' a bath tonight, girls: payday in the mines") and the railroads on the first and fifteenth and many factories paid every Saturday; then too on Saturdays farmers came to town in wagons or on the interurban. Gambling was fast and wide open. In the heart of town right across from the Terre Haute House stood Duncan's place, famed for its stained-glass windows, excellent cuisine, fine liquors, and high-stake gambling. Usually matters ran smoothly in the District, for the entrepreneurs were as interested in avoiding wreckage as the police, but in one brief period there occurred, unaccountably, three ax murders and a flatiron murder. Theodore Dreiser and his brother Paul were born in a shack on the edge of the District. Paul was a rotund straw-hatted sport, and an Evansville madame with whom he lived inspired his song *My Gal Sal.* Gene Debs too, like Dreiser, one of ten children, was born near the District but later he stayed away from it. He once said Paul Dresser "was a sport, and therefore he was out of my class," and he never met Dreiser either. Today a boulevard, power plant, and park near the Wabash River are named for Dresser, but nothing in Terre Haute memorializes either Dreiser or Debs except a bronze plaque to Debs at the Central Labor Union Temple.

Terre Haute was a pork-packing center early. Distillers and brewers came next since corn, water, and coal were plentiful. After the Civil War railroads and coal brought iron and steel industries. Glass and other industries came when natural gas failed elsewhere. By 1887 Vigo County mines alone produced 222,320 tons of coal, in 1905, eight times that amount. Every mine had its town, usually a company town. Shirkieville, Fontanet, Carbon, Coal Bluff, Perth, once boom towns, today are abandoned or nothing but hamlets. The Scotch settled Bicknell; the English, Shelburn; the Welsh, West Terre Haute; the Italians, Clinton. The Austrians and Lithuanians and Slavs came too. Terre Haute had a German-language newspaper by 1870. The coal fields' boom was rather quiet, for many miners arrived with their families, prepared to pick up tools and begin work where they had left off in the old country. It was not adventure that drew them so much as economic opportunity and freedom. In the early 1850's Francis Hulman wrote to his brother: "Oh, Herman, Herman follow my advice. . . . Get Mother's consent and . . . hurry to get here. Here you will have an altogether different chance; you will lead an entirely different life, and be a different person. A man is free here. . . . He is conscious of his own worth and dignity as a man, in this free and happy

America; where ignorance and poverty do not reign. . . . Here tyrants and despots are not. . . . The laws are good and wealth and well-being reign everywhere. You can have a good job in our new business. . . . You can go horseback riding once or twice a week. . . ." Many of the miners, however, did not find life so pleasant.

During the seventies miners and railroaders alike were restless. Miners at Coal Creek struck, and the operators brought in Negro strikebreakers; on April 18, 1878, three of them were murdered. The Noble Order of the Knights of Labor was gaining power. Terre Haute became a center of labor unrest. On August 2, 1881, twenty labor-union leaders, including twelve from Terre Haute, representing fifteen unions, assembled at Temperance Hall; later they formed the A.F. of L. For years the Terre Haute Agreement set the pattern for the national coal industry. P. H. Penna, a shrewd, long-faced miner, organized the Indiana miners, led them into the United Mine Workers when it was formed in 1889, was U.M.W. International President in 1895 and 1896, and the next year went over to the Indiana Bituminous Coal Operators Association. (It has been said the mine workers have been sold out by their own leaders more often than any other workers.)

This, then, was the town where Eugene Victor Debs grew up. He was born here November 5, 1855. His parents had come here from Alsace in 1851, about the time Francis Hulman was writing to his brother. The Debses were very poor. They lived in a little frame house at 447 North Fourth Street. In it they ran a grocery. When Gene was fifteen he had to leave school and go to work. He scraped paint off railway cars at the Vandalia shops for fifty cents a day. He bought his own scraper for a dollar. He was restless. After two years he became a Vandalia locomotive fireman. The railroaders at St. Louis, Terre Haute, Indianapolis, and Evansville liked him. He was friendly, eager, generous. Firing was a man's job, and he was only sixteen but he was tall and lanky and strong. One night his locomotive rounded a bend face to face with the headlight of another; they got her stopped in time. The prairie roadbeds were not ballasted. His mother worried about him, and so, reluctantly, in 1874 he quit firing. His father got him a job clerking at Hulman's.

He spent his evenings hanging around with railroaders. Things were happening. In the hard times following Jay Cooke's failure of 1873, the Brotherhood of Locomotive Firemen arose. A brotherhood organizer hit Terre Haute in February 1875, and picked Gene Debs out of the first meeting to be the secretary of Vigo Lodge No. 16. He also became president of the Occidental Literary Club of Terre Haute. (His father long ago had read Voltaire and Goethe and the story of Jean Valjean to him and, indeed, had chosen his middle name, Victor, out of respect to Hugo.) The club approved his bringing Robert Ingersoll to lecture at Terre Haute but disapproved his bringing Susan B. Anthony. She spoke to a small audience, as did Wendell Phillips, the aging abolitionist agitator who impressed Debs so much.

In 1877 the railroad proprietors cut wages, and the workmen struck, bloodily and vainly. The brotherhood convened at Indianapolis, Debs denounced strikers, and Riley McKeen, president of the Vandalia, congratulated him. Troops crushed the strikes which almost wrecked the brotherhoods. Terre Haute Democrats nominated Debs for city clerk in 1879, and the *Gazette* termed him ". . . a finely built young man of twenty-five . . . active, hard-working, painstaking . . . ambition to succeed. . . . He has a good voice to read the record of the Council and writes a neat, plain hand. . . ." He led the ticket and quit his job at Hulman's but edited the firemen's magazine from his home. The brotherhood appointed him national secretary-treasurer. Dubious honor: the brotherhood was demoralized, its membership low, its treasury looted. Debs induced Crawford Fairbanks and others to sign his bond. In a year the brotherhood had three thousand members. Re-elected city clerk he used his salary to organize the brotherhood. He was traveling everywhere. He went by freight. The boys in the caboose were glad to see him. Sometimes the division heads had him thrown off. They ordered him out of roundhouses. An agitator. One night in midwinter a conductor dropped him off in a snowbank at Elmira, New York, and he fell into the arms of a policeman. He tramped through the yards in rain and sleet at night, hunting a freight. The firemen knew him. So did the brakemen, switchmen, telegraphers, shopmen, track hands. Other workingmen,

not railroaders, heard about him and asked him for help. They
were all groping, the times were troubled, they did not know
what to do. His grip was always packed. He declined a job as
general manager of a newspaper enterprise. He did not like business. To honor him, the brotherhood held its convention in Terre
Haute, and he marched at the head of the delegates, the literary
club, the fire brigade, and the G.A.R. Dan Voorhees and the
mayor praised him, and when he told the delegates that the
brotherhood now had five thousand members, they roared:
"Debs ! Debs ! Debs !"

Elected to the legislature, he nominated Dan Voorhees for
the Senate. He wrote a labor law that the legislature emascu-
lated, and he went back to Terre Haute disgusted and told his
brother Theodore he was through with politics. Theodore was
never far from him, the constant loyal aide on whom Gene
leaned. They looked much alike. Debs was tall, gaunt, high-
domed, and though he was not yet thirty he was starting to lose
his hair. He lived upstairs over a bakery at Eleventh and Wabash
a block east of the tracks. Kate Metzel, born to wealth, visited
his older sisters. Nights that she stayed late it fell to Gene to see
her home. He married her in 1885. Kate was an Episcopalian.
They had a big June wedding and a honeymoon in the East and
a write-up on the society page. They had no children. Kate was
thin-lipped, oval-faced, buxom, handsome, imperious. He called
her "Duckie." Nearly all his life he wrote her mash notes: In
1918 he wrote:

> *Kate is my sweetheart and the idol of my heart;*
> *Faithful, loving, kind and true is my darling wife;*
> *Thanks to God that she is mine, may he bless her noble life;*
> *I will worship at her shrine till in death we part.*

In 1889 he used his building-and-loan savings to build a house
at 451 North Eighth Street. It had eight rooms, a fruit cellar,
mahogany woodwork in one room, eleven-foot, nine-inch ceilings downstairs, a northlit living-room with a fireplace flanked
by bookcases. When his low-brow friends, the railroaders, the
union men, came to the door, Kate opened it a crack on a chain
and turned them away; she admitted them only when they
brought him home drunk. She and he slept in separate bedrooms,

she in the best. His room, with its view of the tracks, was the worst, the only one except the kitchen without a fireplace. Ambitious, she was proud of his presidential candidacy but must have wished it had not been on the Socialist ticket. She was the best looking wife of a candidate in 1912 and knew it. He never stopped loving her. The Hulmans lived four doors from them, and other manufacturers near by. They visited and entertained the Debses. They might not understand a labor organizer, but after all the brotherhood's slogan still was "Benevolence, Sobriety, Industry," and, moreover, these were the golden years; there was room for all.

But Debs liked better to drink with the railroaders in the bars at the St. Nicholas and the other hotels near the tracks. He bought more drinks than he drank; he bought for anybody who had no money. He liked to sing and talk and recite poetry. He liked to meet people in saloons. He was a whisky drinker. He had small patience with temperance people—"this mean and narrow fanaticism." He brought James Whitcomb Riley to town several times, and it amused him that not until Riley's national veneration did he attract a crowd to the Opera House. Riley visited Debs so often that a bedroom was called "the Riley room." When he was there neighborhood children flocked to the house, delighting Debs. He and Riley liked to get in a carriage and drive out to Monninger's Wine Gardens and spend the afternoon drinking at a table in the grove of sycamores and elms and oaks. Riley wrote:

> And there's 'Gene Debs—a man 'at stands
> And jest holds out in his two hands
> As warm a heart as ever beat
> Betwixt here and the Jedgement Seat!

When the police ordered a homeless girl of good family into the District to keep her off the streets, Debs took her home and accused society of hounding her. Strolling on Wabash Avenue, he remarked that it was too hot for a paving gang to be working, and the foreman said if they'd taken care of their money they wouldn't have to work. At noon Debs took them to a cool restaurant and bought their lunch and all the buttermilk they could drink, and one of them asked who he was, and another replied:

"It may be Eugene Debs, they say he does things like this to working men."

He traveled ceaselessly—freights and bunkhouses—organizing. He built the Brotherhood of Locomotive Firemen. The engineers were the aristocrats. The head of their brotherhood said: "No engineer in the country is worth going to jail for." Debs wrote:

> *While there is a lower class I am in it;*
> *While there is a criminal element I am of it;*
> *While there's a soul in prison I am not free.*

America heaved mightily. The Haymarket Riot exploded. Debs lost his belief in "Benevolence, Sobriety, Industry"; where had that got them? The engineers struck the C.B. & Q. Debs called the firemen out too and wrote: "The strike is the weapon of the oppressed." The conductors stayed at work, the engineers lost heart, the Pinkertons broke the strike, the firemen were left out. Debs called for a federation of all railroad workers. The engineers declined. The firemen convened, chanting the roar: "Debs! Debs! Debs!" but Debs was through: Weeping, he quit, this union was not big enough.

In resigning he gave up a four-thousand-dollar-a-year job. He said: "I do this because it pleases me. . . ." The railroad proprietors played off one brotherhood against another. They had formed the General Managers' Association in 1886. Debs wanted one big union. On June 20, 1893, he announced the American Railway Union. To it he welcomed lowly track hands as well as lordly engineers. He said: "If I rise, it will be with the ranks, not from them." In a year the A.R.U. had 150,000 members. Railroads were bankrupt, factories shut, farms foreclosed, soup kitchens busy. In Indiana it was cheaper to burn corn for fuel than to haul it to market. James J. Hill, president of the Great Northern Railroad, cut his employees' wages in August and again in January 1894. When he cut them a third time, in March, only one union did anything about it: Debs's A.R.U. The Great Northern ordered A.R.U. sympathizers fired. In April the A.R.U. struck. Debs asked for arbitration. Hill refused. At Charles Pillsbury's invitation Debs told uneasy members of the St. Paul Chamber of Commerce about the track hands in the shacks out on the plains, and defied Hill. The chamber demanded that Hill, long the Twin Cities' ruler, arbitrate. Instead, at Hill's behest, the Governor of Minnesota called Debs "anarchist," "agitator," "foreigner." Debs replied: "I have never in my life worn the collar of a plutocrat, nor jumped like a jack when he pulled the string as you have done for Mr. Hill. Now, Governor . . . you may, with my consent, take the B Line and go to hell." After eighteen days Hill granted ninety-seven and one-half per cent of the union demands. Pillsbury wanted to banquet Debs. Debs told him to spend the ten thousand dollars on calico for the railroaders' wives. He refused to sanction a union mass meeting in his honor. Next morning he and Theodore boarded a train for Terre Haute. It moved unusually slowly through the yards. The conductor touched Debs on the shoulder. Wondering, Debs followed him to the rear platform. He saw the trackmen who worked in the yards lined up beside the right of way, heads bared, hat in one hand, shovel in the other, standing at attention. They did not roar: "Debs! Debs! Debs!"; they only stood silent as his train rolled slowly past, and some of them wept, and so did Debs.

Proudly he told four thousand people in the park near the Terre Haute House that he had got $146,000 more for Jim Hill's employees without bloodshed. Two months later bayonets glinted in the company town, Pullman, Illinois. As a young mechanic, George Pullman had patented a sleeping car; by 1894 his cars rode the rails of the nation and he was a financial giant. He would recognize no labor unions and he cut wages five times between May and December 1893, the last time by almost thirty per cent. He said hard times were responsible and declared an eight per cent dividend. He did not reduce the rents he charged his employees. A committee of them asked him to restore the cuts. He fired two members of the grievance committee. The men struck. On June 12 Debs's A.R.U. convened at Uhlrich's Hall in Chicago. Debs was in a strong tide. Pullman employees had affiliated with the A.R.U. A minister described conditions in the "model town." Coal miners had helped the A.R.U. against Hill. Debs tried arbitration. Mr. Pullman told the A.R.U. committee there was nothing to arbitrate. On June 26 the A.R.U. boycotted his cars. The General Managers' Association rallied round Mr. Pullman. The boycott became a strike. Debs had not wanted it but he fought for it. By the third day nearly everything west of Chicago had stopped rolling.

Debs kept sending telegrams: "We have assurances that within 48 hours every labor organization will come to our rescue. . . . Labor must win now or never." But the forces set against him were mighty. Grover Cleveland had obligations. His Attorney General, Richard Olney, had been a railroad attorney. Federal circuit judges issued an injunction against Debs under the Sherman Act, which everyone supposed had been intended to restrain capitalists. Cleveland ordered out the troops, and General Nelson A. Miles led them, first paying his respects at the offices of the General Managers' Association. Governor Peter Altgeld had protested that troops were not needed. Debs sent more telegrams, nine thousand in all: "Troops cannot move trains." Five were killed in a battle at Hammond. Mr. Pullman went to the seashore. There were eleven thousand men under arms, three thousand described by the Chicago police chief as thugs and ex-convicts. On July 10 Debs and three others were charged with conspiracy, and released on ten-thousand-dollar bond. Eugene Field sent him a note: "You will soon need a friend; let me be that friend." Debs had a hold on poets. On July 17 Debs and other A.R.U. officials were jailed for violating the injunction. Almost at that hour Mr. Gompers issued a statement: "The great industrial upheaval now agitating the country has been carefully, calmly, and fully considered. . . . We are forced to the conclusion that the best interests of the unions affiliated with the American Federation of Labor demand that they refrain from participating. . . ." Debs said later: "Gompers would not hold his position year after year unless he was satisfactory to Wall Street. . . . Wearing a frock coat and dining with the enemies of the workers." In spite of Gompers, the A.F. of L. in Indiana stood by Debs: it proposed him for Governor.

Clarence Darrow defended Debs: ". . . we shall try to get the general managers here to tell what they know about conspiracy." This proved difficult. Mr. Pullman disappeared. Debs was sent to jail for contempt of court. His parents wired: "Stand by your principles regardless of consequences." He entered the county jail at Woodstock, Illinois, January 8, 1895.

He was thirty-nine years old, tall, thinning down, very bald, with gold-rimmed glasses and creased forehead and staring eyes. At Terre Haute, Theodore would answer the mail. Kate closed up the house on Eighth Street and went to Woodstock. Debs and the seven other A.R.U. men had brought books to jail. The sheriff gave them tables and chairs, and in the corridor outside their cells they studied the social sciences on a strict schedule. Eight men in high-necked collars, narrow trousers, and high-buttoned coats, hair parted and plastered down, purged their contempt for a capitalists' court by diligently reading Ingersoll's speeches, *Wealth Against Commonwealth,* and great piles of tracts that Socialists, anarchists, single taxers, and Populists sent. Victor Berger, the guttural Socialist from Milwaukee, came to instruct them from *Das Kapital.* Later Debs said Berger converted him to Socialism, but it was no overnight conversion. The courts had broken his strike and smashed his union. The courts were the tools of the capitalists; so were the Democratic and Republican parties. Just before the strike collapsed he had said: "I am a Populist, and I favor wiping out both old parties." Much later he said: "How short-sighted the ruling class is." It was the ruling class, not Victor Berger, that made a Socialist of Eugene Debs.

On November 22, 1895, the Sheriff told him he was free. A crowd surrounded him. Somebody cried: "Lift him up so we all can see," and they did and carried him to the railroad station, chanting: "Debs! Debs! Debs!" Hundreds boarded the train, and a band played. When he got off the train at Wells Street Station in Chicago he found a hundred thousand people in the trainshed and in the slush and snow outside. They were roaring "Debs! Debs! Debs!" They were trying to carry him to a carriage drawn by six white horses, but he would not go; he would walk with them. He did—to the Battery D Armory—and he told them: "The theme tonight is personal liberty. . . . Corporations know the price of judges, legislators and public officials as certainly as Armour knows the price of pork and mutton," and he counseled them to turn to the ballot: "It can make and unmake presidents and congresses and courts. . . . It can give our civilization its crowning glory—the co-operative commonwealth."

Then he took a train to Terre Haute, and miners with the Coal Bluff Band waited in the rain to escort him from the depot to his home. That night others took him through streets lit by Roman candles to the Armory, where he shook their hands and said: "Money talks. . . . There is something wrong in this country. . . ."

When he talked like that he was a righteous avenger, a tall, spare man alone on a platform leaning forward and shaking his long, bony finger: "I am not a Labor Leader; I do not want you to follow me or any one else. If you are looking for a Moses to lead you out of this capitalist wilderness, you will stay right where you are. I would not lead you into this promised land if I could, because if I could lead you in, some one else would lead you out."

The A.R.U. came out of the Pullman strike twenty-two thousand dollars in debt. Debs assumed the debt, renounced his seventy-five dollars a month salary, borrowed some cash, and hit the lecture trail with Theodore. People were curious about him. He drew big crowds. He would talk in the opera houses and escape with relief to saloons with railroaders. Those who had struck were black-listed. When he entered one meeting hall, a little fireman escorting him spied a railroader with his hat on and told him to take it off: "Don't you know Gene Debs is here?"

He was stumping for Bryan that year, 1896. Though he had renounced Democracy, the Populists had endorsed Bryan, and Debs was on their side by instinct. Bryan lost. Debs turned Socialist at last. There was no place else for him to go.

But the Socialist Labor Party was too narrow. And so in 1897 he and others, including Berger, formed the Social Democratic Party of America (which, after tortured mutations, in 1901 became the Socialist Party of America). Into it Debs dumped the remnants of the A.R.U. He traveled, spreading the Socialist doctrine. At Muscatine, Iowa, lecture receipts were sixteen dollars, and he couldn't pay his hotel bill. At Perry only seven men turned up for his lecture, all Rock Island officials who had come to see that none of their employees attended. Debs knew who they were. He addressed them on "The Vaunted American Republic Where Intimidation of Employees Prevails."

There was still room for Debs in Terre Haute. It had room for

immigrant miners and railroaders and factory hands, for whores
and pimps and gamblers, for Debs. In 1899 Frank McKeen, a
banker, asked Debs for a copy of the talk that he had given at a
manufacturer's home "as I would like to have it to lay away for
future reading." In reply to a Michigan man who inquired what
Debs was like, the mayor wrote: ". . . while the overwhelming
majority of the people here are opposed to the social and economic theories of Mr. Debs . . . there is not, perhaps, a single
man in this city who enjoys to a greater degree than Mr. Debs,
the affection, love and profound respect of the entire community.
He is cultured, brilliant, eloquent, scholarly, companionable, and
lovable in his relations with his fellowman. . . . he is known as
'Gene.' . . . Some of the richest men here, people who by very
instinct are bitter against Socialism, are warm personal friends
of Mr. Debs. . . ." Even in 1912, after Debs had swung far left,
his old employers, the Hulmans, praised him. His neighbors
thought of him as the man who wept when children gave him
flowers at a banquet, who left the banquet to sit on the curb with
them. As well as indictments of the system he kept writing sentimental verse and prose—on his parents' golden wedding anniversary, childhood, woman,—and indeed it can be said that this
man was influenced almost as much by Riley as by Marx.

He went over to Indianapolis on March 6, 1900, where the
Socialist splinter groups were getting together. He said this was
"not a reform party, but a revolutionary party," and they nominated him for President against Bryan and McKinley. Debs and
the Socialist Labor candidate together polled 127,519 votes,
the biggest Socialist vote up to that time. (He polled four times
that many four years later.) Next year delegates from nearly
every state gathered at Masonic Hall and the Grand Hotel in
Indianapolis.

At the call of Debs, Big Bill Haywood, and others, a convention met at Chicago on June 27, 1905. Haywood, a big one-eyed
lunk of a man, got up and began: "Fellow Workers," and that
was what they wanted to hear. They formed the Industrial
Workers of the World. Debs told them: "They charge us with
being assembled here for the purpose of disrupting the union
movement. It is already disrupted. And if it were not disrupted,

we would not behold the spectacle here in this city of a white policeman guarding a black scab and a black policeman guarding a white scab, while the trades-unions stand by, with their hands in their pockets, wondering what is the matter with union labor in America. . . ."

He and Haywood had caught a vision, though dimly. When Gompers had learned craft unionism in the cigar makers' union, cigar making was a skilled trade. So were most factory jobs. And factories were family affairs. But now the production line was coming. The year that the I.W.W. was founded, U.S. Steel built Gary. The position of the workingman in the industrial machine was changing fast. D. M. Parry understood this. So did Debs. Vast industries used vast quantities of unskilled workingmen. The A.F. of L. wanted craftsmen, nothing more. Debs said: "[Morgan and Schwab] used to oppose trade unions. They don't oppose them any longer." He said: ". . . the Industrial Workers began by declaring that there is nothing in common between capitalists and wage-workers." When he talked like that, they sang:

We hate their rotten system more than any mortals do.
Our aim is not to patch it but to build it all anew.
And what we'll have for government, when we're finally through
Is One Big Industrial Union!

He preached them dignity and a dream: "We want a system in which the worker shall get what he produces and the capitalist shall produce what he gets. . . . When you unite and act together, the world is yours." And he told them: "Stand erect! Lift your bowed form from the earth! . . . Stand up and see how long a shadow you cast in the sunlight!"

They cast a long shadow. It reached from Cripple Creek to the Long Island mansions. On February 17, 1906, Big Bill Haywood and other union officials were kidnapped from Denver and charged with murdering the former Governor of Idaho. Debs, infuriated, wrote "Arouse Ye Slaves":

"It is a foul plot; a damnable conspiracy; a hellish outrage.
". . . according to the words of the slimy 'sleuth' who 'worked up the case' against them, 'they shall never leave Idaho alive.'

147

"Well, by the gods, if they don't, the governors of Idaho and Colorado and their masters from Wall street, New York, to the Rocky Mountains had better prepare to follow them.

"Nearly twenty years ago the capitalist tyrants put some innocent men to death for standing up for labor.

"They are now going to try it again. Let them dare!

"There have been twenty years of revolutionary education, agitation and organization since the Haymarket tragedy, and if an attempt is made to repeat it, there will be a revolution and I will do all in my power to precipitate it.

"The crisis has come and we have got to meet it. . . .

"They have driven us to the wall and now let us rally our forces and face them and fight. . . .

"They have done their best and their worst to crush and enslave us. Their politicians have betrayed us, their courts have thrown us into jail without trial and their soldiers have shot our comrades dead in their tracks. . . .

"Let them dare to execute their devilish plot and every state in this Union will resound with the tramp of revolution.

"Get ready, comrades, for action! No other course is left to the working class. . . ."

This was the farthest left he went. He printed it in the *Appeal to Reason,* a Socialist paper published at Girard, Kansas, of which he had become a contributing editor. His mother, whom he had called Daisy, died. He hastened back to Terre Haute. A few days later he wrote:

> *The grass grows green*
> *Where Daisy sleeps;*
> *The Mulberry tree its vigil keeps*
> *Where Daisy sleeps.*

His father was going blind; Debs read to him. He and Theodore opened an office on Wabash to answer the mail. He slept but five hours a night. He kept his hunting clothes in a third-floor closet and slipped off to the fields whenever he could. But he could not stay long in Terre Haute, he had to go speak for the Wobblies. Darrow defended them. They were acquitted.

The 1908 convention of the Socialist party was coming on. The party leaders, the intellectuals, had misgivings. They were always hovering in the background, playing Rasputin. Debs kept veering from one orthodoxy to another—craft brotherhood, industrial A.R.U., Populism, Democracy, Socialism of so many stripes, I.W.W. That was one reason Gompers hated him. Whenever rank-and-filers, disgusted with do-nothing leadership, formed a splinter group, Debs went along. He stayed close to the poor people, not to their leaders. No single movement, really, was big enough for him. Doctrinaires like Berger did not know what to do with him, but they knew they could not do without him. He was the only one of them who could make people's hearts sing. He was desperately impatient of their factional quarrels, their cold talk of tactics and dialectics. They were always relieved when he hit the road and left them in the smoky rooms. What would he have done had he been elected President? He once confessed he didn't know. He knew what was wrong with the capitalistic system—too few had too much—but as to how to fix it he was vague. About the closest he came was this: "Collective ownership by all of the people of all the means of wealth production and distribution." He wanted his one big industrial union to elect a Socialist administration which would create an "ordered, cooperative commonwealth." This meant planning. Debs never got around to drawing the plans.

At the 1908 convention Berger actually proposed someone else's name; but the delegates answered: "Debs! Debs! Debs!" A week later Debs went back to Girard, Kansas. The shopkeepers were having a street fair, and the crowd gathered about him in the public square. Making it up as he went along, he opened his presidential campaign: "Yes, I am my brother's keeper. . . ."

They were Kansans standing in the sun. "I am opposed to capitalism because I love my fellow men, and if I am opposing you I am opposing you for what I believe to be your good, and though you spat upon me with contempt I should still oppose you to the extent of my power. . . . Here I stand, just as I was created. I have two hands that represent my labor power. I have some bone and muscle and sinew and some energy. I want to exchange the use of these for food and clothing and shelter. But between me and the tools with which work is done there stands a man artificially created. He says, 'No, no!' Why not? 'Because you cannot first make a profit for me.'"

Some of these serious-faced, bony-faced people, or their fathers or mothers, must have driven out of the terrible plains of drought to cheer the Populist platform: ". . . tramps and millionaires." Now Debs told them:

"I know . . . how men become idle. . . . I have never yet seen the tramp I was not able to receive with open arms. He is a little less fortunate than I am. He is made the same as I am made. . . .

"Can you tell me why there wasn't a tramp in the United States in 1860? . . . If human nature is innately depraved and men would rather ride on brake-beams and sleep in holes and caves instead of comfortable beds . . . why were they not built that way fifty years ago? . . . Fifty years ago work was still mainly done by hand . . . and every boy could master the tools and go to work. . . . In fifty years that simple tool has become a mammoth machine. . . . With the machine came the capitalist. . . .

"We are not going to destroy private property. We are going to establish private property—all the private property necessary to house man, keep him in comfort and satisfy his wants. Eighty per cent of the people of the United States have no property today. A few have got it all. . . . We will reduce the workday and give every man a chance. We will go to the parks, and we will have music, because we will have time to play music and desire to hear it.

". . . it does not pay now to love music. Keep your eye on the almighty dollar and your fellowman. . . . Get the dollar and keep him down. Make him produce for you. You are not your brother's keeper. Suppose he is poor! Suppose his wife is forced into prostitution! Suppose his child is deformed! And suppose he shuffles off by destroying himself! What is that to you?

"But you ought to be ashamed. . . .

"Competition was natural enough at one time, but do you think you are competing today? . . . Against whom? Against Rockefeller? About as I would if I had a wheelbarrow and competed with the Santa Fe from here to Kansas City."

On August 31 out of Chicago's La Salle Street Station moved the Red Special—a locomotive, a baggage car, and a combined sleeper, observation, and dining car. The baggage car was crammed with band instruments and Socialist literature. Debs lived on this train for more than two months. The berth cramped his long legs. Sometimes he spoke ten times a day, standing at the door of the rear car, red flags sticking from brackets. Only Bryan's campaign of 1896 and Willkie's of 1940 parallel this one Neither of those men had to worry about money. The Red Special ran out of money on its first swing to the Coast. Zealots, among them Tom Mooney, sold literature and beat the bushes for nickels and dimes. Rich men contributed anonymously. People paid to hear Debs. The Red Special covered twenty thousand miles. At an Iowa hamlet a crowd of farmers stopped the Red Special, demanding to see the hero. When Debs, hoarse from a half-dozen speeches that morning, sent the band out to mollify them with the *Marseillaise*, they only roared his name the louder: "Debs! Debs! Debs!" One might expect him to inflame the urban masses, the Wobblies, and the Western miners. But look at the names of other towns where the Red Special stopped: Joliet and Ottawa, Spring Valley and Muscatine, Evansville and Loogootee,—an American litany. He wrote from Kansas City: "The meetings out here are big as all outdoors and red hot with enthusiasm. Ye Gods!" In Los Angeles he could speak nowhere but the zoo, and when the newspapers called this a suitable forum for wild animals, twelve thousand turned up, to Debs's amusement. He drew a bigger crowd at Evansville than Taft, who spoke there the same night. On election eve he went home to Terre Haute, where Haywood joined him. A latter-day admirer has said: "People yelled like hell for him, then went out and voted Republican or Democratic." His vote showed only a slight increase over that of 1904. (So did the total vote.)

Wherever there was a fight he got into it. When Ortie McManigal and the McNamara brothers, John and James, Indiana farm boys turned steelworkers, were charged with dynamiting the Los Angeles *Times* building and killing twenty-one people on October 1, 1910, Debs hurried to their defense. John McNamara, secretary-treasurer of the structural ironworkers' international, was arrested in its office on Monument Circle in Indianapolis April 22, 1911. Detectives said they found explosives on a farm near Indianapolis and in the basement of the building that housed the union office, but McNamara's landlord said he was a quiet man who took his meals with the family, rode down to the office each day on a motorcycle, voted Democratic, and had never said he hated capitalists. The nation was excited. Steel jobs had been bombed at Indianapolis and elsewhere. The *Brotherhood of Locomotive Firemen and Enginemen's Magazine* called the arrest a "damnable" frame-up. Trades unions at Indianapolis met in the Carpenters' building at 222 East Michigan Street to organize a defense committee. Debs was writing: "All nine members of the United States Supreme Court are corporation attorneys." He called William J. Burns, the detective who hoped to get $250,000 for tracking down John McNamara, a "kidnapper," and Burns solemnly said Debs had employed two hundred men to assassinate him. Darrow was hired to defend the McNamaras. James McNamara confessed. At once Gompers repudiated the McNamaras, the U.M.W. called them "moral degenerates," and the trades unions met once more at Carpenters' Hall: ". . . with them we have nothing more to do. . . ." Never was Gene Debs's fundamental divergence from orthodox unionists more striking: "The McNamaras are products of capitalism. . . . If you want to judge John McNamara you must first serve a month as structural iron worker on a skyscraper, risking your life every minute to feed your wife and babies, then be discharged and blacklisted for joining a union." At Walhalla Hall in Indianapolis Emma Goldman agreed.

When Debs was in Terre Haute the poor came steadily to his door. Some wanted help, some advice, some a handout. Kate was disgusted with his foolish charity. J. A. Wayland, of the *Appeal,* told him: "Debs, you're a fool . . . wasting your valuable time on these human wrecks. . . . Cut it out. . . ." A little later Mr. Wayland killed himself, leaving a note: "The struggle under the capitalist system isn't worth the effort. Let it pass."

In 1912 at Indianapolis the Socialists nominated Debs for President for the fourth time. He more than doubled his 1908 vote. But he would not even allow his name to be presented at the 1916 convention. Perhaps he felt it was useless to run again, perhaps he felt there was no issue: "Wilson yells for undivided Americanism and Hughes orates for undiluted Americanism." No longer was it possible to go down to the bar in the old St. Nicholas and tell stories about Bill Nye to the railroaders and denounce the General Managers' Association and forthwith organize a Socialist local. The class struggle had got all mixed up with making the world safe for democracy. Profits had become

entangled with patriotism. Church investigators found that steelworkers were not earning a living wage in the Calumet, but
there was a war on. Wilson started putting Socialists in jail. In
Terre Haute a banker beat up a German grocer while a cop held
the grocer's arms. A Socialist miner was nearly lynched in the
name of liberty because he refused to buy a Liberty Bond. Debs
told a German hiding from a mob that he'd shoot the first
vigilante who came to the Debs house, and the German reported
it to the draft board. But nobody in Terre Haute bothered Debs.
His views pained his neighbors. But they knew he loved them.
Then the Bolsheviks revolted in Russia. Debs went back to the
platform. He knew he was headed for jail. On June 16, 1918, a
month after Congress tightened the Espionage Act and at the
time that the Second Division was in Belleau Wood, Debs addressed a convention of Ohio Socialists at Canton. The newspapers called him traitor. He continued his speaking tour. The
mayors of Mishawaka, South Bend, and Elkhart announced he
would not be allowed to speak. He spoke anyway. He went to
Cleveland, though warned he would be arrested. He registered
at an obscure hotel and walked the streets, nervous. He made up
his mind to let the police arrest him. They did. He went to trial
September 12, refusing to present witnesses, speaking mildly
and seriously in his own defense, courteously asking the court's
permission to read from Mr. Wilson's book *The New Freedom*
(granted) and to discourse upon wartime profiteering (refused). The jurors—they averaged, says Max Eastman, seventy-
two years and were retired businessmen worth fifty or sixty
thousand dollars each—convicted him. Not a plea for leniency,
but these were his final words to the Court: "Your Honor, the
five per cent of the people that I have made reference to, constitute that element that absolutely rules our country. . . . They
control the courts. . . ." The Judge sentenced him to ten years.
He went home to Terre Haute on bail. A barber there said:
"Well, it's coming along to Easter time, and we're getting ready
for another crucifixion." The Supreme Court upheld the conviction. The District Attorney called from Cleveland. It was time
to surrender. Debs issued a statement: "Great issues are not
decided by courts, but by the people. . . . I despise the Espionage Law . . . and I defy the Supreme Court and all its powers

of capitalism to do their worst. All hail to the workers of America and the world! The day of emancipation is dawning."

A rich manufacturer, Theodore and his wife and daughter, Kate's mother and her wealthy brother called to say goodbye. The parlor was full of flowers. A delegation of Terre Haute Socialists and Central Labor Union members called to ask his permission to hold a demonstration. He told them to wait till he came home. Walking to the depot that night, he stopped at a watchmen's shanty to say goodbye, just as he'd always done when leaving Terre Haute. At the Big Four station about two hundred men, nearly all old railroaders, were waiting. A miner grabbed him hard: "We're with you, 'Gene—by God, we're with you to the last man." Debs said he knew it and kissed him and tried to break away, but they kept yelling: "Debs! Debs! Debs!" They clung to him, and when the train came in he had to tear loose to get aboard. A Negro Pullman porter doffed his cap. Debs took off his own hat. The crowd uncovered. For an instant it was silent. The train started. A soldier with a wound stripe cried out: "Mr. Debs, I went through hell over there for them, and now I'm ready to go through hell over here for you," and the crowd roared, and the soldier cried: "And there are a million more like me," and the train pulled out in the night, headed for Cleveland. He was delivered to the West Virginia State Prison at Moundsville—the Federal penitentiary was over-crowded, full of objectors and Socialists and military prisoners—on April 13, 1919, five months after the war ended.

When he was transferred to Atlanta, a harsher prison, he sternly warned the warden that, an enemy of all prisons, he would watch for "iniquities" here.

The Indiana Federation of Labor did nothing to get him pardoned. The Socialists did what they could. But the Red hunt was on. Led by William Z. Foster the steelworkers struck at Gary and elsewhere and lost bloodily. On May 4, 1919, parading "Gary Reds" were met by armed policemen, deputies, returned soldiers, and a mob that ripped off their red neckties and badges. At Terre Haute on the same May day, Socialists announced they would parade to protest Debs's imprisonment. The authorities said it would be better if no red flags were displayed, and none was. Up at East Chicago where a Socialist parade impended, citizens awakened to find Federal authorities, railroad detectives, steel-mill "home guards," deputy sheriffs, vigilantes, and five hundred armed "special officers" patrolling the streets. The American Legion conferred with city officials at Lafayette and Elwood to prevent speeches urging amnesty for Debs. President Wilson said: "I will never consent to the pardon of this man." Debs refused to ask pardon. "We are confined but they are prisoners. . . . They are waiting for us to relent. Well, we can outwait them." On May Day 1920, Debs and other political prisoners paraded, singing *The Red Flag*:

> *Come dungeons dark or gallows grim,*
> *This song shall be our parting hymn*

and Debs wrote to Theodore: "Just in from the stockade. The band, all convicts, playing some sweet, heart-touching strains. Near two thousand of us convicts pressed closely about the stand. I hope God was looking that way. . . ." The Socialist Party nominated him for president, and the notification committee met him in the warden's office. He proclaimed: "The mission of the Socialist party is to free the human race. . . ." He polled nearly a million votes, the most a Socialist ever polled in the United States.

Two days before Christmas 1921 President Harding decided to free Debs without restoring his citizenship. "The Father of Three Soldier Sons" protested Debs's release in the name of the Unknown Soldier buried at Arlington. Christmas Day Debs wired Kate:

"MY DARLING KATE   GREETINGS AND LOVE TO YOU AND DEAR SWEET MOTHER   THE DAY HAS COME AND OUR BLESSED COMMUNION IS NEAR   A NECESSARY TRIP TO WASHINGTON AND THEN HOME TO YOU MY BELOVED   WITH OVERFLOWING HEART I EMBRACE YOU AND GOD BLESS YOU."

Theodore said later Kate had not visited Debs at Atlanta. While he was there she neglected the house on Eighth Street. He rode the day coach to Washington and gave the Government's Pullman fare to Russian Relief. He went to see Harding, a strange conference surely, and then, pausing in the Union Depot at Washington to make a speech against war, he went home once again to Terre Haute. As the train came into the station, a friend called to him: "The whole state of Indiana is out here." They were roaring: "Debs! Debs! Debs!" miners and railroaders and factory hands. Where but in Indiana would one of their bands have played the *Internationale* and another *Hail! Hail! The Gang's All Here*? Bearing red railroad flares, they hoisted him into a truck decorated with red bunting. This time he accepted the ride gratefully—he was sixty-six, and sick—and they took him home. He kissed Kate and stood on the porch and told the crowd: "I am glad to be back home again. . . . I still have love for my fellow men. . . ."

He was a Hoosier and conscious of it; when Harding did not restore his citizenship, Debs complained: "I am not a citizen of the United States, despite the fact that I was born and reared in Indiana." He was a Hoosier of the nineties, warm, sentimental, generous, possessed of dry wit and stubbornness. It happened that Hoosiers did not follow him on election day; neither did the nation. He usually polled about the same percentage of the total Indiana vote as of the nation's vote. In 1916 he could not even be elected to Congress from the Terre Haute district. He was in the main stream of Indiana protest, the ceaseless quest for the better life begun by Robert Owen, the uprising against authority begun in William Henry Harrison's time. All these have been smothered in Indiana. Yet it cannot be said they failed completely. They left an impress and a heritage,—Debs most of all. He was the greatest of the Indiana protestants, the most effective,

Terre Haute had changed while he was in prison. The world had changed. Mencken's writings seemed to Debs "all so very negative, so hopeless, so pessimistic." Communists and factions of Socialists kept trying to get him to endorse theirs as the true faith; this annoyed him. He lived to lose faith in the Russian Revolution: "Russia has . . . actually swapped dictators. . . . There is not a single one of the actual leaders of the Russian Soviet Government who is a proletarian. They are intellectuals. . . . I am heartily in favor . . . as long as they fight capitalism, but when they proceed to dictate to the Socialist parties of other countries . . . then it seems to me to be time to back up. . . ." He considered John L. Lewis of the U.M.W. a conservative and also a coward for obeying an injunction issued at Indianapolis by Federal Judge A. B. Anderson.

Governor Warren T. McCray of Indiana called out the troops during a coal strike, and Debs, sick, could do nothing. McCray in 1922 denounced Debs to the powerful American Legion at Indianapolis, and the legion resolved to march past Debs's house shouting "traitor." McCray said righteously that Debs had spent three years in Atlanta. Shortly thereafter Governor McCray himself was sent to Atlanta for using the mails to defraud, the first sitting American Governor so convicted. Yet Debs did not oppose McCray's pardon, as McCray had opposed his. Riley wrote: "God was feeling mighty good when he made 'Gene Debs, and he didn't have anything else to do all day."

He was lonely at Terre Haute. His friends were dying. He grieved when a rich man died and told his authorized biographer, David Karsner: "Mr. Ijams . . . was a plutocrat through and through, but he had a heart. We shouldn't forget that many capitalists . . . are . . . creatures of their environment and circumstance." He and Karsner went to a run-down saloon, theoretically closed by Prohibition but once the throne of Buster Clark, king of the District, deliverer of votes, owner of a whorehouse chain. Debs had met him at Atlanta where the reformers had sent him. With Phil Reinbold, once president of the Terre Haute Central Labor Union and perhaps Deb's closest crony in the St. Nicholas Hotel days, they drove to Buster Clark's house near Crawfordsville. Buster was a lumbering giant in a derby and a candy-striped silk shirt buttoned with a big diamond. They talked about prison days. Clark's wife came in, and he sprang up to guide her like a crippled child out to sit in the sun—she had paresis. Debs told Buster: "Your life was shaped for you and mine for me. . . . If the story of Jesus has any meaning at all it is that in the final accounting the so-called sinner will have his day in court the same as the alleged saint. Personally, I hope to find my place among the scorned and shunned outcasts." And Buster replied: "The trouble with you is, 'Gene, you are 2,000,-000 years ahead of your time. . . . Human beings are rotten, corrupt, and that's all there is to it."

Debs lectured a little. He helped unionists when he could. In 1924 the Socialist Party was disorganized; he told his followers to vote for Robert M. La Follette the Progressive. The Indiana Federation of Labor convened at Terre Haute in 1925. For two hours he stood and spoke to the delegates in a public park in the August heat along the river flats, a tall thin man sixty-nine years old. His audience had to stand, and he asked if they were tired. They reminded him he had to stand too. He still could laugh. He said: "The capitalists, professors, preachers, and congressmen were all for the war but not in it. I was against the war but in it. I was conscripted and I think that I should have a bonus."

In the summer of 1926, seventy years old, he was forced to suspend his writing for the new *American Appeal* and take to his sanatorium bed for the last time. He fell into a coma, scribbling a stanza of Henley's:

> *It matters not how strait the gate,*
> *How charged with punishments the scroll,*
> *I am the master of my fate;*
> *I am the captain of my soul.*

He died, with his hand in Theodore's. They took his body back home to Terre Haute and held his funeral on the front porch, and thousands stood in the street and wept. But before that his body had lain in state a few hours at the Central Labor Union Temple. The C.L.U. president had told Theodore: "You will have to give him to us for a while, Theodore. You know he belongs to us."

Chapter 12

WILLIAM AND POWERS HAPGOOD

E UGENE V. DEBS declared: "There is something wrong in this country," and D. M. Parry agreed, and so did William Powers Hapgood, another business owner. No doubt if forced to choose between Debs and Parry, Hapgood would have chosen Debs. But, though rich men called him a Socialist among other things, Hapgood's solution was not Debs's. It was to give his employees an opportunity to run his business and ultimately to own it. He wanted to use his company as "a laboratory in which to test the relations of workers with owners and with technicians." He felt that "a political democracy is meaningless without industrial democracy. It is not enough for a man to vote; his industrial life is more important than his political life."

Born at Chicago in 1872, William Hapgood was reared in Alton, Illinois. His father, a successful plow manufacturer, sent him and his two brothers, Hutchins and Norman, to Harvard at a time when Harvard was turning out questioning young men like Robert Morss Lovett, Robert Herrick, and William Vaughan Moody, a native of New Albany, Indiana. When William Hapgood returned to Chicago, Debs's Pullman strike was on. His friends were Lovett and Moody and others like them. "They all believed a better world could be made," Hapgood recalled in 1946. He got a job as an assistant shipping clerk at Franklin MacVeagh's wholesale grocery house on Wabash Avenue during what Hapgood calls "the glorious days of food adulteration."

He stayed nine years, becoming head of the manufacturing department. His son, Powers, was born in 1899. Hapgood wanted to become an executive; he liked business. MacVeagh, who later became Taft's Secretary of the Treasury, told him frankly he had no future with MacVeagh. Armour and Company "considered employing me but I was too radical." His father bought a small canning plant on South Meridian Street in Indianapolis. This became the Columbia Conserve Company. Hutchins and Norman became journalists, and although ownership of the Columbia Conserve Company devolved upon all three brothers, William ran it, badly at first. He had moved it to Churchman Avenue near the Belt tracks and was just beginning to make money when his father died in 1917.

William had long discussed industrial democracy with his friends and brothers. It seemed unfair to him that just because he had inherited the Columbia Conserve, he should control it. He believed that the workers should determine their own hours of work, incomes, associates, leaders, and the policies of the business as well.

One day in 1917 he called the employees to the plant dining-room and explained his plan. He has since recalled: "Those who understood did not believe me, and very few understood." He formed a committee of ten to run the business. Seven of these were elected from the factory, only one of whom had attended school beyond the fourth grade. All had worked most of their lives. Cynical friends prophesied that "the workers would rush in and destroy everything before they understood how to manage."

The Council, as the expanded committee came to be called, would stay at the plant for supper and then meet around the dining tables. Hapgood installed a blackboard and guided the discussion. For a time the uneasy Council did little. Then, in Hapgood's absence, it reduced the working week from fifty-five to fifty hours.

A Council member pointed out that only a few employees were paid steady salaries. Hapgood felt they must reduce everybody to an insecure wage basis or raise everybody to a secure salary basis. Regularity of employment—and the annual wage—was a perplexing problem in the seasonal canning industry.

Nevertheless, the Council placed all regular wage workers (excluding seasonal "extras") on salary and guaranteed them fifty-two weeks' work a year with no overtime pay, but without deductions for necessary absences and without regard to seasonal inactivity or even a general business slump (plus paid vacations). Hapgood has said: ". . . workers are altogether more entitled to an annual wage than stockholders are to an annual dividend."

What about pay? The Council based it upon need. An unmarried employee in 1930 received twenty-two dollars a week, a married one thirty-three dollars per week, and an additional two dollars per week was paid for each child. The maximum was fixed at a hundred dollars a week—Hapgood's salary—until the lower incomes were increased. Any employee who felt he needed a raise was invited to discuss it with the Council. At once five men and one woman applied. The woman asked three dollars more a week because she recently had become almost the sole support of her parents; the Council decided she needed not three dollars but eight dollars more. It approved the requests of all the men but one, who withdrew his application.

The Council set up a pension plan and sickness and accident insurance and did "everything in its power to relieve the individual employee of worries which he has not the strength to bear alone." Hapgood wrote: "It interests me to hear 'red-blooded' employers denounce this practice as sentimental and destructive of the moral fibre of a worker, and to . . . defend what they are pleased to call the law of the survival of the fittest. But when I inquire if they apply that law to their own children they stare at me in amazement and indignation." He thought the rich rewards of the craftsman period could be restored only if workers looked upon the factory as "their workday home, as a school, as a cultural and spiritual environment." Classes were held in industrial history, elementary economics, and labor problems. Manual workers were trained for "white-collar" jobs; the company sent some to school. The Council abolished the time clock—"Few workers are normally unfair"—and, to the amusement of businessmen, punished two employees by denying them the right to work for two weeks though continuing their pay. Workers shared in the profits. In 1925 Hapgood agreed to give them all

net profits (after dividends) for their use in buying the company's common stock. They did not want to hold the stock
individually—they felt that before long a few would have it all
again—and instead agreed to own it collectively, through trustees whom they would elect. By 1930 the workers owned a controlling interest in the company, and Hapgood expected that
soon they would own it all and the company would be a purely
communal enterprise.

All this time Hapgood was proselytizing among orthodox businessmen. He told them: "I have changed my own spots and I
have seen other employers in the process of changing theirs." He
felt certain the American workman's position was going to
change, perhaps through Socialism, Communism, or the union
movement. He distrusted all three. He thought most union leaders wanted only higher wages and shorter hours, not greater
participation in management: "There is little difference in social
outlook between, say, the president of the United Mine Workers
of America and the president of the United States Steel Corporation." He thought the Russian Communists aimed "to enlarge
and retain their own power." He traveled the world studying
industrial relations. In a cottage in a Welsh mining town he
described Columbia Conserve, and a coal miner replied: "They
will never get off the backs of the workers until they are kicked
off." Hapgood admitted "overwhelming evidence to date is in
support of that," but hoped for a change. He thought that, just
as technicians had achieved technological progress, they could,
if enlightened, better achieve social progress than theorists,
politicians, or revolutionists. He lectured from hundreds of plat-
forms and pulpits. He addressed the Commonwealth Club in
San Francisco and antagonistic steel magnates in a Pittsburgh
club. He kept quoting Lincoln and Jesus Christ, kept repeating:
"The problem is purely one of sympathy and understanding."
His experiment aroused no organized opposition—"we weren't
big enough"—but most Indianapolis businessmen, including
Hapgood's neighbors, disapproved. He was a tall, slender man
of genteel appearance. When he took Emma Goldman to the
Contemporary Club, a fashionable organization of wealthy people, an uproar ensued. Hapgood, chuckling, has recalled: "I
rather enjoyed taking her into those sacred precincts." She was

his brother Hutchins's friend, but she had little interest in Columbia Conserve. Neither did Debs, whom Hapgood met twice and whom his brother Norman visited at Atlanta. Of a Socialist colony that failed, Debs had written: ". . . there is no royal road to the Socialist commonwealth, there is no escape from capitalism for any favored few. . . ." And, indeed, all such good societies in Indiana had failed—Rappites, Owenites, Shakers, and La Grange Phalanx. Hapgood's Columbia Conserve survived as a communal enterprise much longer than they—twenty-six years. This quest for the better life is a leitmotiv in Indiana. We have seen how Owen, also a business owner, first tried to appeal to capitalists' better natures, then turned to political action, and finally to a fundamental reorganization of society; how Debs, a workingman, first tried benevolent craft unionism, then a striking industrial union, then Socialism and one big union that would overthrow capitalism violently if necessary; how Hapgood was early troubled by the Welsh miner's restatement of the question that bothered them all. Let us see where the quest led Hapgood and his son, Powers.

Some who disagreed with Debs thought the good societies failed because of dissension or the fundamental indecency of the common man. Norman Hapgood, William's brother, thought they neglected the need to equal the capitalists' technical skill. Certainly William Hapgood realized that in order for his experiment to impress other businessmen, it must succeed financially. Liberals everywhere used Columbia to prove all sorts of ideological points, Norman Thomas called it the single good capitalistic enterprise. But William Hapgood never forgot that he was competing with a giant, Campbell, and by 1929 the Council had developed "an ability to manage a factory quite as effectively as the best autocratic plants are managed." That year the net profit before taxes and depreciation was nearly $121,000 on a capitalization of about $257,000 common and $55,000 preferred, and Hapgood wrote: "I should be embarrassed [except] that all the surplus . . . goes to the workers." They planned to cut prices to help consumers. They lent money to an enterprise that pursued "liberal" labor policies, lent $10,000 to a co-op faced with a mortgage foreclosure, and donated "large quantities of soup to people in need, such as starving coal miners, the oppressed strikers of Danville and the flood sufferers of Southern Indiana."

As the business depression began in 1930, however, pressure was greater on Columbia than on more orthodox companies, for it was committed to discharge no one even though there was no work to do. In 1931 Hapgood urged a reduction of all salaries. "During the long and painful discussions . . . it was very clearly shown that few of the workers had really come to understand their status as owners." By June 30, 1933, the workers were drawing only 50.7 per cent of their 1930 salaries and on several paydays had received nothing at all. Meanwhile, salesmen recruited from the manual workers had bungled a new sales program. (Hapgood concluded technical problems must be dealt with by specialists.) And Hapgood's son Powers was conducting a widespread publicity campaign the expense of which was opposed by workers already disgruntled at salary cuts. They criticized his father, and it was little short of tragic that Powers had brought the leaders of the dissidents into the plant. In order to understand this controversy, which almost destroyed the company, we must know something of Powers Hapgood's career. And it repays study anyway, for, as a sincere consuming quest for a faith, it has few parallels.

Powers attended Phillips Academy at Andover. Midway through Harvard and interested in economics and sociology, he told a leftist woman lecturer that he was confused, and she advised him to "go earn your own living so your old man won't have to pay your rent." He took extra courses and was graduated in three years, in 1921—a classmate was Thomas S. Lamont, later a Morgan partner—and, with twenty dollars in his pocket, caught a freight west. He worked in an iron mine at Hibbing, Minnesota, on the Northern Pacific Railroad, in a Montana sugar beet factory, and then in Montana and Colorado coal mines. He joined the U.M.W. He wrote an article for the *Nation* comparing union and nonunion mines. A New York research bureau hired him to investigate workmen's compensation in U.M.W.'s District 2. He decided to dig coal "and take my chances on being elected organizer." He was big and strong and eager, a hard-mouthed man with soft eyes. On April 1, 1922, he was appointed a union organizer near Wilkes-Barre, Pennsylvania. Three weeks later he was arrested, the first of thirty-six arrests (up to 1946). That spring he was arrested about ten times. "I'd just go into a town to organize it, the mayor and chief of police would tell me to leave, I'd say I wouldn't, they'd put me in jail, and then when John Brophy didn't get my call up at district headquarters at Clearfield he'd send his lawyer out to look for me. I was usually out within 24 hours." On one of the first occasions he "started talking to my jailer about idealism. And I started talking about Jesus. And he said, 'Listen, you know about Daniel in the lions' den. Well, the lions weren't scared of Daniel, were they?' " John L. Lewis called a nationwide coal strike. The companies put thugs on Powers's trail. He went to a company town where the evicted strikers were living in three hundred tents. He was shocked when they wanted to blow up a bridge. He advised against it, but it was blown up anyway, and a dozen innocent men were sentenced to ten years (and pardoned later).

Twenty-five years later Powers could laugh at those early experiences. Not then. That terrible strike lasted from April 1 to mid-August. Against great opposition Powers and other young men had organized nearly a hundred thousand miners in south-western Pennsylvania, using as a slogan: "No settle till all settle." But Lewis sent the men back to work in Indiana, Illinois, Ohio, and the Pittsburgh district for the same companies Powers's men were striking. These men lost their strike, and, like other young men in the U.M.W., Powers broke with Lewis.

After another year in the mines he went to Europe. He studied the Labor Party of England, coal-mine conditions there and in Wales, in the Ruhr, and in Siberia. He was gone two years, supporting himself by working in the mines. "Oh, it was very interesting," he has recalled. "But I didn't like the dictatorship, so I wouldn't join the Communist Party." But, "I wanted to join something," so when he returned to America in 1926 he joined the Socialist Party. He worked two years in Pennsylvania mines. U.M.W.'s headquarters, like those of numerous other union internationals, were then in Indianapolis. At the 1927 convention there, Powers, twenty-seven years old, managed John Brophy's campaign to succeed Lewis, and on Sunday three of Lewis's henchmen beat him up in a hotel room. The police arrived; Powers recalls: "It's the only time in my life I was ever glad to see a cop." However, one of his assailants said Powers was "a Com*mun*ist, he's the delegate from Rooshia," and the sergeant locked Powers up with pleasure. At the trial next day about two hundred of his partisans and one hundred of Lewis's crowded into the dingy attic-like municipal courtroom in the police station. When the sergeant testified that Powers wanted to continue the fight and have the sergeant referee it, Powers's boys cheered raucously. Powers took the witness stand and, interrupted frequently by prolonged cheering, made a half-hour speech on the blessings of the Russian workers—the six-hour day, the five-day week, one hundred per cent salary compensation for an injured married miner and seventy-five per cent for an unmarried one. And indeed, when Powers described how he had been injured by a rock slide, these miners knew he was one of them; he always seemed that way to them, just as Debs had to the railroaders, in spite of his Harvard accent and well-cut clothes and well-stocked mind. The judge became interested in Russia and rendered judgment: "Don't have any more fights on Sunday afternoons." Four fights started on the narrow stairs leading from the courtroom. The delegates trooped back to Tomlinson Hall. The credentials committee refused to seat Powers. He rose in the back of the hall and started to thread his way through the yelling delegates, waving his credentials over his head; but on the way "Lewis's boys jumped me and I took another trimmin'."

That same year Powers spoke in behalf of Nicola Sacco and Bartolomeo Vanzetti in Chicago and through the Pennsylvania coal fields. At the climax he went to Boston and got arrested four times in a week and met a young woman, Mary Donovan, who was secretary of the defense committee (he later married her). When Sacco and Vanzetti were electrocuted, it seemed to him and to her and to many people like them that the lights had been turned out everywhere. Powers went to work in a mine owned by Josephine Roche, one of few Colorado mineowners to recognize the U.M.W. Lewis revoked his union card. Miss Roche offered him a foreman's job, but he refused. That would put him on the side of management. Then she offered him a job on neither side, as assistant mining engineer, and he took it.

In 1930 U.M.W. men in Illinois rebelling against Lewis asked Powers to help. He did but soon Lewis put down the rebellion with a court order.

Powers had entered the U.M.W. a young man of high hope. Now though only thirty he was disillusioned. "The A.F. of L. is very discouraging," he has said. In the fall of 1930 he went to work at his father's Columbia Conserve. He and his father had been extremely close. When Powers had been a boy his father had taken him on long trips in the Canadian wilderness. He reared Powers to think independently, and although Hapgood himself put his faith in educating employers, he never opposed Powers's devotion to militant unionism. Powers sometimes considered his father too tolerant, too gentle. Sometimes Powers would accompany him on his trips to lecture on Columbia Conserve. Once on the West Coast while William Hapgood was addressing the Portland Chamber of Commerce, his son was exhorting some Wobblies in an I.W.W. hall. They went down to San Quentin together to visit Jim McNamara, the Indianapolis dynamiter, and one of his co-conspirators, Matt Schmidt. (Schmidt had fled to South America after the *Times* bombing, and, Powers recalls, had returned furtively to stay with "Uncle Hutch," that is, Hutchins Hapgood, before he was finally jailed.) At San Quentin, Tom Mooney immediately launched a lengthy lament on his persecution. When he had finished, Schmidt, who had listened patiently, said to McNamara: "Thank God we're guilty Jim, we don't have to do all that." Powers always has enjoyed the freemasonry of protest. Jim McNamara died at San Quentin; his brother John died on a farm near Indianapolis, but not before he had been charged frequently with using threats to persuade Indianapolis contractors to hire only union ironworkers.

When in 1930 Powers joined Columbia, its financial difficulties were about to begin. He brought with him John Brophy and his own brother-in-law Dan Donovan, both unionists. These men and their friend, Leo Tearney, led others in the plant who suspected that William Hapgood had turned autocratic capitalist and who demanded that the company restore wage cuts instead of spending money for publicity. When a Council member attacked Norman and William Hapgood's integrity, a vituperative discussion ensued, and William Hapgood wrote: "Some of the workers were on the verge of hysterics."

In the midst of this, Powers ran for Governor of Indiana on the Socialist ticket, against the advice of his uncle Norman, who felt this would only sharpen the Columbia controversy. At that time Democrats had nominated Franklin D. Roosevelt for President and Paul V. McNutt for Governor; University Square near the Circle was full of unemployed, farmers were muttering about doing something about the bankers, and the coal miners were striking. At the Dixie Bee mine south of Terre Haute the owners sent nonunion men underground, and the strikers kept them there. They lay in the cornfield and poured bullets into the tipple from high-powered rifles. Governor Harry G. Leslie, in mid-campaign, sent the troops. Machine guns were mounted on the hillsides, and a man was killed and seven wounded. Powers campaigned at strikers' picnics. He polled 18,735 votes (Thomas had polled about 4,000 four years earlier and polled about 4,000 four years later; Debs's peak was 37,000).

Powers returned to Columbia Conserve. It was nearing dissolution as a co-operative. His friends Brophy and Donovan, experienced in labor politics, were attacking his father vigorously. Hapgood characterized them as extremists and impractical theorists. They replied that they needed money for their babies. (Columbia wages still were above average.) The company virtually ceased functioning. Hapgood wrote: "I have changed my mind about the wisdom of letting all the workers . . . decide by majority vote what shall take place." On January 30, 1933, when the Council "could not bring itself" to fire Brophy, Donovan, and Tearney, Hapgood did so. Powers had supported his father against them during their attack on the publicity campaign, but now he felt they had been dealt with in an autocratic manner and he told the Council so. His father walked out. Powers quit the company. So did about a dozen others. Desperately, his father requested the aid of Sherwood Eddy, Jerome Davis, Paul H. Douglas, and James Myers. They proposed, and the Council and the board of directors accepted, an agreement defining the powers of each, dealing with financial questions, and providing for the reinstatement of Brophy,

Donovan, and Tearney. Soon Hapgood demanded that the Council accept his resignation or fire Brophy and Donovan again. The Council split, but fired them. Telegrams, statements "for the record," and long, tortured letters were tossed back and forth among Hapgoods, the Council, and the Committee of Four; everybody went to great pains to get the record straight. William and Norman Hapgood wrote long pamphlets. Journals of opinion joined in. The Committee of Four charged Hapgood with autocracy. The Council chairman resigned, convinced that workers must help themselves. The agony was compounded because of the company's policy of baring its innermost secrets. A supporter wrote to the company secretary: "Dear Sir: I am so much disgusted with the treatment of the Hapgood family by employees . . . that I ask that no more of the reports be sent me." Hutchins wrote: "Our moral to be drawn from this correspondence is that when men are in the midst of a struggle, they do not understand what their own ultimate goal is." But he was in Provincetown; in Indianapolis, Powers and his father had not spoken to each other for a few days and still could not discuss Columbia. Hutchins wrote to William: "There was no idea of 'class' in your experiment. . . . Your son, an idealistic and earnest young man, courageous and strong willed, had . . . as a miner become . . . 'class conscious.' There is an employing and an employed class to him, and their interests are necessarily antagonistic. . . . [But] you saw that your experiment . . . would go to smash unless you could rid the business of these agitators, among whom was your noble son. . . . It is difficult for a father and a man to be put into a more painful situation. You did what you were compelled to do. . . . your son felt you were wrong in principle and he could not compromise. With time and experience he will change his mind."

By that time, late 1933, the quarrel had subsided, for it had become apparent that unless the antagonists did some work there would be nothing left to quarrel over. The company had lost $86,500 in the fiscal year 1932–3; it lost $46,000 in the next six months. After the truce the company began to show a profit, and the profits went to the workers. However, the poisonous split between workers and employers remained. Powers's unionist friends had applied to the A.F. of L. for a charter. The A.F.

of L., holding that they were really owners, refused. The employees organized a CIO local; the company paid the dues of some, but membership dropped so low that the charter was revoked. In 1942 while Hapgood was trying to work out a new guaranteed annual wage plan, employees struck, to the amusement of businessmen. They returned to work after a week but filed suit for back pay against the trustees who held the workers' common stock, a sixty-one per cent interest in the company. The Marion County superior judge dissolved the trust and ordered the stock distributed individually to all who had worked at Columbia since January 1, 1925, when the trust was established. This destroyed the co-operative plan. Columbia Conserve became a capitalistic enterprise once more.

After a brief wartime shutdown caused by the poultry shortage, the factory reopened with nearly all new employees. They organized an A.F. of L. local. According to Hapgood, "they wanted time and a half for overtime and a raise in pay and besides they wanted to go back to the old full-time salary plan —all the benefits of our old salary plan together with all the protections of the union." In 1946 he negotiated with a pair of Chicago CIO organizers. By that time his son Powers had become regional director of the CIO at Indianapolis.

After leaving Columbia in protest in 1933, Powers had gone to Kentucky as an organizer for the Amalgamated Clothing Workers, then to Massachusetts as an organizer for the Socialist Party. He went to Arkansas in 1935 and organized the Southern Tenant Farmers Union and then drifted back to his father's plant at Indianapolis as a migrant tomato worker. About that time a general strike, the first east of the Rockies, occurred in Terre Haute. Since March 1935, employees had been striking the Columbian Enameling and Stamping Company; on July 18 it imported about fifty out-of-town strikebreakers. The A.F. of L. demanded they be withdrawn. They weren't. The A.F. of L. pulled everything in town. Governor McNutt sent the troops. Picketing was forbidden, mass meetings broken up, and 1,800 pickets dosed with tear gas. A professor, J. R. Shannon, an independent man who later bought Gene Debs's old home to live in it and preserve it, was ordered off the streets by what he calls "a young tin hat," and taken at bayonet point to the city hall and locked up. Waiting to be "mugged" and interrogated, he sat in a "dungeon" reading an article in *Harper's Magazine* on how to raise roasting ears in the basement. Next night he was released. Meanwhile Powers Hapgood and other Indianapolis Socialists decided to make a free-speech fight. They sent Leo Vernon, a University of Wisconsin professor, to Terre Haute. On Saturday afternoon he spoke from the courthouse steps. Only about two hundred showed up. The guardsmen put him in jail. Sunday morning Powers drove over and told the sheriff he wanted to provide bail for Vernon. The sheriff arrested him. The commanding major accused him of planning to make a speech at Sullivan. Powers admitted it, and the major asked if he didn't know Sullivan County was under martial law. (It had been for three years, ever since the Dixie Bee trouble.) Powers replied: "Yes, but I didn't realize martial law meant fascism," and, he said, the major answered: "Well, we don't have fascism in the United States but we do have it in Vigo and Sullivan Counties and I'm the dictator." Powers refused to leave town. The major told him to stay till he rotted. Powers's wife came down and nearly got jailed. The affair was attracting national attention. Norman Thomas, head of the Socialist Party, telegraphed Governor McNutt in protest. Powers and Vernon were released. With local union leaders they held a mass meeting at the courthouse; ten thousand people attended, and Norman Thomas was the principal speaker. The guard only watched. At Powers's suggestion picketing was resumed at the stamping mill. After three days, he, Vernon, and a Unitarian minister interested in Socialism were arrested by two policemen and put into a squad car, Powers in front. Powers says the lieutenant called him a "God damn unAmerican bastard." Powers replied: "I'm a better American than you are and I'm not a bastard." They stopped in an alley and the lieutenant told Powers to repeat what he had said. Powers did. The lieutenant hit him in the nose, and the professor and the minister protested that that wasn't a very nice thing to do. The sergeant pulled a gun. Powers was still denying he was a bastard; the lieutenant blacked his eye, then they drove to the station. There Powers tried to fight the lieutenant but a big, fatherly Irish captain intervened: "Son, I don't blame you, but it never pays to argue with a cop." Three lawyers bailed them out next morning. A little later John L. Lewis set up the CIO and charges were dismissed. Powers always thought Lewis was responsible. For Powers, like other of Lewis's old enemies, joined the industrial CIO. "He took a lot of his bad boys back to help him," Powers has recalled. Powers, like Debs, long since had found craft unions unsatisfactory. He went back to the U.M.W. for a few months, then early in 1936 became a CIO organizer and in 1941, regional director in Indiana, an office he still held early in 1947.

Long before, he had made peace with his father; they had agreed not to discuss Columbia controversies. He kept out of the negotiations between his father and the CIO organizers (who worked out of Chicago and were not responsible to Powers). None the less, it was a somewhat uncomfortable situation, for Powers was living with his father on a 630-acre farm. In the spring of 1946 while Walter Reuther, head of the United Auto Workers, was demanding that General Motors show him its books, Hapgood offered the CIO organizers Columbia's books: "If you can't understand them, take them to somebody who can." He could be acid if he thought his motives misrepresented or his past record disregarded. He said: "They wanted a fight, not cooperation." One of them told him: "All we're interested in is a fair day's pay for a fair day's work," but Hapgood replied: "No, we're interested in more than that." Later he said: "I would like to spend the remaining years of my life in doing what I can to develop a far-reaching agreement with the CIO." He was an old man, seventy-four, seated in a wicker chair in a big, bare office that once was a part of the Council room. He was leaning forward on a cane hooked onto a string around the chair, his manner still vigorous, his back bent, his white hair drooping over his forehead, the skin loose on his hands and his lean face. He had an intensity about him, and his voice was sharp and hard, his mind incisive. He came to the office every day for several hours. He was blind, and his wife was only strong enough to read to him for short periods. Of the experiment to which he had devoted his life, he said: "I don't know that we convinced anybody that a producers' cooperative would work, don't even know that we convinced ourselves." He had finally signed a contract with the CIO, but it was not satisfactory to him—it didn't give the workers enough. He wanted to reopen it—"But the union will have to send some organizers in who understand that all management is not deceptive—though I realize most management is. I wish we could get Walter Reuther in here to deal with. He says he understands management. We'd test him out in this office," and he banged the floor with his cane.

Powers, however, explained that Reuther's union was not involved. Powers avoided discussing this and past differences in his father's declining years. He was busy with union affairs. None the less, he took time to talk over the old days with battle-scarred union men, mainly miners. He enjoyed telling tales about deputy sheriffs and company men who have asked in amazement: "What's a nice young Harvard guy like you doing mixed up with a bunch of radicals?" He always seemed a rather light-hearted revolutionist. Both he and his father appeared scarred. They had chips on their shoulders, they were a little embittered and, especially Powers, very wry. They reached the same conclusion about Indiana: that it was a little more "liberal" than the deep South, a little less "liberal" than the Northwest, that it was, in short, "about average."

PART SIX

Four Gentlemen from Indiana

Chapter 13

PROLOGUE: THE 1920's

T HE GLORY of the 1890's faded fast, and today to many
Hoosiers the 1920's, not the nineties, are the good old days.
Manufacturers were making large profits. Debs and many labor
leaders had been trampled underfoot by the wartime patriots.
Governor McCray called for volunteers to dig coal, and sent the
troops in to protect them. He was a national hero. Did other
problems arise? Did a judge call the automobile "a house of
prostitution on wheels"? Did ministers fret about "the younger
generation"? Did reformers object to "corrupt politics"? The new
enlightenment provided a ready answer: the nature of things
was to blame. Money was plentiful. A Muncie auto dealer was
advertising: "Hit the trail to better times," and touring had replaced bicycling. True, the auto industry was moving to Detroit, but though Indianapolis lost thereby, towns like Anderson
gained, for General Motors planted a colony there, and nobody
saw reason to mourn this advent of absentee power. It still was
true that an ambitious, young, local man of good family but
modest means could borrow from a bank and start a store or an
alley machine shop with every expectation that he would become
an influential member of the country club, Rotary, Masonic order, chamber of commerce, Methodist Church, and Republican
Party—he might even end up a philanthropist. The steel industry of the Calumet was fast providing a new economic base.
Gary became a marvel of the new age by rebuilding its downtown district. Did not brand new buildings signify excellence

in all things? Just as in the nineties, every town yearned to be
a city, and to the members of every chamber of commerce there
seemed no end in sight to the wonders that money and enterprise might work. Citizens read reports on the town bank with
solid satisfaction. Lions, usually younger and less affluent than
Kiwanians or Rotarians, lunched in Y.M.C.A.'s or church basements or hotel private dining-rooms and sang unashamed:

> *For I'm a Lion a roarin' Lion,*
> *That's why I'm fighting, fighting, fighting all the time.*
> *The King I'll be—of Industry—*
> *That all the world may know our power and immensity.*
> *I'm here to say—we have our way—. . . .*

Or:

> *Hello, Bill! Hello, Hank!*
> *Howdy, George! Ha-yah, Frank,*
> *The Lions are meeting this noon*
> *The gang's all here, lots of fun,*
> *Business too, will be done; . . .*

To Hoosiers the tomb of Tutankhamen briefly seemed as real
as the spring formal at the country club or the baseball game
across town; Samuel Insull's magic as substantial as the red
brick factory that had risen where the tracks crossed Main
Street. Playing the game in the office as on the golf links was
the only ethic. For Indiana was George Babbitt's spiritual home,
and young men (that is, those who read Mencken as scripture)
could localize in Hoosierdom nearly every scene and character
of Sinclair Lewis's *Main Street* and *Elmer Gantry*.

The old remained to mellow the new. Up at Winamac a
bride was injured when, slipping away from a "belling party"
with her groom, she leaped from the buggy as it tipped over
into a ditch. Bankers fraternized virtuously with clerks. People
lived well. On the Tippecanoe River some Winamac businessmen built themselves a poker lodge. Brush the magician mysti-
fied a large audience at the Winamac Chautauqua; other
attractions included a touring *Mikado*, violin solos and a concert, readings "of high class," and a program by the Ladies'
Rainbows Saxophone Band. Though people came to the Old

Settlers' Reunion in automobiles, it still was Old Settlers', complete with selections by the Winamac band, a speech by the judge, horseshoe pitching, foot racing, and contests to select the handsomest baby, the oldest lady settler, and the old settler having the most grandchildren present. The *New York Times* reported that more than fifty-five per cent of Indiana people owned their homes (36.9 per cent in the nation), that Indiana still admired above all others Ade, Tarkington, Nicholson, and Kin Hubbard, that policemen drawled and slouched, and that resplendent doormen at Indianapolis hotels were "not many years removed from the barnyard."

The old-time religion retained a powerful grip. At the cavernous Tabernacle in Indianapolis, E. Howard Cadle was president of the Gypsy Smith Choir, and Billy Sunday exhorted the old folks. Twenty-five years later many people, fondly remembering the Tabernacle or peaceful afternoons at Winona Lake, venerate Billy Sunday. Before he is canonized it might be well to examine his ideas and his style. On May 2, 1921, he told a large crowd:

"America is going crazy over pleasure and the whole world is, too. If we keep going the pace we are now going and if the mental unsoundness in this country keeps pace with the increasing population, in 250 years every man, woman, and child in America will go nuts. . . . To my mind the most useless thing on earth is the thing they call a society woman. Some of you old birds don't like that, I see. I am afraid to make you laugh, for some of your faces might break. You know I think God must have liked fun, judging from the fact that He made the monkey and some of you. . . . If the devil were his father and Emma Goldman his mother and hell his home, the kaiser is so lowdown he would rebuke his father, deny his dam and would bring dishonour on his birthplace. . . . I can no more imagine a man loving a north or a south of this land than I can imagine his loving the 'gee' or the 'haw' side of his wife better than the other. I have no use for the I.W.W., Bolshevists or Socialists. To me they are simply like blow flies on meat. They are ulcers to progress. If that bunch got into power they would repeal the laws of nature. They would try to make chickens give milk, make cows lay eggs and they would try to make yesterday be day after tomorrow. . . . No flag is greater than the people who live under it. There is no liberty where might takes the place of right.

179

What would become of this country if Debs were to be President, Victor Berger secretary of state and Bill Haywood attorney-general? When the Socialist party nominated Debs, who was at the time serving a sentence in the Federal penitentiary, it spat on every star in the American flag. If that crew got in charge of this land hell would have a public jubilee and heaven would hang crape. . . . [The country] shall be overrun by that crew from Europe who still smell of the steerage. . . . They can go back to the country from whence they came, and we will stand on the Statue of Liberty and wave good-by to them and sing 'Praise God From Whom All Blessings Flow.' You can't ride blind baggage on the gospel train. If capital and labor would stand at the grave of Washington and shake hands, the devil would bank his fires and hang crape and hell would be for rent before the Fourth of July. A pessimist is a man who wears both belt and suspenders. America is the corncrib of the world. . . ."

He praised John L. Lewis as a conservative. He roared: "I have championed the cause of the union man all my life, but I'm dead against the radical in whatever form he may appear. He's the bird I'm after. America, I call you back to God! . . . Every woman in Russia between the ages of 14 and 45 is a common prostitute under the Soviet system." Of him Debs said: "I wish I had the physical strength to . . . meet that vulture on a public platform. . . . God damn him! . . . Billy Sunday is a good investment to the railroad company and the mine operators." Ah, indeed the twenties were the good old days; indeed God was good to Indiana.

Of course, the twenties are not the good old days to the farmers. The farm depression of 1920–1 was terrible. I. H. Hull, a portly round-faced man today president of the Indiana Farm Bureau Cooperative Association, recalls: "I had a marsh farm up in La Porte County. I waded around in mud till I got web-footed. I had a baby, I was farmin' fifty-four acres. In nineteen and twenty the banker called me up one day and told me I'd have to take up my note coming due and he'd never talked that kinda language before. So I shipped my five cars of cattle and hogs up to Chicago. When I got there it looked like ten thousand other fellas had done the same thing. Well, I didn't get enough outa my cattle and hogs to pay my note. So I had my year's work for nothing." Of one farmer, Hull has said: "He was so blue he wasn't even painting his house or nailing up the roof boards on his barn." In December, Hull, a big man in a cowhide coat, and some other farmers held a routine federation meeting at South Bend. Somebody brought up fertilizer prices, just published and higher than ever. They sat around all day, trying to figure out what to do. "We decided to have a strike," Hull has recalled, laughing aloud. "We wrote down to the Federation at Indianapolis. Well, our strike didn't amount to much, it was in the winter, and then it came round to corn plantin' time and we had to have our fertilizer." But the new federation, anxious to attract members, tried to buy co-operatively from the monopolistic Big Six fertilizer manufacturers. When one of them said he wouldn't sell to "any bunch of scab farmers," the federation bought four thousand tons of fertilizer from an independent and sold it for less than half the monopolists' price. This was the beginning of the modern co-operative movement in Indiana, a movement that, avoiding politicians with panaceas and hewing closely to an economic line, has grown to gigantic stature and may be viewed as the most recent manifestation of the golden thread, the recurrent communal effort to set up the good society.

But in the twenties only half the population lived on farms, and the other half carried more weight and had more fun. Near Evansville, horse racing, aided by a legal fiction, came to Indiana to stay. Stuart Walker's Portmanteau Theater played repertory to big crowds in Indianapolis and Indiana towns. Musicians were recording some of the early hot jazz that later became collectors' items. Down at Bloomington, Hoagy Carmichael, his mother a movie-house ragtime pianist, was enrolled in Indiana University but he spent less time in classrooms than in blind pigs and graveyards and dance halls, playing jazz and inventing nonsense rhymes with some musicians who called themselves the Bent Eagles. Soon he wrote *Star Dust*. E. G. Spink promoted the Spink Arms Apartment-Hotel in Indianapolis and the rococo Spink-Wawasee Hotel on the shore of Lake Wawasee. Every town had its "fast crowd"; Stutz Bearcats and Duesenberg Specials were their home-grown trademarks, Cincinnati and Chicago and Palm Beach, as well as the local country club, their habitat, and one aged man, remembering, has said:

181

"God damn we had more fun in them days than young folks has today. My advice to you young man is, don't pass up anything, you might die young. Me, I never passed up a thing." People were drinking Jasper corn whisky, made in the southern hills by moonshiners driven there from Kentucky by the Night Riders, whisky distilled in abandoned farmhouses or in the hills and hollows around Terre Haute by miners left behind when the mines closed down, and whisky imported from Chicago. Bootleggers guaranteed that two drinks of white mule would kick you into a police station, three into a hospital, and four into your grave. The war had given victory to the ancient temperance forces, but restless young men turned to bootlegging. In Terre Haute, though bawdy houses no longer were sedate, the District survived. In a single political cleanup some hundred and fifty public officials, gunmen, and other town characters, including the mayor, were convicted. Terre Haute became a crossroads for gangsters. The Egan Rats were running booze over from St. Louis, the Capones were running it up from Florida, and they met at Terre Haute and across the Wabash. On many a night along the road, flaming liquor trucks lit up the sky, funeral pyres for driver and guards. Machine-gun and shotgun warfare began in the Calumet. Gary and South Bend and Evansville all had big districts where whores and gamblers operated with police blessing. Bill Armitage, an ex-saloonkeeper and gambler, a man of fancy clothes and many diamonds and cynical views, bossed Indianapolis. Policemen were sold like bananas, by the bunch; councilmen, commissioners, and others were as cheap. County officials kept getting indicted in connection with the sale of surplus war materials. Large bundles of cash bounced around city hall—thirty-five thousand dollars, in one instance, to have all bids rejected on a big sewer job. Now and then newspapers forced a city engineer or a whole board of works to resign, but sometimes the newspapermen covering city hall were dealt in. Nobody cared much anyway, there was always more money. By manipulation, breeders of purebred cattle were luring gullible farmers into paying prices far too high. Governor McCray, a gentleman farmer whose prize bull Perfection Fairfax sired a lucrative herd near Kentland, got into debt. His politician friends raised pools for him, and he used his office as Governor to borrow money from banks all over the state, placing what turned out to be, when farm deflation came, a fictitious value on his assets. And his downfall, heaped upon growing corruption, fertilized the soil in which the Ku Klux Klan grew and flourished.

Indiana since the 1917–18 war is a bewildering place, filled alike with gentle, contented rural folk and with wicked schemers. Perhaps we can in part describe Indiana, perhaps we can explore the recent Hoosier character, by examining four men and the conditions that surrounded them—D. C. Stephenson, Grand Dragon of the Ku Klux Klan; Court Asher, publisher of a venomous newspaper; Ned Gorrell, publisher of an ordinary country weekly; and Ralph F. Gates, the man the Hoosiers elected in 1944 to govern them. In the minds and deeds of these men is reflected varied Indiana. Beyond doubt, D. C. Stephenson and what he stood for dominated the Indiana of the 1920's.

Chapter 14

D. C. STEPHENSON, KLANSMAN

O<small>N</small> A<small>PRIL</small> 2, 1925, D. C. Stephenson was arrested. It is almost impossible twenty-odd years later to recall how incredible that seemed. David C. Stephenson, Grand Dragon of the Ku Klux Klan in Indiana, had said with reason: "I am the law in Indiana." Less than a year earlier the Klan had won political control of the state. It claimed a membership of nearly half a million. On occasion it took over good-sized cities to hold its awesome parades, it burned its fiery crosses almost nightly, it made the laws in Indiana, and it enforced them. Its ruler was Stephenson, a man probably without precise counterpart in American history.

But a determined, outraged father, George Oberholtzer, swore out a warrant for the arrest of Stephenson, charging him with assaulting Madge Oberholtzer. Twelve days later Madge Oberholtzer died, and the charge became first-degree murder. With this indictment began the end of Indiana's experiment in home-grown dictatorship. By a wonderful irony Stephenson, leader of an organization sworn to uphold virtue and smite immorality, was brought to trial for a crime involving gross moral turpitude.

Madge Oberholtzer was the daughter of a thoroughly respectable family in Irvington, an upper middle-class section of Indianapolis. Her father was in the railroad mail service. She had attended Butler College in Irvington and a business school, and she had taught in a rural school and had done secretarial work for a couple of Indianapolis business houses before going to work "at the Statehouse," as her father put it. In Indiana the Statehouse is Mecca for ambitious folk of all kinds. Madge worked for the State Superintendent of Public Instruction. In 1924 she was a rather pretty girl of twenty-eight, unmarried. She once had been engaged but "the young man had to go to the war." She was five feet, four inches tall, weighed about 145 pounds, and her father testified: "I don't think there ever was a more healthy looking girl than she was."

She was murdered in March 1925, not long after she had met Stephenson. He was then about thirty-three years old, though most people thought he was much older, an impression he encouraged by asking his followers to call him "The Old Man." He was handsome, with blond hair, thin, plucked eyebrows, a thin mouth, narrow, steady blue-gray eyes, and a ready smile. He was squat and powerfully built. He dressed conservatively and looked like, say, a banker. Most people seem to remember him as a suave man of the world, a behind-the-scenes manipulator, but one man recalls the day when, folksy as any baby-kissing candidate, he walked coatless into a resort hotel dining-room in northern Indiana and joked heartily with vacationing Hoosiers. Then, that evening he distributed fistfuls of ten-cent tickets at the lakeside dance hall and stood beaming on the sidelines while the young people danced. (But later that night, long after the folks had gone to bed, Stevie, as his intimates called him, came roaring into the hotel grounds in a fast car, and he needed the assistance of his bodyguards to get upstairs. The Klan raided blind tigers relentlessly, but Stevie liked a drink, indeed, evidence hinted that he once had been treated for alcoholism.)

When he met Madge Oberholtzer he had been in Indiana only three years, but his rise had been spectacular. A few months earlier he had managed Ed Jackson into the Governor's office and he was the most powerful man at the inaugural banquet at the Athletic Club on January 12, 1925. Madge, in her controverted deathbed statement, claimed she met Stephenson at the banquet, and it is easy to see why, young and ambitious and on the fringe of politics, she did not refuse flatly when the great man asked her for a date. After all, they had been properly introduced. He telephoned her insistently and she dined with him at the Washington Hotel where he had a suite; he called for her in his Cadillac. Later she attended a party at his house "with several prominent people when both gentlemen and their ladies were present." This house, only a couple of blocks from the house where Madge lived with her parents, was "one of the show places of Irvington." It was here that the party which ended in murder began. On Sunday evening, March 15, 1925, Madge returned to her own home about ten o'clock. Her escort departed and her mother told her that somebody had been telephoning for her from Irvington 0492. Madge called the number and Stephenson answered and, telling her he was leaving for Chicago, urged her to come to his home on a matter of great importance. He sent his bodyguard for her—Earl Gentry, a big ex-cop who smoked cigars. He and Madge walked to Stephenson's house. "I saw Stephenson and that he had been drinking. . . . So soon as I got inside of the house I was very much afraid." The housekeeper was not there. Stephenson was not married at that time. They took Madge to the kitchen and Earl Klenck came in. He was a deputy sheriff and another of Stephenson's henchmen. "I said I wanted no drink but Stephenson and the others forced me to drink. I was afraid not to do so and I drank three small glasses of the drink. This made me very ill and dazed and I vomited."

Stephenson told her he wanted her to go with him to Chicago, but she refused, being "very much terrified." He told her: "You cannot go home." The men selected guns from a dresser drawer. Gentry arranged for a drawing-room on the midnight train to Chicago. They all got into Stephenson's automobile and drove to the Union Station, stopping en route at the Washington Hotel to pick up the tickets.

They took her into the compartment (or drawing-room) and Gentry climbed into the upper berth, her deathbed statement continued. "Stephenson took hold of the bottom of my dress and pulled it up over my head. I tried to fight but was weak and unsteady. . . . What I had drunk was affecting me. Stephenson took all my clothes off and pushed me into the lower berth. After the train had started Stephenson got in with me and attacked me. He held me so I could not move. I . . . do not remember all that happened. He chewed me all over my body, bit my neck and face, chewed my tongue, chewed my breasts until they bled, my back, my legs, my ankles and mutilated me all over my body."

The next thing she remembered was being wakened next morning. "Stephenson was flourishing his revolver. I said to him to shoot me. . . ." They took her off the train at Hammond about 6:15 a.m., just before the train crossed the state line into Illinois. They walked the block from the depot to the four-story Indiana Hotel. Stephenson was wearing a cap, a pair of laced boots, khaki trousers, and a closely fitting black sweater. He needed a shave. The party was assigned to rooms 416 and 417, adjoining rooms but without a connecting door. In room 416 Stephenson gave the bellhop a half dollar and ordered breakfast. The boy left. Madge begged Stephenson to send a telegram to her mother. He dictated it: "We are driving through to Chicago will take train back tonight," and Gentry said he would send it.

"Stephenson lay down on the bed and slept. Gentry put hot towels and witch hazel on my head and bathed my body to relieve my suffering. . . ." Stephenson wakened and "said he was sorry, and that he was three degrees less than a brute. I said to him, 'You are worse than that.'" The bellhop brought up their breakfast and Stephenson, standing shirtless beside Madge, who sat dazed on the edge of the bed, tipped him a dollar. Stephenson ate heartily, Madge only drank coffee.

Stephenson's chauffeur, "Shorty," came in; he had driven Stephenson's car up from Indianapolis. "I said to Stephenson to give me some money that I had to buy a hat. 'Shorty' gave me $15.00 at Stephenson's direction and took me out to the car." She bought a small black silk hat for $12.50. Then "I said to 'Shorty' to drive me to a drug store in order that I might get some rouge. We drove to a drug store near the Indiana Hotel and I purchased a box of bi-chloride of mercury tablets."

Back at the hotel, the men got some more liquor, and Madge asked permission to go into room 417 to rest. Stephenson said: "'Oh no . . . you are going to lie right down here by me.' I waited awhile until I thought he was asleep then I went into room 417 [alone]. There was no glass in room 417 so I got a glass in 416 . . . I laid out eighteen of the bi-chloride of mer-

187

cury tablets and at once took six of them. I only took six because they burnt me so."

Now she lay down on the bed "and became very ill . . . vomited blood all day." About 4 p.m. Stephenson found her, and she told him what she had done, adding: "If you don't believe it there is evidence on the floor and in the cuspidor . . . the cuspidor was half full of clotted blood." He made her drink a quart of milk and told her they would have her stomach pumped at a hospital, where she could register as his wife. "I refused to do this as his wife. . . . Stephenson said that the best way out of it was for us to drive to Crown Point and for us to get married . . . I refused. Stephenson snapped his fingers and said to 'Shorty,' 'pack the grips.' Stephenson helped me downstairs. I did not care what happened to me."

On the 175-mile drive to Indianapolis they removed the license plates. "All the way back to Indianapolis I suffered great pain and agony and screamed for a doctor. . . . They refused to stop. I begged and said to Stephenson to leave me along the road some place . . . Stephenson said he thought I was dying. . . . I heard him say also that he had been in a worse mess than this before and got out of it. Stephenson and Gentry drank liquor during the entire trip. I remember Stephenson having said that he had power and saying he had made $250,000. He said that his word was law."

They reached Stephenson's house in Irvington late that night, and Madge's mother was at the door. One of them stalled her and they concealed Madge in the loft above the garage. (Stephenson ordinarily slept there, a friend of his has said, avoiding the house out of fear of attack.) Stephenson told Madge: "You will stay right here until you marry me." She remembered little more until the next morning when, about eleven o'clock, Klenck took her home. He carried her into her house and put her on a bed. Coming downstairs alone, he met a woman, Eunice H. Shultz, who lived with the Oberholtzers. She asked him who he was and he said: "My name is Johnson, from Kokomo . . . I must hurry. . . ."

Upstairs, Madge "was groaning, very pale, could hardly speak. . . . She said 'Oh I am dying, Mrs. Shultz.'" Her alarmed parents, who had been out hunting her, returned home and called the family physician, Dr. John K. Kingsbury. They already had consulted their attorney, Asa J. Smith; it was he who later took from Madge the dying declaration that wrecked the Klan in Indiana. Several physicians attended Madge, and her brother gave blood for a transfusion; but she died April 14, and her father charged Stephenson, Gentry, and Klenck with murder.

D. C. Stephenson's origin is clouded. Probably he was born in Texas in 1891 and spent some of his boyhood in Oklahoma. A printer's apprentice, he became a second lieutenant during the 1914–18 war. Beautiful women were important in his life (he married at least two before he was thirty). Honorably discharged from military service, he moved to Evansville where he took up his life work.

Now, the original Ku Klux Klan, organized in 1865 by bored Civil War veterans and perverted into an instrument of Negro terrorization, was dead by 1872. The Klan of the 1920's owed its tenets to Know-Nothingism, and its name, regalia, and some of its outlandish terminology to the Reconstruction Klan. Founded in Georgia in 1915 by Colonel William J. Simmons, the modern Klan didn't amount to much until 1920 when two press agents took it in hand. The original leaders were replaced in 1921 by Hiram Wesley Evans, a Dallas dentist who as Imperial Wizard was by turns D. C. Stephenson's mentor and his implacable enemy. Under Evans, Klan membership rose to an estimated six million in 1924. That year the tide of the national Invisible Empire reached high watermark. The date coincides precisely with the high watermark of Stephenson's own career in Indiana.

Indiana—perhaps because it represented a cross section of the United States—was fertile ground for the Klan. The war's backwash favored its growth, but so did other conditions. There was the boredom of the small towns. There was the old tradition of intolerance—before the 1914–18 war you could hear whispers that every Catholic church was fortified and built on a hilltop to command its town with firepower, and you could see roadside signs at village outskirts: "Nigger, Don't Let The Sun Set On You Here." Although thousands of Europeans had come to work in the steel mills and coal fields, Catholics, Jews, and foreigners were oddities in central Indiana. The old stiff-backed yeomanry, the farmers and the small-town merchants, were set in their ways, resentful of outsiders. In 1918 Mark Sullivan watched the revered G.A.R. come down to the railroad station at Peru to see draftees off to another war, and when a fellow passenger asked in a foreign accent: "Who are them old guys?" Sullivan understood hundred-per-cent Americanism. And now in 1920 the postwar scramble for jobs was on, with foreigners and Negroes competing with returning veterans. Hoosiers were sick of world problems, they were hell-bent for normalcy. Any organization sworn to uphold hearth and fireside and womanly virtue, "Americanism" and law and order, was assured of welcome. The Klan waged righteous war on Bolsheviks, Catholics, Jews, Negroes, bootleggers, pacifists, evolutionists, foreigners, and all persons whom it considered immoral. It worked closely with the potent Anti-Saloon League and it revived the moribund Horse Thief Detective Association, a Civil War "regulator" group that now became the Klan enforcement arm, a formidable vigilante organization that entered private homes without warrant and got to be the bane of petting parties on lonely country roads.

In Evansville, D. C. Stephenson set about organizing the war veterans and entered the 1920 Congressional primary as a wet Democrat. The Anti-Saloon League licked him; he promptly became bone-dry and Republican. He joined the burgeoning Klan, taking with him his beloved veterans. He was a personable man and an eloquent speaker. Hiram W. Evans may have met Stephenson earlier in Texas. In 1922 he gave him the job of organizing the Klan in Indiana, and before long Evans added twenty other states from Maine to Nebraska. For a time Stephenson maintained headquarters at Columbus, Ohio, but soon he moved to Indianapolis, where meanwhile he had gone into the coal-and-gravel business. He sold Klan memberships for ten dollars each, of which he kept about four dollars. The white robes and peaked caps, manufactured for a dollar and ten cents, cost the members from five to ten dollars. In eighteen months, it has been estimated, Stephenson made between two and five million dollars. He hired full-time organizers, some of them stock-and-bond salesmen or Florida real-estate promoters, and he encouraged rank-and-file Klansmen to obtain new members by giving them a split of the initiation fee extracted from each "alien" admitted to the Invisible Empire. Among his most diligent proselytizers were Protestant clergymen. People of all kinds joined eagerly—power-hungry ward heelers and men from the criminal classes, prominent businessmen and bankers. Your nextdoor neighbor might be a Klansman and you never would know it even after an application for membership had been mailed to you at his instigation. The application, on stationery bearing pen and ink sketches of Klansmen on white-shrouded horses and headed "Imperial Palace, Invisible Empire (incorporated), Aulik of the Imperial Wizard," contained twenty questions, including these: "Are you a gentile or jew?", "Do you believe in White Supremacy?", "What is your politics? . . . religious faith?"

The Klan had more than the usual amount of the abracadabra common to secret orders. It suited the Hoosiers fine. The klaverns might meet once a week, the local leaders might meet almost nightly. Many of their meetings were simply poker sessions in the clubroom above the store overlooking the square, but many were more serious. Every now and then posters would appear mysteriously on telephone poles at rural crossroads, posters announcing a konklave, or a klavalcade, a parade. At the appointed time, usually just at dusk, the robed and hooded marchers formed near the outskirts of one of the small cities on the Indiana plain. They came from miles around. In orderly procession they marched into town, and the street intersections were patrolled by brother Klansmen who had usurped the police function. Why could they get away with this? Simply because they were in truth the law. The mayor was Klan elected; so were the city councilmen; so were the sheriff and the prosecutor. No one viewing a parade could laugh at the Klan's absurd posturings. There they were, the hundreds, perhaps thousands, of marching men, all clad in white from head to foot, no leaders, no flags, no drum-and-bugle corps, nothing but silent men marching in the dusk—that, and a silent, awed crowd of onlookers. Through the town they moved, perhaps pointedly passing the Negro district or the home of the Catholic priest, and on out to the side of the country road where in the gloom of the evening they set up their wooden cross on a hillside and soaked it with kerosene and fired it for all to see. Perhaps they took in new members, who, kneeling before this blazing symbol of terror, swore secrecy and obedience until death.

The Klan seemed omnipotent and omniscient. Its armed investigators, some of them thugs from Herrin, Illinois, raided blind tigers. Klan members issued warnings to nonmembers who, neighborhood gossip said, were cheating on their wives. It warned that the Pope was on his way to America. Once a mob of fifteen hundred, exhorted by a Klan speaker, actually met a train at North Manchester and forced the single frightened passenger who alighted to prove that he was not the Pope. The Klan spread fast. By 1924 it claimed from a quarter- to a half-million members, more than a tenth of Indiana's total population.

Stephenson, an adroit opportunist, seized on Governor McCray's conviction as proof that the duty of the Klan was plain: to purify, to purge Indiana politics. A former Exalted Cyclops of the South Bend klavern said that he understood the Klan was building a political machine to control the United States, that "we planned to extract Catholicism from the schools as a dentist would extract teeth," that at least one local klavern broke up when the Klabee, or treasurer, could not account for the funds, that Klansmen who had been planted on every newspaper in one of the state's largest cities regularly furnished to Klan leaders advance proofs of editorials and news stories before publication.

Thus while the rank and file played ghost, their leaders had more serious aims: money and political power. They got both. Stephenson maintained an expensive yacht and owned interests in various business enterprises. Did a Knight who was a chiropractor by day want to get his profession legalized? Stephenson would put a bill through the legislature. When a bill that would have abolished Madge Oberholtzer's job came before the legislature, Stephenson killed it for her.

He could be a man of the people when he chose. Once at a downstate farm home he "got down on the floor and crawled around with the baby"; he had come dressed in hunting clothes to arrange for a rabbit hunt on Thanksgiving, almost an annual rite on Indiana farms. He promised to go fishing with one of his downstate organizers, and when in the summer evenings he drove through his realm, he would park his Cadillac slantwise at the curb on the square and chat about crops with the klavern leaders who left the corner drugstore to stand with one foot on the running board.

But he also moved in a fast circle in the capital city—a circle of cocktail parties in hotel suites and dinner parties in the hotel roof garden above the city, a circle that met in a smoke-filled room when the Legislature was in session. A circle, in short, that he must have denounced many times in flaming speeches to the rank and file in the country districts.

And he also could be spectacular. When, on July 4, 1923, two years after he joined the Klan (his phenomenal career was surprisingly brief), he assumed office as Grand Dragon of the Realm of Indiana, he arranged at Kokomo the greatest konklave ever held in Indiana. After the Knights had assembled two-hundred-thousand strong (his estimate), he swooped down from the sky in a gilded airplane, stepped from it clad in resplendent robes, and pledged his unfaltering leadership. When he departed majestically, the hysterical multitude threw at his feet coins and jewelry.

He knew all the tricks. He called himself the foremost mass psychologist of his time—a claim that cannot be dismissed lightly—and he kept before his desk a bust of Napoleon. His ambition was to be President of the United States. He had his eye on the Senate seat of Sam Ralston, whose health was failing fast in 1924, and on the 1928 Republican presidential nomination. Who dares say with certainty he would have failed? No one had laughed when he explained to the throng at Kokomo that he was late because he had been consulting with President Harding on high matters of state, nor when, frequently, he kept callers at his office waiting on the pretext of speaking long distance with the White House.

Having built his organization, Stephenson led it into the political campaign of 1924. Already he had made deals with some of the bosses. The Klan crossed party lines. It voted for its own members and its friends, whether Democrats or Republicans. But by and large the Klan won power by using the Republican

Party, probably because the Republicans were already in control of Indiana, and Stephenson, instead of trying to lick 'em, joined 'em.

Before the polls had been open long on that primary day in May 1924, it was apparent that something new had come into Indiana politics. Negro leaders had double-crossed their race and thrown support to Klan candidates. The Klan was supporting Ed Jackson (Republican) for Governor. He was nominated. Stephenson dominated the Republican Party.

But only four days after the primary it became known that Stephenson and the Klan leaders were at odds. The leaders claimed he was banished from the Klan for conduct "unbecoming a Klansman" and involving a manicurist. Stephenson said he had resigned earlier because he didn't like the way the national leaders stirred up religious and racial hatred and used women to frame their political enemies on Mann Act charges. On April 7, 1924, that is to say: "On the Deadly Day of the Weeping Week of the Appalling Month of the Year of the Klan LVII," His Lordship, H. W. Evans, Imperial Wizard, had signed an edict ordering the Evansville klavern number one to try Stephenson and had addressed it to "All Genii, Grand Dragons and Hydras, Great Titans and Furies, Giants, King Kleagles and Kleagles, Exalted Cyclops and Terrors, and to All Citizens of the Invisible Empire, in the name of the valiant and venerated dead."

Could such stuff be taken seriously? Indeed, it was the opening of a fight for big stakes involving ultimately, perhaps, the fate of the nation. To Cadle Tabernacle at Indianapolis, Stephenson summoned Klansmen from every Indiana county in an effort to sever the Indiana realm from the "domination" of Evans and Walter F. Bossert, who was an imperial representative and a Republican politician. Stephenson said: "God help the man who issues a proclamation of war against the Ku Klux Klan." The gathering elected him Grand Dragon. (Grand Dragons always had been appointed at national headquarters.) He said: "We're going out to Klux Indiana as she's never been Kluxed before."

Everybody was politicizing in this crucial election year. Indiana Klansmen had rival Grand Dragons, Bossert and

Stephenson, and the politicians were nervous. Who really controlled the Klan vote? One night late in May the Klan paraded in strength through Indianapolis, starting on Indiana Avenue, heart of the Negro section, and thousands of citizens watched soberly. Nationally, the Klan claimed the power that blocked Al Smith's nomination. Ed Jackson stumped Indiana in Stephenson's car. Strife within the Klan became vituperative and deadly. The campaign ground on to election day. On that day the Klan elected "most everyone that was elected."

Now to Stephenson's elaborately appointed eight-room office suite on the third floor of the new Kresge Building, came a steady stream of legislators and other state dignitaries. Stephenson himself rarely was seen in the halls of the sepulchral Statehouse, but his men were there. He was desperately busy. For years criminal prosecutions and frame-ups had been common in Indiana politics. But now matters were approaching the flash point. Stephenson said the Klan leaders from Atlanta were trying to frame him on a morals charge. A woman who said she was his first wife from long ago came to Indianapolis and sued him on March 18, 1925, for desertion and nonsupport, and it was said that her expenses were paid by Stephenson's Klan enemies. Curiously, only the day before, Madge Oberholtzer had taken poison in the hotel room at Hammond.

Madge Oberholtzer's father said: "Neither faction of the Klan is mixed up in this. I am going through with this uphill fight for the sake of humanity—for the sake of other fathers and their daughters." Stephenson's secretary, Fred Butler, said: "We've always landed on our feet, haven't we?" Stephenson, in a dark suit and pearl-gray hat with turned-up brim, told a reporter: "I'd give anything if I could get away from the Ku Klux Klan."

Friends of Stephenson have argued that he, a shrewd man fully aware of the many enemies who confronted him that critical spring, would not have been indiscreet enough to get drunk and assault an innocent maiden. With what glee his enemies must have read the newspaper accounts of his arrest! As the trial began Stephenson declared that the murder charge was part of a gigantic conspiracy fostered by the Imperial Wizard. Was it a frame? Well, the chief evidence against Stephenson was Madge Oberholtzer's "dying declaration." Asa Smith took it from Madge, and he was a reputable lawyer with a substantial civil practice.

But was it possible that Smith was made an innocent party to a conspiracy? That would mean that Madge Oberholtzer lied in making her dying declaration. This Stephenson's partisans charged. A booklet published in his behalf in 1940 attacked the dying declaration at various points. For instance, why did Madge make no outcry or effort to escape? Again, although "terrified" and "very ill," she was able to note such details as the fact that Stephenson's revolver was pearl-handled but did not recall that the Pullman porter (as he testified) brought sandwiches to the compartment. Again, the newspapers reported she bought the hat and the bichloride of mercury at stores in the hotel building, which she would not logically have used a car to reach, as she said she did. (And it is a curious fact that the state introduced no witness to testify he had sold her either poison or a hat.) The pamphlet questioned, among other things, whether in those days in Indiana a woman of the virtue claimed for Madge Oberholtzer would have gone voluntarily to a bachelor's home at ten o'clock at night, whether she could have been "forced" to take three drinks. The pamphlet asked whether she would have gone unguarded from the hotel room where her abductor slept to an adjoining room to take poison instead of escaping and whether she would have swallowed the poison and vomited all day alone in the room without seeking aid. Nevertheless, Judge Will M. Sparks admitted the declaration and said: "[Its] credibility and weight are wholly for the jury." And this Indiana judge told this jury of ten farmers, a businessman, and a truck driver: "The certainty of the declarant's belief that he or she is *in extremis* and that in a very short time, those immortal and spiritual elements which inhabit the body will forsake it, to encounter the dread possibilities of the unknown and supernatural world beyond the grave, is deemed to furnish a sanction equivalent to that of a solemn and positive oath administered in a court of justice." As to the statement's details, one must remember that, when she made it, Madge Oberholtzer was in pain and she was dying. Of course Madge's statement was not subject to cross-examination.

But the question of Stephenson's guilt involves broader issues. For certainly this was no ordinary murder case—that is, death did not immediately follow the act of violence charged, and indisputably Madge took a deadly poison by her own hand. This raised the question: what, precisely, killed the girl? The state's medical experts contended that she died of a pneumonia infection caused by the bites on her breast, that she would have recovered from the mercury poisoning and ensuing nephritis, and that Stephenson's delay in providing medical treatment contributed to her death. The defense claimed simply that she had committed suicide. This had been the verdict of the coroner, Paul F. Robinson, and he testified for the defense at the murder trial.

The trial was venued to Noblesville, a small county-seat town not far from Indianapolis. Thus Stephenson, charged with heinous crime, came back from the wicked capital city to the country folk whence sprang his original power. Neither Stephenson, Klenck, nor Gentry took the witness stand. The defense established an alibi for Klenck (he was discharging his duties as deputy sheriff at the time of the attack). Its witnesses testified that Madge had known Stephenson a little longer and a little better than her dying declaration indicated, but that was all. The court refused a defense offer to prove that Madge had visited a married man at police headquarters and that his wife had caught them. Attacking the point in the dying declaration where she related that Stephenson and Gentry had stopped at the Hotel Washington to pick up the railroad tickets, one witness testified that he had seen her sitting alone in the car and that she seemed under no duress.

The trial lasted more than a month; the transcript covers 2,247 pages. Judge Sparks, charging the jury, said it was possible for one person to drive another by fear to suicide, and that this would amount to felonious homicide. But in such cases the suicide must have been a reasonable step taken in well-grounded fear of immediate violence and must have been the natural consequences of the "unlawful conduct" of the person who caused the fear. These questions were for the jury, which also had to consider Madge's past relations with Stephenson and her chances of seeking help during the abduction, for the question of whether she went to Hammond willingly was crucial. If she assented to the "humiliation" that drove her to suicide, then of course no homicide had been committed. But if she had been assaulted forcibly, then the jury had to determine whether suicide was a logical consequence, that is, whether, to a virtuous woman, death might be preferable to dishonor. If it so determined, it should convict. If the defendants, having abducted Madge forcibly, willfully kept her prisoner in the Stephenson garage and withheld medical attention, they were guilty of murder. Judge Sparks defined second-degree murder as unpremeditated homicide committed "purposely and maliciously," and he defined malice as not simply ill will but as "any wicked or corrupt motive." It was of second-degree murder that the jury convicted Stephenson. Klenck and Gentry were acquitted. And Stephenson was sentenced to life imprisonment.

What would happen now, politically? Stephenson went to prison boasting that Governor Jackson would pardon him. He didn't. Ordinarily Klansmen went on holding their meetings as always, but the professional politicians were quick to read the omens. They who so recently had welcomed Klan support now shunned it desperately. The Democrats feared that the Klan would move in on them. A Democratic boss said: "We don't want the poisonous animal to crawl into our yard and die." Democrats sensed a new political weapon. Clearly the political machinery that had controlled Indiana so tightly was flying apart. For years to come "Stephensonism" would be a label fatal to any Indiana politician. They all knew it; they scurried to cover. The fearful politicians heard rumblings from the penitentiary at Michigan City. Stephenson, embittered by Governor Jackson's refusal to act, was going to blow the lid off. Finally the storm broke. Stephenson disclosed the location of two "black boxes" containing his private papers. The Indianapolis *Times* launched a crusade. Stephenson played ball: "I have been railroaded to prison to protect others." It became plain that Stephenson for years had collected evidence against the politicians he corrupted. Three Marion County grand juries conducted the investigation. Witnesses disappeared. The black boxes disgorged. Mayor John L. Duvall was indicted for violation of the Corrupt Practices Act; February 4, 1931, he began serving a thirty-day sentence. Six members of the Indianapolis council, indicted for receiving bribes, paid small fines on minor charges and resigned. The entire city administration had been overturned. The *Times* produced a $2,500 check (among others) drawn by Stephenson in favor of Ed Jackson during the 1924 campaign. "After three weeks deliberation" Governor Jackson explained that the check was payment for a riding horse named Senator which had choked to death on a corncob. Finally came evidence purporting to show that Jackson, while a candidate, had offered a bribe of money and immunity to Governor Mc-Cray, then under indictment. Jackson was indicted; he pleaded the statute of limitations and was saved. The former Republican State Chairman went to Leavenworth on a conspiracy charge. Other officials were indicted. Judge Clarence W. Dearth of Muncie was impeached; he had once threatened a newsboy peddling an anti-Klan paper; he barely escaped removal from office.

The pot had boiled over. For its part in building the fire under the Klan, the Indianapolis *Times* won the Pulitzer Prize in 1928. By 1928 the Klan claimed only four thousand members in Indiana. Is the Klan dead in Indiana? Probably only a few local groups survive. On July 2, 1934, a fiery cross burned at Kokomo. Throughout the 1930's—the Democrats were in power—the Klan was political poison. Among the men washed into local offices by the Republican tides of 1940 and 1942 were a number of Klan holdovers. In 1944 Robert W. Lyons, a millionaire chain-store lobbyist, was elected Republican national committeeman, and a member of his own party denounced him as a onetime Klan intriguer; he resigned.

Stephenson in 1947 was still in prison, having carried his case unsuccessfully through more than thirty appellate actions. He has claimed that Klan death threats prevented him from presenting an adequate defense and, recently, that he has been kept a "political prisoner" by "the machinations of Robert W. Lyons." One newspaperman has said: "Stephenson is the hottest thing at Michigan City—if you paroled him it'd be worse than getting caught stealing ten thousand dollars." Stephenson himself once wrote this note to a newspaperman: "I should have been put in jail for my political activities but I am not guilty of murder." Many Hoosiers agree.

The Indiana cast of mind that made possible Stephenson's success by no means changed when he went to prison. Nor did all his henchmen lapse into obscurity. One was Court Asher, a reckless young man from the southern Indiana hills. After the Stephenson debacle he landed on his feet. He became a national figure of sorts during the debate over foreign policy in the late 1930's and early 1940's when Indiana gained renown as a home of isolationism. Let us see what kind of man Court Asher was, let us trace the progress of his thought.

Chapter 15

COURT ASHER, ISOLATIONIST

O<small>N</small> S<small>UNDAY</small> afternoon before Labor Day 1946, after the chicken and the roasting ears and the watermelon had been eaten, the kinfolk dismantled the tables and with the planks made a speakers' platform in front of the ancient red brick schoolhouse on the hilltop. About a hundred people had come to this Asher-Long family reunion in the southern Indiana hills. No formal program had been arranged, so the chairman just called on people to come up and do some stunts. Most did what they always did at the reunion—one lady gave an impersonation of an old maid, another read *The Barefoot Boy*, a man and his wife sang *My Jesus Gave His All* and *Old Shep*, a little girl played *Silver Threads Among the Gold* on a saxophone, a man told a Jewish joke. A man who had been in the Army recounted his experiences ("If anybody tries tell you it wasn't rough you just look 'em in the eye and tell 'em he's a liar, it was plenty rough"), and one of the Ashers, Court Asher, perhaps the most renowned member of the clan present, made a little speech. A small, compact man in a tight double-breasted city suit, he climbed the schoolhouse steps, took off his snap-brim hat, and said with disappointment that he had expected more than two hundred to attend this first reunion since the war.

The children playing in the goldenrod beside the fence grew noisy, and Asher raised his voice. "This beautiful valley is rich in lore," and he waved a hand at the Jurdon Valley planted to corn below, green and brown in the September sunlight, with sycamores gleaming white on the far hill beyond. "You should love your ancestors," and he called forth the old family names—Bobby Asher who had come here from Kentucky in 1812 before Indiana was a state, and his own grandmother, Betsy Asher, born here in 1830 and wed to Tup Long, the patriarch buried back of the cabin on the ridge. Far off a rooster crowed twice. Asher was saying: "Aunt Dove: How many of you remember her?" He had a glibness other speakers here had lacked. Sometimes it was plain he had progressed beyond the narrow confines of Redbird Holler up the valley where he was born. "Jurdon has a lot to be proud of. We're clannish, always have been. I've sailed the seas, traveled the globe, been on the hot desert sands, been in the Klondike, and I've been where the bright lights shone, but my heart has always been in the hills. The flint-hearted cities with iron streets—they go around there mad at each other, they haven't the brotherly love we have, they hate each other," and he talked on for fifteen minutes.

It seemed strange to hear Court Asher speak ill of hate. He was once a Kleagle in the Ku Klux Klan, he had recently advocated the Klan's revival, and in his newspaper, the *X-Ray,* he was tirelessly demanding the "extermination" of "red rat Communists" and "Red Kikes."

Court Asher has been by turns a machinist, bootlegger, Klan undercover man, newspaperman, politician, saloonkeeper, and publisher. Not until he opened the columns of his *X-Ray* to people like Father Charles Coughlin, Representative Clare E. Hoffman, and Elizabeth Dilling, did he achieve national prominence. He knew Coughlin, Gerald L. K. Smith, and Mrs. Dilling, and he has a high regard for Martin Dies, before whose Congressional committee he testified, but he always stood a little apart from the tenuous network of people who, ranging from downright Bund members to honorable newspaper publishers, sought to persuade America to stay out of the war, and he despised William Dudley Pelley. After Japan attacked Pearl Harbor, Asher continued his onslaught against Jews, Communists, "Mr. Van Rosenfelt," "Vendell Villkie," and "The Jew Deal," and he was indicted, along with twenty-seven others, for sedition. The charges against all of them were dropped later. His life has been threatened numerous times in Muncie, and

such radio commentators and newspaper columnists as Walter
Winchell and Drew Pearson have attacked him verbally. His
X-Ray, suppressed briefly during the war by Federal authorities,
has been denounced as a scurrilous blackmail sheet and has
been supported by hundreds of zealots. He has been accused
of conspiring against the nation's safety and has been defended
as a patriot laboring to save the republic from destruction by
the "red Jew" conspiracy.

He was born in the Morgan County hills below Martinsville
April 24, 1893, the youngest of ten children. As a boy he trapped
along Indian Creek and Ghost Creek and Jurdon Creek, selling
rabbit skins and short-stripe-skunk skins for a dime and star-
skunk skins for a half dollar. He gathered and dried walnuts and
sold them for fifty cents a bushel in town, and his Fourth of
July money came from blueberries at a dime a gallon. He earned
twenty-five cents a day hewing out crossties with a broadax.

His father died when he was one, his mother when he was
eight. He went to live with his widowed grandmother in Martinsville, the county seat seven miles north. There one of Asher's
schoolmates and neighbors was Paul V. McNutt, later Governor
of Indiana and High Commissioner of the Philippines. McNutt,
son of the local judge and banker, lived in a large house on
broad, shaded Washington Street. Laughing, Asher recalls: "We
use to rock him home from school ever' noon." Asher had to
work. "Grandma had four orphan kids, she took in wash, and I
done anything I could." He earned four dollars a week in Hiram
Pearcy's livery stable near the courthouse, bedding down the
horses and sweeping out. He earned fifty cents a week plus tips
cleaning spittoons and shining shoes in Billy Rudicel's barber
shop.

Martinsville lies in the broad, flat Indian Creek valley, which,
though not "the best land the crow ever flew over" that Asher
calls it, is rich. But the hills begin a few miles south and the
soil there, except for the bottom land in the narrow valleys, is
poor. The hill people overproduce children and underproduce
crops. They live in poverty. Other Hoosiers ridicule them as
hillbillies, which they resent bitterly. When the children of these
people are forced off the farm, as Asher was, they tend to become
village urchins. "Hell, I never had no education, never went

beyond seventh grade." After Asher left school he began to fear he would be placed in an orphanage. So, at fifteen, he caught a freight. In Philadelphia he got a job washing dishes in a workingman's restaurant. A man who ate there, a foreman at the Baldwin locomotive works, gave him a job as an apprentice machinist at five cents an hour. He paid a nickel a night to sleep on newspapers spread on the floor in the Newsboys' Home. His apprenticeship lasted three and a half years. He worked an additional year and a half. Then, restless, he became a boomer machinist. "I went all over the world—Erie, New York, Brooklyn, St. Louis, Illinois, Indianapolis, Detroit." Indiana was the place for a machinist, the Speedway was new. One cold night in 1914 the freight Asher was riding stopped for water in an Indiana town, and the brakeman threw him off. He walked down the railroad tracks to a saloon. The bartender gave him a shot of whisky, lent him a quarter, directed him to the Warner Gear factory down the tracks, and told him he was in Muncie. He got a job. In a boardinghouse he met the landlady's daughter, a large, handsome farm girl named Opal Miller, whom he married. They have no children. Intensely loyal, she has stuck with him through all his adventures.

In the Army he served as a technician with units engaged at St. Mihiel and the Argonne and was discharged as a first sergeant. He received a partial-disability pension for a mental disorder. His offhand, exaggerated account of this has produced the tale that he received a medical discharge as a psychotic and is "not right," but in speaking for the record now he is inclined to minimize the whole matter.

After working briefly in Cleveland and Indianapolis machine shops and on an Indianapolis newspaper under the veterans' vocational training program, he returned to Muncie. Like many ex-soldiers, he was restless and tired of being poor. "I didn't have nothin' but my uniform." He was a good mechanic, and a bootlegger offered him twenty-five dollars a trip just to keep the car going. Asher was quick to see the big money in booze. He saved enough to buy a motorcycle with a sidecar and started bootlegging for himself. He bought a car and soon he was running liquor into Muncie and Indianapolis from Cincinnati, Pittsburgh, and Miami.

This inevitably involved Asher with local politicians, police-men, and criminals. Few of the new-risen factory cities were more corrupt than Muncie. Asher carried a gun and grossed a thousand dollars a week. Arrested several times, he was not convicted. Playing politics—the politics of "protection"—he made many enemies. Belligerent and outspoken, he made other enemies for varied reasons. They framed two bank-robbery charges against him, he claims. Asher, a desperate vindictive man, tried to break into the house of a customer with whom he had quarreled, was trapped by detectives, tried to shoot his way out, broke a leg, was jailed, beat a burglary charge, and in re-taliation informed on forty-five persons with whom he was in-volved in the liquor traffic. This resulted, late in 1921, in Asher's only jail sentence—sixty days—and fines or sentences for most of the others.

Although the night Asher got out of jail he walked into the Muncie police station carrying a jug of moonshine and bragging he'd bootlegged from jail, he hadn't liked jail at all. His troubles multiplied. He was three times convicted of bootlegging by Muncie courts but won appeals in the Indiana Supreme Court. His mounting "protection" and legal costs were draining away his profits. He became convinced the Klan had packed a jury and convicted him of bootlegging (not an uncommon practice). Klansmen beat up a friend of Asher's. One night soon after, Asher went to the fairgrounds, where a konklave was scheduled. He had a pistol and was determined "there wouldn't be no Kon-klave." A friend introduced him to D. C. Stephenson. He told Asher the Klan needed men like Asher and offered him a hun-dred dollars a week plus expenses as an investigator with the rank of Kleagle. "Steve showed me what their principles were. And it was more than I'd ever dreamed of makin', except at boot-leggin'."

Asher investigated local klaverns to determine whether they were loyal to Stephenson. He served as Stephenson's bodyguard and traveling companion and slept in his home. After Stephen-son's political victory of 1924, he and his favorites were living in expensive hotel suites, drinking good liquor, driving fancy cars, and keeping fancy women. How much did they care for the Klan principles? Looking back in 1946, Asher said—remember, his forebears were Southern—"When I was in the Klan I never paid much attention to that Negro and Jew stuff except for white supremacy, and the truth is I was makin' good dough and I saw what a hell of a political organization the Klan could become." He opposed the Klan's anti-Catholic attitude, not as unethical, but as politically unwise.

By the time Stephenson was sent to prison, Asher had become associated with the state Republican Editorial Association and was writing special articles for several newspapers including, he says, the *Chicago Tribune.* Some of his articles dealt with corruption in Indianapolis; the mayor sued for libel. Retaliating, Asher was instrumental in bringing to light Stephenson's "black boxes"; as a result (as we have seen) the mayor and others went to jail and a Muncie judge was impeached (earlier he had convicted Asher of bootlegging).

One time, Asher says, he and Hildy Johnson and other Chicago newspapermen immortalized in *The Front Page* got thrown out of the Morrison Hotel in Chicago for engaging in a singing contest. He recalls with pleasure that "there was bonded whisky runnin' down the corridor" outside the hotel rooms of the newspapermen during the trial of a Cincinnati bootlegger. "God damn, them was good days," Asher recalled in 1946, sitting on the Claypool Hotel mezzanine in a rather seedy suit and runover shoes, his hair partly gray. "The best days I ever had, maybe."

He bought some real estate in Muncie, pyramided it, and became a professional bondsman. The depression ruined him. During this period, and earlier, he was suspected of a number of shady activities in Muncie, but nothing was proved. When the Prohibition amendment was repealed, he borrowed ten thousand dollars and opened in Muncie the Wigwam, a fancy saloon near the courthouse. He netted eight or nine hundred dollars a week, perhaps his greatest prosperity. But he backed losing candidates in the election, and the winners refused to renew his liquor license. Asher went to see Paul McNutt, then Governor, and, according to Asher, McNutt told him he would have to "get right" with his local organization. This was impossible: Asher long had battled the men in control of it. So he went back to Muncie, sold at auction fifteen-thousand-dollars worth of saloon fixtures for $428, and started the *X-Ray* to get even with the Democratic machine that he considered had ruined him. "And I drove Doc Bunch [then mayor of Muncie] out of office at the next election and I beat him the next time too. I've seen 'em all upset, every one I've ripped into, except Roosevelt. And he died."

The first issue of the *X-Ray* appeared September 11, 1937, carrying the slogans *A Beacon for Taxpayers and Honest Labor* and *Truthful, Courageous, Impartial, Fearless*. Most of the front page of the four-column, four-page paper was devoted to a general statement of policy and charges that Mayor Bunch was running a corrupt wasteful machine financed by "so-called donations from saloons and other dens of iniquity." The inside was mostly filler. "The paper wasn't much back in those days," Asher has said. "I hadn't got into national stuff yet." A signed editorial on the back page said: "I intend to operate this paper honorably, fearlessly and for the best interests of the community. I intend to turn the X-Ray on all forms of political graft and corruption, to fight for the interests of organized . . . labor. . . . I will take orders from no one. I will never degrade my paper to a scandal sheet. . . . If I receive contributions, advertising and subscriptions, I will keep this paper going as long as I have a crust of bread. . . . notify me at my home 814 W. 12th St., Muncie, Ind., and I will call for your ad or contribution. I have not the funds to afford a phone. . . ."

In the early issues Asher concentrated on Muncie affairs. He attacked the "great profits" of the local gas company, and recurrently, political favoritism in the granting of liquor licenses. When the Home Owners' Loan Corporation, a Federal agency created in 1933 to rescue small home owners from debt, foreclosed the mortgage on his home, Asher called HOLC a "Simon Legree," "a scheme to save the banks and money lenders." He took up the cudgels for a family of nine that was evicted, and against a loan shark and a project to widen a street and turn it into "a speedway." In 1946, recalling an attack he made in those days on a proposed city ordinance to license plumbers as a "health measure," Asher said: "Sure, healthy for the politicians. But it's gonna be unhealthy as hell for this little feller got a little shop out in the backyard, trying make a living." Time and again Asher took the part of the underdog.

On January 8, 1938, his banner headline read: *WE NEED A RESURRECTION*, and the story, his first dealing with a national issue, was a straight Republican-Party-line blast at pump priming, waste, corrupt administration of relief funds, tax burdens on industry, and government meddling. Now the *X-Ray* originally had been financed by some old Klan friends of Asher's and some Muncie politicians who opposed the Democratic Party in power. Asher, feuding with McNutt, espoused the Republican cause as the Klan had done earlier. After leaving the saloon business Asher had worked for the local Republican organization and, he says, the state one, and for individual candidates. Through the spring of 1938 Asher devoted more and more space to national affairs, and much of his material appeared to have been written by Republican publicists. He expanded his circulation. He began to get the ads of all political candidates ("they was scared not to"). He backed Raymond Springer for Congress. The issue of May 21, 1938, carried the first piece by Representative Clare Hoffman, a leading Republican isolationist. Asher says Hoffman had heard of him through Congressman Springer, who sent the *X-Ray* to Hoffman.

On June 18, 1938, Asher filled the front page under the bannerline *Red Communism*. This was Asher's first assault on the "Red Menace," and it must have startled his Muncie readers. He has explained: "I had Doc Bunch beat here and I was goin' to start fightin' Communism." It was really Dr. William A. Wirt who, unknowingly, first started Asher thinking about the danger of revolution. Dr. Wirt was the Gary school superintendent who charged in 1934 that he had been told by New Deal brain trusters that "Roosevelt is only the Kerensky of this Revolution." Asher recalls: "I took it up on the floor of the Legion in Muncie." Though this gregarious man is an inveterate joiner and belongs to "every fraternal order in Muncie—Eagles, Moose, Elks, everything," he expends most of his fraternal energy on the V.F.W. and the Legion, has held offices in both, and spends his spare time playing cards or drinking at their halls. He always has approved of their resolutions against "Communism" and for "Americanism." It was natural that Dr. Wirt's charges should interest Asher. He sought more information from a former Muncie newspaperman, Walter Steel (or Steele), who became an isolationist publisher; from Father Coughlin's paper, *Social Justice;* and from Carl Mote. Mote, another former Muncie newspaperman, had become a wealthy utility executive. He sent for Asher about 1939 and Asher went, he says, to his home in Indianapolis, where Mote revealed to him the New Deal's conspiracy to over-throw American institutions. "He laid it down to me that Cough-lin was right. And he was." Mote gave him an armload of "lit-erature" to take home, and Asher printed it in the *X-Ray*. All at once Asher began getting massive stacks of "literature" from all over the country. From then on he was on the mailing list and he was in the thick of the struggle over just who was going to save the republic and how. Colonel Robert R. McCormick, of the *Chicago Tribune,* led this crusade, and a raggle-taggle host yam-mered at his heels and on his flanks. Asher says he has met Colo-nel McCormick but he does not pretend to intimacy. Although some of the isolationist leaders maintained close liaison, their followers were loose-knit at best. Asher denies he was intimate with any of them. Pelley visited Muncie, but Asher disliked him and had little to do with him. Some isolationists found Asher hard to get along with. Often he wouldn't even answer their let-ters. He is a suspicious man, a man with a dark background who has had much trouble, and usually he prefers to go it alone. He even broke with Coughlin finally. About 1943 Asher appeared on a platform with Gerald Smith and others. (Smith, once an Indianapolis pastor, had gained prominence as an associate of Governor Huey Long of Louisiana and, by 1943, as an evangeli-cal isolationist.) "I never had no more to do with Smith. He was takin' in too much dough." Asher never made much money out of isolationism, Jew baiting, Roosevelt baiting, or Red baiting. Once he asked Smith and Mrs. Dilling, who seemed affluent, for help, but they didn't even answer. He concludes they are not sincere, but are money-mad. No other well-heeled organization, like the National Association of Manufacturers, has ever backed him; he says rather plaintively: "I never got any of that big money. And I don't know why either. My support's been right here in Muncie." Muncie manufacturers have not supported him, he says. But Muncie politicians have. His paper sells for a nickel. He gets small individual contributions from scattered zealots. The paper nets him about seventy dollars a week. His automobile, house, furniture, and clothing all appear to bear this out. There was more money in bootlegging, Klan work, and saloon-keeping.

However, he attracted attention. The Dies committee on unAmerican activities called him to testify. "Martin Dies treated me, O Jesus Christ, I never met a finer fella in my life. I went down in the cafeteria, had lunch with Springer, and Martin Dies and two other members of the committee. I learned things down there in Washington I never knew existed." He returned to the holy crusade with renewed strength. In a 72-point headline he demanded:

IMPEACH ROOSEVELT!

His paper on April 1, 1939, was sprinkled with headlines like: *Does Roosevelt Want a War? Looks That Way!* and his editorial, displaying his love of the rustic, was a model of isolationist expression. A kindred aspect of the Midwest isolationist mind appears here: *Jew York As National Home Suggested For Jew Deal Government.* Leading isolationists, including, Asher says, some Congressmen, had told him that "the Jews was connected with Communism, that they was the head of it. Sidney Hillman. They was using labor movements to promote it."

He aroused reprisal. In meeting it, he abandoned the fine, canned phrases supplied by others and in an article on January 25, 1941, he revealed the true Court Asher speaking in anger:

> "Both last week and this week a Jew voice called me on the phone; called me vile names; declared he intended to kill me; spoke of my mother (dead 46 years) in vile and vulgar terms . . .
>
> "I asked him in the phone conversation if he was a 'Kike'; he became very abusive, that is, over the phone from his place of safety. Just a dirty, stinking, yellow coward, too yellow to face me in person. . . .
>
> ". . . Well, I travel the streets of Muncie alone. . . . Try your luck, but be sure of your effort, for if you fail and I get my hands on you there will be 'fresh fish' in hell and it will be you. . . . I call on my blood relation in Bell and Harlan County, Kentucky, to take notice.
>
> "I am the grandson of Blevins Asher and Nancy (Huffman) Asher; grandson of Martha (Asher) Goodwin, Son of Issac and

Ida (Goodwin) Asher; great grandson of Dill Asher who with his brother Bob Asher, settled in Kentucky with Daniel Boone, after the Revolutionary War. Granny Asher taught me the prayer of the Asher Clan. It was,

"'Lord if ever become a coward and fear any man, beast or devil; take me from this earth so I will not disgrace the name of my family.'

"There are more than 200 Ashers, descendants of Dill and Bob Asher in the Kentucky mountains. In the Asher veins flows as pure a blood as ever honored any nation. I am one of those Ashers.

"And now I say to those Ashers in the Cumberland and Blue Ridge mountains that, I might be killed in a sneaking and cowardly manner by this Jew or one of his ilk and if I am so killed; my spirit along with those of our departed kin, will listen from my grave for the word . . . that the sneaking cowardly murderer who took my life has been brought to book for his foul deed. . . ."

In 1946 Asher recalled, smiling a bit: "They got to calling up too often. It was scaring my wife." Threatened often as an editor he never has been assaulted. Though rather small, he is a strongly knit man with powerful arms and shoulders; friends consider him an excellent street fighter, physically without fear, hardened by the life he has led.

The top headline in the issue dated a day before Pearl Harbor was: *PEOPLE NOT WITH YOU, MR. ROOSEVELT.* The next —and first wartime—issue carried a confused lead story, and Asher wrote editorially: "The X-Ray feels called upon to make its position clear. . . . We would have considered it none of our (this country's) business had Japan attacked . . . any foreign possession, but when these imps of hell, sneakingly, cowardly, treacherously and with premeditation drop bombs and murder our soldiers, attack the soil of the United States Government— well, then THAT is the business of EVERY American. . . ." Nevertheless Federal authorities scrutinized the *X-Ray*. Asher began to print small U.S. flags on page one, but in May his second-class mailing privilege was suspended. It was restored after a hearing in Washington. (He thought it "peculiar" that editorials reprinted from the *Tribune* and Hearst should interest postal authorities, and he published letters, of which he is extremely proud, from the Congressional and university libraries asking for, or acknowledging receipt of, files of his paper.) However, he was recalled to Washington for questioning by Prosecutor William Power Maloney. He was indicted along with 27 others, including Mrs. Dilling, Pelley, and Viereck, for conspiracy to commit sedition. His paper was out soon: *NEW DEAL POWERS GIG THE X-RAY EDITOR.* (Asher in 1946 laughed and said: "That was a dandy. That word gig—I kinda like it. I usta gig fish when I was a kid.") The story began: "The New Deal in a Gestapo manner has struck!" It defended his right to criticize, and jibed: "Answer that one Maloney—Baloney." (Another time he defiantly told Federal authorities to "slap it on your sore heel.") None the less, Asher became cautious for a time, flaying Doc Bunch more vigorously than Roosevelt. His circulation took a nose dive. Nervous subscribers told him FBI agents had questioned them. Asher regarded this as a deliberate, unfair attempt to put him out of business. Aroused, he returned to the assault on Winchell ("the Jew Stink Bomb of the Air"), "a local Sheeny," Pearson, Roosevelt, CIO leaders, and assorted "Jew Communists." The hysterical sedition trial ended abruptly when the judge died. There was a second indictment and then a third, in which Asher was not included. The last was dismissed in the fall of 1946. By then Asher was inclined to speak lightly of the indictment, and his attacks on the old bogeymen displayed the old vigor. Also, he enlarged his list to include OPA, "Pee Wee Truman and his Jew Deal," "Un-Rah," and the United Nations. However, in 1946 he was devoting considerable space to attacking the state Republican administration (some of his ammunition appeared to have been smuggled out of the penitentiary to him by D. C. Stephenson). After he was indicted, Asher was not on the Republican payroll; this might have had something to do with his feud with the administration (remember, his old enemies were Democrats). In 1946 in the *X-Ray* Asher announced a Klan revival in Indiana aimed not at Negroes and Catholics but at the "machinations of Communistic JEWS." Asher reported: *"The Klan Rides Again"* as early as 1939. Privately Asher admits he has no high regard for the Klan as such and does not believe it could be revived effectively in Indiana. In 1944 when a Muncie mob went after a Negro suspected of rape, Asher, though he flagged the story, printed nothing to inflame race prejudice.

Asher writes all the headlines and much of the copy for the *X-Ray*. "I've written that paper on the linotype, without usin' a typewriter first." His office is the high-ceilinged parlor of his modest two-story frame house in a workingman's section of Muncie. He works in an old-fashioned upholstered chair with a typewriter on a low stool in front of him, surrounded by a litter of correspondence from admiring subscribers—"here's one old woman sent me a dollar; she writes me ever' week"—and great heaps of magazines, mats, newspapers, and printed matter from the propaganda mills. "I use a lot of stuff from the *Tribune*," he has said. "Especially stuff from foreign countries. I never had no other way of gettin' the information." Sometimes he seems to regard himself as a sort of interpreter between the common man and the press lords. At work he is likely to take off his shirt and shoes. His arms are tattooed. Reading, he wears horn-rimmed glasses low on his nose, peering through them as though with some difficulty. His eyes are quick and wary, his face leathery and lined, his wiry brown hair is graying, brushed sideways. He has a prominent gold tooth. An extremely nervous man, he chain-smokes strong cigarettes, can take nothing for breakfast but strong black coffee or a shot of whisky or both, drives a car jerkily, talks and moves rapidly. He drinks heavily and at length on occasion, but he works hard, sometimes all night on deadline. Beside his chair is a radio; he likes to listen to Winchell and Pearson. On the wall hangs a cheap banner: "Remember Pearl Harbor," and a picture of Asher in the uniform of a buck sergeant in the 1917–18 war. In a bookcase in front of his chair is his editor's library—a set of Ridpath, its binding cracked, which he bought at auction ("Ridpath—that's my main grab when I wanta find out somethin'"); scores of Haldeman-Julius Little Blue Books ("I get a lotta information outta them; Holy Jesus they's a lot of information in them if you can just pick out the right one"); a set of the Little Leather Library ("here's a lotta Browning's jewels; then I got Flaubert, DeMaupassant, Oscar Wilde, Hugo, Schopenhauer, I got 'em all"); a number of odd volumes, including books by Marie Corelli, Vash Young's *A Fortune to Share*, *Elmer Gantry*, the Bible, a dictionary, *10,000*

Jokes Toasts and Stories. Occasionally he gives his *X-Ray* articles tone by quoting a famous secular writer, but more frequently he quotes the Bible, usually to prove something about Jews. His prize possession is his file of the *X-Ray.* Some day he will give it to a library, but only "if I'm sure it's some place where they won't get 'em out." That evil mysterious "they," the plotters who have been after him all his life, crops out constantly in his conversation.

Asher is extremely busy. Sitting in his editorial chair in 1946, he said: "I been away two weeks, haven't even listened to the radio, I got to get over to Indianapolis and check on what's going on. But my God I got a paper to write tonight." His paper is printed in a job shop at Centerville; he goes there Thursday night to help make up and set type. Friday it is distributed and Asher disappears for the week end. Critics say he goes away to collect a cash payoff, or hide. Actually he goes down to the Jurdon hills. Asher insists he has avoided publishing scandal, unlike so many editors of small blackmailing weeklies. "When you start hammerin' that personal stuff you're punishing a man's wife and children; you got no right to do that."

If Asher had been shown to have been on the Nazi payroll, those who know him best would have been flabbergasted. One has said: "I think Court is completely loyal. It's just that somebody took advantage of his ignorance." The same inner drives which sent him to jail as a bootlegger sent him twenty years later to the Federal dock accused of sedition. He was a poor boy. He had to live by his wits. Something in his nature would not let him be content with plodding along as a machinist. A pure opportunist, he tried for the big money in any field of endeavor that presented itself—bootlegging, the Klan, politics—and in all he naturally made enemies. His newspaper gave him a weapon. And more—a justification. In it he found use for the two mainsprings of his character: opportunism and an underdog's vindictiveness. In the thirties the views of the Republicans and isolationists fitted his. Isolationism is a type of patriotism. Your high-octane patriot loves his country so intensely that he cannot see beyond it; just so Asher loves the Jurdon hills. The Republicans hated the Democrats; so did Asher, for they had put his saloon out of business. And so on—he slid into line. But

214

some of his fellow crusaders may have had further motives which he did not fully understand. Once they had lit the fuse they scarcely needed to do more, Reds and Jews became his personal enemies. The viciousness of his attacks was boundless, for he is by nature a street fighter, not a duelist with a rigid code of honor. Asher probably never knew a Communist, and he has said: "Some of my best friends have been Jews"—and he named them. Once he had adopted these ideas he could not shake them off. He is quick to analyze a complex situation, arrive at an answer frequently wrong, and stick to it stubbornly. He is a victim of the *idée fixe*. At his family reunion in 1946 he blamed the small crowd, which disturbed him greatly, on the committee's failure to provide chairs, and before the afternoon was over he was talking of almost nothing else, with nearly pathological repetition. Just so easily have larger ideas been implanted in his mind.

Muncie newspapermen who are ashamed of Asher consider his influence negligible. Some Muncie people think of him only as an eccentric. However, state CIO leaders credit him with encouraging suspicion and race hatred among Muncie workmen. His influence goes far beyond Muncie. The *X-Ray's* circulation in 1946 was at an all-time high—9,000, Asher says, with a national subscription concentrated in California, Chicago, New York City, and Detroit. Poison spreads fast. Many people to whom Asher's extremist expression is repugnant sympathize with some of his views. That he influences his loyal subscribers cannot be doubted. In the Indiana hills, where his paper is widely read and admired, a gaunt old man said: "You know that big print under your picture Court, I never let that go by, O, that really knocks the sox offa 'em." He meant the editorials.

Frequently Asher publishes long hymns to the rustic or to the old days. (One must remember James Whitcomb Riley's hold on Hoosiers.) Asher has written: "The farmer and the farmer's wife . . . had a good grip on things . . . the plot of ground beyond the farm up on the hill, where they would lie down in quiet graves and rest among relatives and friends, neighbors all, until the blowing of the trumpet. . . . Ah, me, in these Satanic days when the Jew Deal edicts and commands are that we must relinquish all that is sacred. . . ."

215

Every summer he suspends publication for two weeks to vacation in the Jurdon hills. He has his eye on a piece of land there. At the reunion, standing on the hilltop by the schoolhouse, he said: "God damn this is a pretty valley. Here's where I wanta come back here and live." He likes publishing and politics—he is never happier than when he has stirred up a ruckus, and his eyes flash with delight when he says: "I'll have a *Con*gressional investigation goin' yet on this god damn liquor thing"—but withal publishing has become burdensome. "Hell, I been fightin' all my life. I'm tired of it." He would like to sell out for fifteen thousand dollars and live in the hills and write for magazines or start a business in Martinsville. His wife wants him to.

Many elements of the Hoosier character are exhibited in Court Asher. Yet some of them seem heightened, distorted, while other Hoosier attributes are wholly lacking. Asher cannot be termed a representative man of Indiana. For every editor like Asher there are in Indiana a hundred editors of a different sort, editors of country weeklies published in small towns, editors who write more about family reunions than about Communism. One of these is Edmund C. Gorrell, of Winamac. Asher grew up in the poverty-ridden hill country; in his youth he wandered rootless through the new factory cities; he became a publisher almost by accident, to vent an underdog's wrath. Gorrell, on the other hand, grew up in a print shop, surrounded by better soil, savoring the Indiana heritage not only of rusticity, but of gentleness. His town, Winamac on the bank of the Tippecanoe River in northwestern Indiana, was in 1946 one of the few Indiana farm towns almost untouched by fifty years of change. Not in Asher, but in Gorrell, and in Gorrell's town, one could still recognize the Indiana idea.

Chapter 16

NED GORRELL, COUNTRY EDITOR

By noon on a hot August Sunday in 1946, automobiles were thick in the park beside the Tippecanoe River. Boys, bicycles cast aside, were idly dangling fishing lines into the brown water from the high, swaying footbridge that led to Winamac just across the river. The crowd was gathering, some at green picnic benches, most around the dance pavilion, a concrete slab enclosed by white, latticed walls. Lettered on the doorframe was a sign warning: "No Spiking"; but that would be no problem today, for this was the band reunion. Ladies were sorting the big market baskets of food the people had brought, and men were arranging tables and chairs.

Old men were clasping hands and holding on while they peered into each other's faces, exclaiming: "Now I got you! I couldn't for a minute, but I did"; kidding each other: "Were you ever a member of the band? Then get outa the park!" (how many had thought they'd never see *that* face again?). Edmund C. Gorrell—everybody in Winamac calls him Ned—cleared a space for himself and said grace. Then lines formed and began to move leisurely past the long tables laden with meat loaf, baked chicken, fried chicken, potato salad, yellow tomatoes, red tomatoes, pickles, cole slaw, chocolate cake, angel-food cake, cookies of all kinds. And men, knives and forks and spoons sticking out of their breast pockets, were carrying heaped plates to the long, green tables where their wives sat chattering.

Ned Gorrell was the editor and publisher of the weekly newspaper of Winamac, the *Pulaski County Democrat*. His father, like Booth Tarkington's Gentleman from Indiana, had dropped off the 5:18 train and taken over the paper. That had been fifty-five years earlier, in 1891, and Ned Gorrell had never worked anywhere else. In 1946 he was sixty-seven years old, a leading citizen of Winamac and leading country publisher of Indiana, a "small-towner by birth and preference" in his own words, a solidly made gray-faced man with thin, tight lips and friendly eyes, a man of terrible temper and strong principles and uncompromising virtue and yet of considerable tolerance, a moral force, a firm believer in the future of his town and the essential goodness of human beings, a contented man. Inevitably, he once had played in the band, but he would have been here anyway for he is involved in Winamac; when he dies, he will be missed more than most men are missed. He would have known people at almost any table in the pavilion; he happened to find a chair with these: a farmer and his wife and awkward son, a big, heaving, white-haired woman in a shapeless dress, a thin, tailored woman from Hawaii who was a former resident and her father who was still a member of the town council of Winamac. The white-haired woman was saying she'd like to go to Hawaii sometime "but they'll have to bring it over here—too much water between it and me." The farmer's wife said: "I'd like to go to England before I die, fly maybe," but her husband had a friend who had an airplane, "he was flyin' around the country and hit some wires." Their son said: "Wait'll I get my pilot's license, Mom, I'll take you," and she said: "All right son, we'll fly to England and leave Dad to take care of the farm." Dad said: "If anything happens you're done." Gorrell said it was the same on a ship. The farmer said: "Never been on a ship either." They wrangled on amiably. Every now and then someone would say: "It's nice to live in a small town." The white-haired woman made her living nowadays keeping boarders. One traveler had told her of his lake-front estate near Chicago. "He was trying to cook me good. I guess he just thought I was pretty low. Said he was selling the big place, cost too much to keep up, had to pay his servants ten dollars a day apiece. I just let on like that was just ordinary. Me! I have help once a week and it pret near breaks me up. But I never let on. He said his first wife was an opera singer with the Metropolitan Opera Company." "Well," said the farmer's wife, "I wouldn't like that cause I don't like opera." "I do," the white-haired woman said. "Oh I like some of it. But not when they get to screechin'. I druther hear men sing than women. I don't like hillbilly music either." The white-haired woman said: "They have the best opry from Nashville, Tennessee. I had a Socony-Vacuum man the other night and I told him I'd have to admit I liked to stay up till ten-thirty to hear that even if it kilt me. And he said so do I. So we stayed up," and she looked around the table almost defiantly. "He'd been down there. He said the one I like so well, the bass singer, use to be with the Metropolitan. So you see *we* know good music too," and she laughed—deep, mannish laughter. The talk shifted aimlessly. This was what they had come for—to eat, to be together, to hear the comforting sound of each other's voices. Now and then one would nudge another and nod toward somebody passing and whisper hoarsely: "Who's *that?*" and this would begin a long conversation: "That is *too* the other Dilts boy's wife, cause *they're* the ones has the baby." "Well they look alike, her build and all, kinda chucky." Gorrell told about a boy who hit a Pacific beach and found two copies of the *Pulaski County Democrat* in the sand.

Outside the pavilion a boy and girl about fourteen were playing catch, and she was kidding him, and he was blushing. Their parents had spread a picnic lunch near the uproarious, circling, ringed trapeze pole. Gorrell was putting his silverware and coffee cup back into his basket. Others were shoving the tables over against the latticed walls and arranging folding chairs. Men with band instruments were arriving, one trying to balance a tuba while shaking hands with an old friend. Gorrell was moving in the crowd, talking to a member of the State Board of Accounts who used to lead the band and now had come back to direct the reunion concert; to a stringy man in white shirt and bow tie ("You didn't play in the band, you lived in the country and didn't get in to town much cause you didn't have a pair of shoes"); to a woman who said: "Wasn't that a swell sermon this morning?" (Gorrell mumbled something and grimaced as she moved on—he'd missed church. "When the minister takes a

vacation I figure I can too," but it made him feel guilty); to a
leading citizen whose father built Keller's Hall. Keller was talking about the days when they used to peel off and go swimming
in the river—"that was before the bathing suit was invented"—
about the town—"we never have a boom, we just go along the
same old meter"—about this park—which he and Gorrell and
other leading citizens had given to Winamac—"it's a blessing to
the community to have a place to play." And Keller talked about
farming: "This is a good feeding section, feed a lotta hogs and
cattle, we think that makes the best type o' farmin', we believe
in that." He was a bulky man in a white shirt, a banker. "They
brought Kentuckians into the muck fields and they've regretted
it. Troublesome. They need 'em for the onions, potatoes, mint,
get down on their hands and knees and weed 'em. There was a
few Mexicans but they all left. Only four, five Negro families in
the county. All pretty good class of niggers. Good people, glad
to have 'em." He glanced at the young people walking past.
"They're all good American kids. We like that better. There's
few foreign-born around here." His grandfather who settled
here was a German-American.

A few women in the crowd wore tweedy skirts and fuzzy yellow sweaters, and their tanned men wore gabardine. But most
of the women wore shapeless dresses, and the men, shiny stiff
suits. The band leader was announcing: "All musicians please
take your places." Years ago the town band had been composed
mainly of merchants; by now it had become a high-school band,
but today the old-timers had returned. Seated in a semicircle
facing the perspiring conductor, they kept tootling and telling
each other: "I haven't had a horn to my lips in ten years," and
somebody in the crowd yelled: "All right you've practiced long
enough, now play us a tune." They did *Stars and Stripes Forever*,
and at its end somebody yelled: "Yippee," and someone else
called: "Boy have you got a bass drummer!" Children were
climbing on the lattice-work walls and in the overhanging trees.
The kids screamed at the marches, but what made the old folks
smile was a medley, spiced with cornet and trombone solos, that
included: *Love's Old Sweet Song, When You and I Were Young,
Maggie, Little Brown Jug, Believe Me, If All Those Endearing
Young Charms, Pop Goes The Weasel, My Bonnie Lies Over*

The Ocean, Home, Sweet Home, and, as a grand finale, *Auld Lang Syne.* When the little man beating hell out of the bass drum missed a beat, he grinned at the conductor and pretended to be dodging a blow. Gorrell, sitting in a corner with perspiration beaded on his bald head, holding his Panama hat on his lap, his short legs spread, said: "Teach a boy to blow a horn and he'll never blow a safe."

Across the river Main Street ran up the hill to Front Street, probably the town's original street and renamed Riverside Drive about 1941 by clubwomen who considered Front Street "too common a name" and perhaps suggestive of vice. On Saturday afternoon Gorrell left the *Democrat* office on Main Street whenever he could and mingled with the crowd. He liked the sight of people, the sight of the buildings he had seen nearly every day for fifty-five years. He never could talk enough about them. "The town moved west from Front Street after the railroad came through," and he gestured toward the tracks a half block from his office. "Johnny O'Connell built a saloon in the sixties or seventies, three blocks from the main business district, and people said he was crazy, it was too far away, and now it's right in the heart of town. Or it would be—it's torn down, there's an A & P store there now." He was walking toward the courthouse, where farmers were sitting on the curbing. At the corner he came to the Keller Block: "Dr. Henry Thompson used to own this site. He was another one that had faith in the town. This was just a brush pile then and old Doc Thompson—he used to put a patient on the dining-room table to take his leg off—he said he wouldn't sell out till someone would buy and build." A little later J. D. Vurpillat built the even grander Vurpillat Block across Market Street, with a slate mansard and a tin roof. The corner office in the Keller Block is, inevitably, occupied by a dealer in abstracts, insurance, and real estate. Winamac's third imposing structure is at this same intersection, facing the courthouse: the Frain Hotel, also with a mansard.

Gorrell turned onto Market Street, its sidewalks thronged, past the open orange doors and the neon bear of the Bear Cat hardware store where a phonograph was blaring out jazz, past the only downtown saloon with a hard-liquor license, on down to

221

the newsstand. Here the *Democrat* was on sale—it has an almost unbelievable street sale of 235 copies to people who want it Thursday night, not Friday, for its ads, who don't want to lay out two dollars for a subscription, or who are embarrassed to go to the *Democrat* office because their subscription isn't paid up —and men were playing cards and drinking beer. Gorrell doesn't drink—"I never did and I don't see any reason to start now"—but he visits in here anyway. The place was smoky and dirty and filled with a low roar of voices, men standing packed together, men in working clothes, many of them farmers, and you had to push your way to the small homemade bar. A young farmer in overalls was saying: "That bull's a pretty dang good bull. I ain't never seen a bull fill out like that one. I told the fella, when his ink run out like that you know, I didn't think he was so good, but a fella tells me he's an Angus-Holstein, a cross-breed, and they're all like that. He really puts a hump in their back." His friend nodded and drank his beer: "Ain't one outa a dozen these days is any good." Panama hats and overalls and khaki pants and suspenders and blue shirts buttoned but unadorned by ties, narrow-brimmed felt hats above lean, brown faces and scraggly necks; round tables with pinochle players, unshaded lamp bulbs hanging from the ceiling by large-linked chains intertwined with the electric cords—Gorrell turned his back to the bar and laughed and said: "I like to play sixty-six or rum here, spend a dime a tab for a coke or a cigar. I suppose church people'd say I shouldn't, but the women play cards for a dollar prize, one woman told me: 'I just have to win because I give the girl a half dollar to stay home with the kids.' Let's go take a walk."

He walked to the Rexall drugstore in the Frain Building. It smelled of chemicals, the wall behind the cigar counter was lined with shelves holding large glass-stoppered jars, and above these were black glass panels lettered in gold leaf: "Humphreys' Homeopathic Specifics." Gorrell sat at the soda fountain and ate a dish of ice cream. The clerk was saying a man still could get a few squirrels and rabbits on the plains hereabouts, but the quail were about all gone and the fishing wasn't what it used to be. Gorrell said: "I hate to take life, don't even like to fish.

222

I'd be a vegetarian if I had to slaughter my own meat." An implement dealer came in, and they discussed the city's plans to trim the overarching maples and to reverse the goosenecks on the street lamps beside the courthouse—"light up the sidewalks, automobiles don't need lights anyway, just the buggies did." Gorrell crossed the street and went back to the *Democrat* office.

His daughter Janet, a small, freckle-faced young woman of about twenty-six who appeared younger, looked up from sorting subscribers' cards and said a couple of men had been in to see him—they'd drop back. On the counter were a stack of *Democrats* and of farmers' almanacs. Gorrell's own office was a cubbyhole under the stairs, partitioned off with composition board. He put his hat on a filing case and sat down at his desk, which was piled with correspondence, proofs, mats, exchange newspapers, throwaways. He had some writing to do, a piece on small-town doctors which an editor friend down at Indianapolis had requested. Gorrell typed vigorously, using two fingers and clenching his teeth so that his undershot jaw stuck out. He had made his desk himself because he couldn't buy one that satisfied him. He quit writing to make notes for "a little talk" on Monday at the twenty-sixth anniversary meeting of Kiwanis at Peru. In 1921, due mainly to Gorrell, Winamac became the smallest town in the United States to have a Kiwanis club. "It was a challenge," Gorrell recalled. He was proud of his twenty-five years of perfect attendance. "I haven't missed a week. Not always at Winamac, of course. Hell, I been to Keewanis meetings from Detroit to New Orleans to St. Petersburg, Florida." Gorrell, a Kiwanian, Mason (he wore a Masonic pin in his lapel), alternate delegate to the 1940 Democratic national convention, several times delegate to the state convention, state-prison trustee and onetime member of the State Clemency Commission, in 1945 president of the Hoosier State Press Association, tourist—Gorrell had acquired a reputation as an after-dinner speaker, he had "been in every county in Indiana except Franklin and Perry, both down on the River," and he could "call someone by name in sixty-seven counties—newspaper, politics, Kiwanis, somebody." He was insatiably interested in what people were doing: "I estimate that about every seventh time the office

223

phone rings, somebody at the other end is asking me to attend a gathering of some kind. The social contacts thus offered are nearly always enjoyable."

One might divide his activities into going out to meet the town and receiving the town at his office. To his office comes a steady stream of people: a lady publicity chairman with a pencil-written "little piece for the paper," a merchant buying advertising space, an irate farmer who wants Gorrell to "say something in the paper" about city hunters that break down fences and shoot cows (he is glad to do so), a merchant with plans to remodel his store, a householder indignant about speeders, a widow with rooms to rent, a man who wants to sell a litter of pups, county politicians, town officials, subscribers with complaints or compliments, the lean, stringy town auctioneer who wants to show Gorrell the new sale barn with tin roof glittering above high-topped corn—one can but suggest their variety. Many business callers stay to talk, and this he likes best, though he keeps saying how busy he is (and, chuckling, wonders why he is when he employs more help than most country publishers). Usually the talk is about politics, crops, or just about the town. He likes to recall the early railroad days, when the Monon was known as "the road that ran through five college towns and had a penitentiary at each end." He has read a good deal of both state and local history, and people ask him to settle arguments.

Gorrell is fond of quoting an old-timer who said: "The Almighty must o' made Pulaski County along on Saturday afternoon, when He was gettin' kinda tired." Even the best soil in the county is rather thin and the rest of the land, early ridden by ague and malaria, is composed of yellow sand ridges, sloughs, and swamps. Though settled late, however, Pulaski was one of the first counties to have a county agricultural agent. "It's been a godsend." About 1915 I. J. Matthews, the new county agent, came into Gorrell's office and said he needed help in selling farmers on Purdue University's recommendation that they treat their soil with lime and raise alfalfa. Gorrell printed articles that Matthews wrote, published front-page lists of farmers who cooperated, publicized "alfalfa tours" of leading citizens who went junketing in model-T Fords, and when a county commissioner scoffed at liming soil, showed him how limestone dust blown from a road had improved a corn crop. Alfalfa brought milk cows, and Gorrell is proud of his part in developing the local dairy industry. "Diversified farming is our salvation here," he has said. Only in recent years has Purdue taught farmers to raise peppermint, onions, and potatoes in the black mucklands, once considered worthless. "Peppermint's terrible stuff to raise—gotta pull off the runners like strawberries and bury them in trenches to make a new field, got to do it on your knees." Gorrell has visited Fowler, Attica, Lafayette, and Kentland to study methods of breeding and growing hybrid seed corn. He has interested himself in checking erosion. "The pioneers came in and saw the level land and cut the trees off and pretty soon the fertility got thin. The land's so flat they had to dig drainage ditches, and that takes off the topsoil." Every term of court hears drainage litigation, and the Monon Ditch was in controversy for many years. The question of drainage goes to the heart of Indiana society, Gorrell thinks. "If I own a high place and you own a low place, to what extent am I obligated to take care of the rain that falls on my land and runs off and floods yours? The Illinois theory is, it's just too bad. The Indiana theory is that every man is obligated to take care of the water that falls on his land, and if it runs onto lower land he must pay his share to get it on out."

Gorrell has said: "All we got is the farms around here. No coal comes out of here, we got no manufacturing. Hell, my automobile grew out of the ground around here, these printin' presses grew out of the ground around here." He said nobody in town was rich. "Everybody made it a dime here, dime there. We don't go runnin' to some big property owner to see whether he approves of this or that." The history of towns fascinates Gorrell. "One beauty about Winamac is it's just been a slow steady growth—we just live off each other." Rensselaer, founded about the same time, grew to twice Winamac's size; Belfast and Strawberry Ridge, founded a little later, have vanished altogether. From time to time a commercial club has been organized at Winamac—Gorrell has headed three—and each whooped mightily that industry must be brought to town, but none was, yet the town has survived. La Porte lured factories that employed some sixteen thousand people, and what happened? The Allis-Chalmers strike knocked it flat in the spring of 1946. Gorrell

thinks Winamac never will die, nor will it change greatly. This
is all right with him. He told about strolling through Indianapolis with a friend who said he'd recently turned down a good
job in Greensburg because Greensburg was too small. Gorrell,
reminding him that on their stroll he'd met only one man he
knew, said: "What's the difference between being in Greensburg
and meeting ten people and knowing them all and being in Indianapolis and meeting a thousand and knowing ten?" Telling
this story, Gorrell chuckled and said: "A fellow says, a hick
town is a place where the folks call up the doctor to ask whether
the new baby at the Joneses is a boy or a girl, but to me, a hick
town is anything smaller than the town you live in." He admits
that Winamac has its share of small-town backbiting and snob-
bery—clubwomen who refer to other clubs as ones to which
"anybody can belong"—but he considers this human frailty
found anywhere.

In 1941, celebrating his family's fifty-year ownership of the
Democrat, Gorrell claimed proudly that the *Democrat* was Winamac's oldest business institution. In 1937 the *Democrat* obtained permanent possession of a trophy awarded by the Hoosier
State Press Association to what it considered the best weekly
newspaper in Indiana. Gorrell's shop is clean, well lighted, and
fitted with new equipment, an outstanding country weekly shop.
He is proud of it. He tries to keep more birth than death stories
on page one, uses a cleaner make-up, better copy, more local
news, and more local pictures than most country weeklies. He
maintains an unusually good newspaper library, including a record of local births, deaths, and marriages, an extensive biographical file, local histories, voters' lists, census and school records, a file of cuts, bound volumes of the *Democrat,* and not least
important (he points out) a Bible.

His father, Joseph Gorrell, bought the *Democrat* with money
earned editing other country weeklies. He was a rather salty
man. (He may have inherited this quality from his own Irish
father, also an editor, who, taking charge of one Indiana paper,
announced: "Politically, we shall be independent; on all other
matters we shall endeavor to tell the truth.") When a light lady
named Em horsewhipped a citizen, Joseph Gorrell wrote a story
calling her a "voluptuous female with a reputation like a glue

factory," and she threatened to horsewhip him too. In describing a stabbing he wrote: ". . . had the stroke been more parallel with the ribs . . . the chances are that there would have been a funeral with Leasure in the front wagon." In 1891 when he brought his family to Winamac, there still was ill feeling because hogs had been ordered off the streets. The *Democrat* was four years old, a precarious venture. He began filling page one with local news instead of boilerplate or ads, although sometimes half the locals were stirring accounts of how subscribers had paid up their dollar subscriptions. Ned Gorrell set his first type when he was seven years old, standing on a packing box to reach the type case. He learned to "mind his p's and q's" when he dropped letters on the floor and discovered p's, q's, d's, and b's were almost indistinguishable, and he learned how to spell whisky from a tramp printer: "We drink it with ease but spell it without."

Joseph Gorrell was an ardent, even violent, Democrat. When Bryan's train on the Panhandle paused briefly at Winamac, the silver-tongued orator, hoarse and wearing a skull cap in the cold breeze, addressed a crowd estimated by Gorrell as ten or twelve thousand, including seventeen Winamac schoolboys, sixteen wearing silver sashes and carrying the American flag and one wearing a sash of gold and carrying the British flag. Bryan carried Pulaski County by 619, and Gorrell wrote: "Think of it! A majority of 619 'anarchists' in Pulaski County! Here's to our fellow 'anarchists.' If it is anarchy to believe that the glorious United States can run her own sausage grinder, without allowing any gol-durned 'furrin' nation on earth to do the 'stuffin',' then you and we have the disease in the thirty-third degree, with slight chance for recovery." (Faced with this from so long ago, who can say Court Asher is wholly a sport, an atypical Hoosier?) People debated the morality of dancing; Joseph Gorrell defended it. He may have reprinted, not written, this doggerel that captured the flavor of the times:

> "The summer girl's the girl for me, arrayed in swiss and dimity, with sailor hat and airy clothes, and freckles on her sun-burnt nose. The bloomer girl I rather like, as speeding past upon her bike with trousers fastened at the knee, a beauteous, well formed l—gacy. The hammock girl is also sweet, with dainty tan shoes

227

on her feet, although perhaps beneath her tans there be corns big as pecans. The picnic girl my love can win, with jelly on her dimpled chin; she charms with her coquettish tricks, then steals away to search for ticks. When she de-ticks her lovely form she comes back looking red and warm; in disarray her clothes are hung, her handsome hair has come unbung. But lovelier far unto my eyes is she when, startled with surprise, with tears she begs me to ransack, and find the bug that's down her back. Yes, there are girls I can't abide—they in their mother hubbards hide; for whether they be lean or fat one cannot tell where they are at."

When rumors reached Joseph Gorrell that a man had opened a whorehouse in town—he called it "a house of decided 'ill-shape' to put it by no stronger term"—he suggested the man should be "drummed out of town astraddle a rail, with a few touches of tar and feathers to keep the cold out." A group of wealthy citizens obtained an injunction restraining the city from surfacing Main Street with crushed stone; Joseph Gorrell printed a drawing of a mired dray and captioned it: "Rapid Transportation on Injunction Street," shaming the litigants into withdrawing opposition. When a gravel road was proposed, a farmer declared that "the whole thing is just a scheme of the blacksmiths to make more horse-shoein'." Joseph Gorrell, noting Winamac's muddy streets, filth around the hitching posts, unsanitary outhouses, and the lack of fire protection, tirelessly advocated improvements, although quietly; and his son has done likewise.

After finishing high school, Ned Gorrell chose to enter the newspaper shop rather than a college. When he was twenty-one, he became his father's partner; six years later he became editor. In 1925 Joseph Gorrell died, and his son wrote editorially: "Yes, we will get by, just as millions of other men have done. Yet ahead there stalks the spectre of that quiet desk once so surrounded by bustling activity; of that vacant chair once so responsive with appreciative smiles; of that 'wait-till-I-ask-Dad-about-it' satisfaction never to be realized again."

In 1941 Ned Gorrell, ruminating on his half century's work on the *Democrat*, wrote a book. Still unpublished five years later, it was a folksy compendium of reminiscences, prejudices, and observations; it exhibited his mind and faith. He wrote a good deal about newspaper publishing, especially its mechanics. He jibed at "fashionable" protests over high taxes, for taxes, he said, financed progress. He reveled in progress, he attributed it to "American genius." He recalled the time that George Ade, as was his annual custom, brought a party of Chicagoans to Winamac for a fishing trip on the Tippecanoe and found that all the arrangements as to boats and bait had been made. Indeed, they had been made too well, for, due to a telegrapher's error, a Chicago bait company had shipped not the "two hundred grass frogs" Ade had ordered but two hundred gross of frogs, or at least all it had on hand, and they were all over the Winamac railway station in boxes, crates, cans, kegs, and at large. Gorrell recalled the summer afternoon when his daughter, two and a half years old, gave him a fresh pansy and a dog-eared card, an eight of hearts. He stuck the flower in his lapel and put the card on top of his desk, and a few hours later she died. He moved the card to the upper left drawer: "Sometime in the future other hands than mine will clean out the drawer and throw the card into the waste-basket." Gorrell wrote that he had grown up with but one boy who "was the envy of all the other lads in school because he went to his dad's office each evening and got a nickel just by asking for it. That boy grew up without learning to work, and doesn't amount to a tinker's dam yet today." He complained about children who "sass" their parents, "unsportsmanlike booing" at basketball games, women with bare knees, "road hogs," drinking at football games. "Yes, I'm old-fashioned. . . . If we have to go back to the old McGuffey idea to reinstate [courtesy] let's start." He wrote about the town of Santa Claus, Indiana: "Ah, folks, we *need* Christmas . . . need it to pry us once a year out of the twin ruts of Selfishness and Narrowness, for a brief spin on the pavement of Thoughtfulness and Generosity." He spaced his chapters with paragraphs apparently modeled after Kin Hubbard's Abe Martin sayings:

> Interviewed on his one-hundredth birthday, Grandpappy Stout was asked if he could think of many things that are the same today as they were when he was a boy. Yes, he could—high taxes and low prices of farm products.

Chemists can name many by-products of gasoline. So can doctors and undertakers.

"All I know about chaos," explains Dad in reply to Sonny's question, "is that it is either something the country faces or something that somebody is going to bring something out of."

Gorrell wrote of a woman who lived near Clifty Falls in Indiana and went to Switzerland, where she met a Frenchwoman who always had wanted to visit Clifty Falls. He disliked radio commercials, big city newspaper syndicate salesmen who "can dope out what the country weeklies need most," small city newspapers that neglect local coverage, Prohibition (unworkable though praiseworthy), the "nauseating display" of Hollywood marital troubles, drunken driving, public-opinion polls, sensational big-city journalism, and writers who portray farm life "at its worst."

He wrote: "I defy you to go into any public gathering in these parts today and separate, by either appearance or demeanor, the country folks from the town folks. If there are any real smart-alecs in the crowd you'll likely discover that they are nitwits from some city who have come out expecting to hear the natives say 'gol durn' and 'by cracky.'" Quoting a city writer's lament that boyhood had been stripped of charm, Gorrell offered to show him a "sand-hill den of a group of modern Huck Finns" and two eight-year-olds who started down the Tippecanoe on a raft stocked with crackers, cookies, and a Bible in search of Treasure Island, which they hoped to find near Lafayette. Once the president of the New York City Kiwanis Club told Gorrell: "You fellows can do far more for Winamac than we can do for New York. . . . When we try to do something, it creates about as much stir as pouring a tub of water into the ocean." Gorrell wrote:

". . . the nearest approach to contentment is to be found in these modest centers . . . a place where we have our friends, the Almighty's greatest gift to humanity. . . . Sham and pretense . . . must of necessity be thin and easily pierced. . . .

"We have but few bustling factories, belching out smoke at the chimneys and Bolshevists at the back doors; no tall office buildings, housing big business and pale cog-in-the-wheel clerks; seldom a spreading university, turning out trained engineers, trained accountants, trained Etta Bita Pi enthusiasts.

"Instead, we live in an atmosphere dominated by home loving, wife and husband loving, children loving, business loving; a place where a neighbor's a neighbor whether he works or plays golf; where a man's a man, whether he be a banker or a blacksmith.

"Where we walk a few blocks along pleasant streets to our work in the morning. Only five minutes or so between the breakfast table and the work shop.

"The small town is a place where we walk home for a noonday meal with the family; where we breathe air uncontaminated by that modern stuff called 'smog'; where we drink water pumped from spring-fed wells and unsullied by chemicals; where we eat pure food, fresh from the farms and gardens; where most people own their own homes and the verdant lawns that surround them; where we have efficient local government because the officials feel responsible to the personal acquaintances who elected them; where we walk back home at the close of a day's toil to an evening of—what, comfort? Ah, there's the fly and the essence in the oil of contentment.

"Shall it be a movie? . . . There was shown in my home town the other evening a talking picture that opened the following week for its first run in one of Chicago's leading Loop theatres.

"Shall it be a basketball game? . . . A visitor from a large city . . . beamed as the crowd leaped to its feet and roared when the home team scored . . . and he shouted in the ear of his companion: 'Great Scott, Jim what community spirit!'

"Shall it be a game of bridge for the evening? Like as not, unless friend wife has her dates mixed on which club meets tonight, or unless she has to attend a Sunday School teachers' meeting, or a session of the committee to make out a program for her reading club; or unless friend husband has to meet with a committee from his luncheon club, or his church board, or has promised to take part in degree work at lodge, or must lend a hand at a political caucus; or unless the oldest daughter can't stay at home with the younger children because she has to practice for a school play, or go to a young people's conference, or play the piano for the boys' glee club. . . .

"If it be summer, shall we enjoy a drive . . . cross the bridge at the edge of town and take the winding road along the river? Can we time the trip so the moon will be slipping up over the eastern hills about the time we reach our favorite 'big tree'? Can we stop at the bend in the creek and let the children play on the sandy bank? Can we linger in some moonlit spot and listen to the night birds, and whiff the odor from new-mown fields, then circle back home past the gladiolus gardens?

"Riches in all these things? No. Fame or power? No. Contentment? Yes. It's reflected best, perhaps in the plaint of a homesick youngster in one of the poems of our beloved Hoosier, James Whitcomb Riley, who wanted to go

> . . . *back to Griggsby's Station,*
> *Back where the latch string's a-hangin' from the door,*
> *And ever' neighbor round the place is dear as a relation—*
> *Back where we ust to be so happy and so pore!"*

So Gorrell ended his book.

In 1887, some Winamac men, like eager Hoosiers in so many towns, drilled a well, seeking gas. They had visions of an industrial boom. But they struck only artesian water. Later they learned that the gas field extended no farther north than Logansport. Regretfully they accepted this. Winamac remained a farm town. But the artesian well became the town's water supply, the fountainhead. People sent barefoot children to it at daybreak, bearing jugs to fill with its pure, cold, undefiled water. And the well became a kind of town social center, a fountainhead even, of a different sort, and it remains that. Townsfolk brag about it to strangers, as they brag about the changeless quality of Winamac. But an outsider, a tramp printer, hearing of the drilling and tasting the sulphurous water, said: "Artesian well, hell. They hit a sewer."

Ned Gorrell lives not far from the well, in a frame house with a garden in the backyard. Late on a Sunday afternoon in 1946, his older daughter Bess and her husband and child came up to visit from Indianapolis; several years earlier Bess had married a city doctor. In the living-room, with its dark woodwork and its flowered draperies, Gorrell sat quietly in a dark corner, fingertips together, looking old. Mrs. Gorrell came in from the kitchen, removing her apron, a small, intelligent, friendly, freckled woman with a wry wit. Janet, the younger daughter, announced dinner was ready—chicken, roast pork, mashed potatoes, green beans, onions, tomatoes, olives, lettuce heaped on a large platter, cake and coffee, all passed from hand to hand. Gorrell, from the head of the table, encouraged his son-in-law to talk. He was recently out of the Army. He told some stories about his practice, including one about a man whom he referred to as "an unpleasant Armenian," glancing sideways at his daughter, who was four. They all talked about the *Democrat;* Janet, who is its news editor, said she guessed "some day it'll be Gorrell and daughter." At Bess's insistence, Gorrell told a favorite story about a town character called Jake, who used to come into the *Democrat* office and talk endlessly. One day Jake said: "You know I'm crazy," and Joseph Gorrell, busy, said absently: "Oh, I guess not," and Jake said indignantly: "I am too. Damn their ornery hides, they proved it on me." They had too—had persuaded the courts to put him in an asylum. A few days later an attorney had been surprised to meet Jake on the street at Logansport. They had a few beers together. Finally Jake said: "Well, I guess I better be gettin' back out to the asylum." The lawyer said he'd been wanting to ask about that. Jake said: "Sure. The sheriff brought me down here this morning, and we stopped for a drink, and well, I can drink a little more than the sheriff can. So we had some more drinks, and when we left he couldn't drive, so I drove him out to the asylum and I told them: 'Here's your man' and gave 'em the papers and the sheriff, and come on back to town to have a few more beers." The attorney got a hack and took Jake out to the asylum; they found the sheriff, sobered up, arguing desperately.

About 11 o'clock after some evening callers left, Gorrell said he was sleepy. He was going to spend the night in their cabin a few miles out of town on the Tippecanoe River. Mrs. Gorrell wanted to go, but she was afraid she'd have to get up and get breakfast and come in to town when her husband did—she liked to sleep mornings now that the children were grown. Driving out to the cabin, Gorrell was saying: "Aren't the black top roads a wonderful thing?" so proudly you'd have thought he invented them. The road lay along the river, dipping through hollows and riding flat plains where a mist lay in the moonlight in the fields. Gorrell was saying he and his wife had to go up to Chicago soon to get her binoculars fixed. They went to Chicago oftener than to Indianapolis. He turned off the highway into a narrow, rutted lane through thick second-growth maples, and soon the headlights shone white on the walls of the cabin.

This really was Mrs. Gorrell's cabin, he explained, unlocking the door and turning on the electric lights. She'd wanted one all her life, he had had his eye on this piece of land and he bought it without telling her. When the title was cleared, he took her downtown and, still teasing her, picked up the deed and drove her out to the land, high on the river bank. Years earlier she had drawn plans for a dream cabin, but she long since had put them in the attic; now she got them out. The war interrupted construction but—and he winked—"our friends helped us out, and we got her finished." He did a lot of the work himself, built the cupboards and the beds and paneled the interior in knotty pine. "I had more fun with it before it got finished."

The night was full of scratchings, night noises in the woods. In the cool morning when he arose, there was a mist on the river. You could hardly see the sycamores on the bend, and when a square-ended boat full of fishermen floated out of the mist, some cranes flapped lazily up from the water. "Cranes," Gorrell said. Under the trees beside the cabin were some benches and rocking chairs, glistening with dew. Gorrell stood on the high river bank a long while, looking down. He said: "I just like to sit on the bank and rock and spit." Then he got into his car and drove to town.

Though one might contend that Ned Gorrell is the Gentleman from Indiana at his best, one cannot maintain that he is "the typical Hoosier" of today. He is, rather, the outsider's idea of a Hoosier, an idea that is sadly out of date; Gorrell stands (a trifle desperately, one sometimes suspects) for something that is passing fast in Indiana. And indeed it would be hard to find in any one man all that is Indiana today. Ralph F. Gates, however, exhibits both the old and the new. Perhaps the Hoosiers elected him their Governor because so many of them could see themselves in him.

Chapter 17

RALPH F. GATES: GRASS-ROOTS GOVERNOR

R ALPH F. GATES, a Republican who was elected Governor of Indiana in 1944, is a medium-sized, vigorous man of fifty-four who gives the impression of being a little younger and a good deal larger than he really is. On such important occasions as the annual Beefsteak Dinner at the Columbia Club, his chunky body looks constricted in a dinner jacket; standing behind a speakers' table, peering down through the lower part of his glasses to read a speech, he seems to have no neck, only a fold of fat below his chin which spills down onto the white front of his shirt. At such times, though he looks not unlike a sea lion, he is a figure that inspires confident satisfaction in any banker or manufacturer. At work in the Governor's office in his shirt sleeves, however, he is all plain, intelligent Hoosier, a friendly sympathetic man to whom anybody can take his troubles. While drinking with some politicians in a hotel room, he is downright jolly, handsome in a rough, unadorned way, with iron-gray hair that keeps falling down over his forehead, a lumpy, rugged face, a quick, easy laugh, a boyish way of glancing up at you from under shaggy eyebrows, a deep, rasping voice that trails off at the ends of sentences, and clothes that nearly always look rumpled.

From the ornate blue and gold ceiling of his office in the Statehouse hangs a heavy crystal chandelier. Rose draperies

235

adorn the windows, and the floor is carpeted in deep blue. On a cabinet near the Governor's desk are a picture of Senator Raymond Willis, a "labor-management charter," some symbolic plaster elephants, and a framed certificate attesting that Gates has been an American Legion member for twenty-five years. The Governor's large desk stands before a window overlooking the statue of Oliver P. Morton. Gates keeps the desk tidy. While talking to a caller he likes to lean back in his swivel chair and clasp his hands behind his head and gaze out of the window, eastward. So doing, he gives an impression of great strength solidly rooted. However, the first impression that anyone forms on meeting him is one of tremendous energy. He thinks fast and moves fast. Anxious to see anybody who wants to see him, he makes many more appointments than he can possibly keep, which annoys his political strategists, who are kept waiting in the anteroom. He is likely to open a conversation with any caller by saying rapidly: "I'm covered up today, completely covered up." He is always popping in and out of his office, walking rapidly across the anteroom, glancing at the long bench where callers wait, jabbing a finger at one and booming: "Just one more minute now." On one summer day before the 1946 elections a tall, thin nervous man with long, black hair and a scholarly but determined manner came into the anteroom carrying a bulky petition for a place on the ballot for the Socialist Labor Party (a petition made necessary by an American-Legion-sponsored law that makes it difficult for protest parties to get on the ballot). Some of the bored callers watched this man with amusement, but the Governor's executive secretary, Ruel Steele, an urbane, tight-jawed, well-groomed young man in a white shirt, accepted the petition gravely and crisply explained the law to the petitioner; Gates trotted across the anteroom, blinking at the petitioner, then hurrying back to his private office, and the contrast between the two men was inescapable. A few moments later Gates was saying impatiently to a telephone caller: "I know, I'm sorry, I was in Chicago. It's that extra five per cent —what's the attitude on it? What's been done in the other states roundabout us? Do you know? You get that dope and let me know." He hung up, making notes for a telegram; the phone rang. His wife had taken their daughter Patricia, a coed at Indiana University, to the doctor. Gates said something about "those little pains she thought she had," and laughed.

Before he became Governor he was a small-town lawyer and banker, almost unknown to the people at large. Nearly every politician in the state knew him, however. He has been for many years a member of the Rotary Club, Chamber of Commerce, American Legion, Masons, Elks, Moose, and Presbyterian Church in his home town, as well as of the Columbia Club of Indianapolis. He travels ceaselessly about the state, inspecting state property, talking with administrators, and making speeches that deal about equally with the perils of Communism and the glories of Indiana's park system. He overlooks no opportunity to present himself to the public. All this activity strengthens his political connections (he is said to be one of the few men who has actively campaigned for Vice President of the United States). Such activity, however, is not burdensome to him; he enjoys it. This is one way of saying he is a natural politician. He ordinarily finds it difficult to pass up an invitation anywhere; he likes people a great deal, and most people, on first meeting, like him.

Ralph Gates was born February 24, 1893, at Columbia City, the seat of rural Whitley County, in northeast Indiana. About 4,500 people live in Columbia City. Nearly that many lived there in 1900. A few years ago an advertising brochure said that 706 families lived in their own homes while but 432 rented, that only six houses were valued at more than ten thousand dollars, that all industries "have been conducted on the open-shop basis," and that "there are no parochial schools in this trading territory."

On a hot Wednesday afternoon in July 1946 the coolest place in town was O'Daniel's Walgreen Agency drugstore on the Courthouse Square. Merchandise cluttered the floor and counters in the center aisle. In the window of Flox's Dep't Store a hand-lettered placard urged: "Be Sure to visit Tri Kappa Rummage Sale and Refreshment Stand First Door East of Citizens Bank." Several cars bearing out-of-state license plates cruised slowly past; to the top of one was lashed a rowboat. A shock of cane fishing poles, two stories high, stood in front of Schrader's furniture store, their slender tips waving slightly. Across the street was a sporting-goods store with a large replica of a fish casting a shadow on the sidewalk, and in this shadow stood two men, talking. "We caught them bass on a little hook like that farthest one there, only 'twas smaller, just wiggled along in the water. In the boat, you use a boat, and you have your motor on the back of your boat. It costs $1.50 an hour, they was four of us used to go and that way it'd cost us about seventy-five cents apiece for half a day." Nearby was a narrow, two-story flat-roof red brick building; its glass show window resembled a store's but the sign on it read: "The Farmers Loan and Trust Co"; this was the Gates's bank. Upstairs on a white-framed bay window was lettered "Gates & Gates" and "Attorneys." Watermelons, marked "98¢," were heaped in front of a grocery. This was Van Buren Street, the main street; the business district was four blocks long. Along the curb, six to a block, stood ornamental lamp posts painted aluminum and topped by clusters of five round white globes. The stone-slabbed sidewalks were worn smooth and concave. In the Secrist Cafe, which, with its soda fountain used as a bar, resembled an ice-cream parlor, a fat girl in slacks was saying to two young factory workmen in tight T-shirts: "Jes' Chris' I woke up this morning at twenty minutes after six." In another varnished booth sat an old farm woman in a wide-brimmed flowered hat, a flowered dress, rimless glasses, her elbow on the tabletop, her finger crooked on her chin just below her lower lip. With her sat two old men in suspenders, eating with their hats square and firm on their heads. The farm woman's voice was querulous, sing-songy, sad: "Coulda been worse. Well, you'd oughta be thankful, anyways." Picking their teeth, she and the two men went out and walked a half block to the courthouse square.

Here cars were parked solidly, people in them waiting for the concert to begin. Big brass horns glinted dully on the bandstand on the lawn, and from the bandstand roof fluttered the flags of America and of a rural high school. Through the leaves of the maples and the weeping birches the turrets of the courthouse aspired to the evening sky. Along one curb stood a few neglected hitching posts. Young girls were parading around the lawn, arm in arm in groups of four or five; older couples stood about near the courthouse steps waiting patiently; boys raced whooping among them all. The lights along the eaves of the bandstand winked on. A state-police car cruised slowly past. Across the street some traveling salesmen were sitting behind the windows in the lobby of the Hotel Clugston, watching the scene without expression. The concert began with *The Star-Spangled Banner;* no one got out of parked cars. Out in the street a local policeman was saying: "Last few years a band concert don't seem draw a crowd like it did." He waved to a man he knew in a double-parked car. "I let 'em park that way. I found out it's not always so much what you say as how you say it." He talked about Old Settlers' Day: "It's to make money for the Legion. Lotsa folks come back. If you're around this way glad to have you, drop around."

In the darkness, the band had finished playing, slowly, *A Pretty Girl Is Like A Melody,* and now came a cornet solo, quavery and uncertain. In the Clugston lobby a man was studying the intricacies of a pinball machine beneath a picture of Theodore Roosevelt. The four faces of the courthouse clock were lighted. Outside of town a string of roadhouses was crowded with tourists. In the window of one were two signs; one sign advertised Old Settlers', and the other read: *"We Cater to WHITE TRADE only."*

This, then, was the town where Ralph Gates grew up. His family originally came from Manchester, England. A few years ago Gates photographed the old homestead at Manchester, Pennsylvania, and hung the picture on the wall of his law office in Columbia City. Before he became Governor he liked to take his family on long automobile trips, visiting the Lookout Mountain battlefield, where his grandfather fought, national parks, monuments, and historic sites, and places in the family's past. These are mainly in Pennsylvania, Ohio, and Indiana. His father, Benton E. Gates, cleared land in Kosciusko County, built a cabin, and started farming and reading law at the county seat, Warsaw. He moved to Columbia City not long before Ralph was born. He practiced law at Columbia City, became agent for the Ohio Farmers Insurance Company, bought and traded farms, and in 1907 organized the bank at Columbia City and subsequently two other banks in outlying county towns. He was a rather quiet man with a wide forehead, slow-moving, deliberate of speech. Today his four sons, all energetic men who have worked hard and in close concert and yet have never seemed to get quite caught up, are unable to understand how their father managed his enterprises single-handed. He always made his sons work on the farms: "My Dad was the kind of a fella if you wanted something you had to work for it."

In 1909 Benton Gates bought the building on Van Buren Street which today houses both bank and law office. It was new then, built for a fine saloon, with cherry woodwork and high tin ceiling. Benton Gates was Republican county chairman, and the back room of his law office became county headquarters. He once was beaten for prosecutor by a single vote—a lesson Ralph never forgot—and the only public office he ever held was that of deputy prosecutor. Politics fascinated him but about 1914 he withdrew from it because it was interfering with his business. Columbia City's great hero at that time was Thomas R. Marshall, a lawyer and Democrat who was elected Governor in 1908 and Vice President in 1912. Ralph Gates was always hanging around headquarters, watching the euchre game. He and his brothers wrote insurance and ran legal errands for their father when they were still in high school. But Ralph enjoyed more checking the poll books at the courthouse. In 1946, asked about his early life, he replied: "My father was county chairman for ten years when I was a boy. Which gives you the background on that."

Ralph Gates was the second of four brothers; by age they ranked: John, Ralph, George Scott, and Benton Earl. Ralph and John ran a lemonade-and-popcorn-and-peanut stand at Old Settlers' Day, making a whole tub of lemonade out of three dozen lemons and sometimes clearing sixty dollars; when a city ordinance imposed a ten-dollar fee upon concessionaires who were not war veterans, it was Ralph who suggested taking in a new partner, a venerable Civil War veteran. Ralph Gates was a high-school debater at a time when debates drew crowds as big as track meets. His coach recalls him as serious, solid, equally good at looking up and presenting facts. He graduated from high school in 1911; at the University of Michigan he took undergraduate work in accounting and received his law degree in 1917. In August he entered the Naval Reserve as an ensign and went overseas in December. He was promoted twice, assigned to desk·jobs, and discharged in 1919. He went back to Columbia City, helped form the Ray P. Harrison Post No. 98 of the American Legion, married a schoolteacher from a nearby smaller town, Helene Edwards, whose father had amassed a competence, and became his own father's junior law partner. His father's former partner, David V. Whiteleather, had pleaded the cases that Benton Gates painstakingly briefed; now Ralph Gates took over the pleading.

However, as Ralph Gates has said, he "only had the privilege" of practicing with his father nine months. His father's illness and death in 1922 placed a heavy burden upon Ralph Gates. With the guidance of his older brother John who was running the bank, the insurance business, and the abstract business, Ralph took over most of the legal work. In the early 1920's, the Gates law firm was one of three leading ones but there were six other established firms, plus transients, to serve this town of 3,500. Gates was fortunate. Because his father had practiced here so long, he could count on a sizable business in probating wills. He appears to have been best known for settling cases, both civil and criminal. Once he narrowly escaped becoming involved with the Ku Klux Klan. Though he didn't know it, a client of his was a Klansman and a Klan membership fee was to be deducted from his legal fee. An older man warned him and he withdrew. Probably eighty per cent of Whitley County men once belonged to the Klan.

Most lawyers who practiced with Gates agree that he might have become a successful trial lawyer, but he went into politics instead. Politics always had interested him more than anything else. He soon was able to devote all his time to it because Scott was running the bank, leaving John more time for law. By the mid-twenties he had become known in his district through the Legion, the Rotary and similar clubs, his family connections, and his legal practice. He built a district organization among his friends. In 1926 he became Republican chairman of what was then the Twelfth District, now the Fourth. Among his father's political cronies had been Governor James P. Goodrich, Jim Watson, and Will Hays, Republican state chairman and later the movie censor. They helped Benton Gates's son. His father took him to his first Republican state convention in 1920, and

Ralph Gates has missed none since. In 1928 he was a delegate to the national convention and has missed none of those since.

Since the Civil War, Whitley County had been unpredictable politically. The whole district was difficult. It embraced eight counties, not only rural areas but also Fort Wayne, second largest city in the state, with a heavy factory vote. As district chairman, Gates helped arrange a compromise between the quarreling rural and urban politicians. The task of the district chairman is to quell rebellion, compromise quarrels, appease enemies, cement friendships, ceaselessly prod the precinct, ward, and county leaders to maintain enthusiasm, however dark the outlook (as in 1934, for the Republicans), and, above all, to deliver the vote. Gates gained a reputation as one of the most successful district chairmen in a state renowned for successful district chairmen. One man, asked to explain this, said: "He is a good mixer. He has an intuition for picking good men. He never broke his word. He likes the mere act of organizing, whether it's for himself or not. And do things move when he gets to going." Although political enemies say he is the ruthless boss of a tough machine, one man has said: "He very seldom just goes up and whams a fella in the nose and drives him away so they can't confer again. He usually argues and talks and talks." Another has said: "The rural man who can lead the rural areas into battle—and at the same time speak the language of the cities— has a very strong position." Just before Gates was nominated for Governor, the mayor of Fort Wayne made noises like a candidate. Gates told him he had a good job—heck, what more did he want? It is in hotel-room caucuses that Gates always has operated most successfully. Once after he became Governor local jealousies had stalemated plans to establish a state park, a pet project of Gates's. Attending one of the numerous almost hopeless meetings, Gates saw the difficulty at once, told everybody he wanted a committee of three appointed "to go out and get that land and get started," and after trotting back and forth among the antagonistic groups for an hour, he had selected three men whom the crowd approved. An aggressive man, he backs a decision hard once he has made it.

In 1928 Gates decided to pursue his political career through American Legion channels. Since 1920 the Legion probably has been the greatest single continuing political power in Indiana, except for the two parties themselves; its national headquarters are at Indianapolis; is has proved a springboard to high office for many men, including Paul V. McNutt, and on several occasions it has been said that a little coterie of Legionnaires ran Indiana (McNutt was abetted by one, and many people believe Gates is surrounded by another). Certainly it was through the Legion that Gates rose to the Governorship. In order to appear above politics, however, the Legion forbids a political chairman to hold high Legion office. Therefore in 1928 Gates relinquished the Republican district chairmanship; a year later he became Legion district chairman. Two years later he was elected state commander. He made the most of this opportunity, driving about fifty thousand miles to visit nearly every Legion post in the state.

He had to shelve all his plans, however, the next year. As he has put it: "All hell broke loose in the banking business." For a time he traveled the state, trying to help save banks for his friends. But he soon had to try to save the Gates banks. He did, and it was one of his greatest accomplishments. He knew most of the depositors from politics or the Legion; he persuaded nearly all not to withdraw their funds, a difficult feat. He has said: "I want to give credit where credit is due. I don't think very many banks would a pulled through at all had it not been for President Roosevelt's moratorium." He and his brothers raised twenty-eight thousand dollars personally, they got a hundred-thousand-dollar RFC loan, and during the week-long bank holiday, Gates was in Indianapolis three times and Chicago four times but he slept at home every night. He has said: "You look back on that period all in a daze." No depositor in a Gates bank lost a dime, no stockholder was assessed, and there was no run. All other banks in Columbia City either failed or went through reorganization. Scott and John dealt with the debentures, Ralph dealt with the depositors. They lost the $120,000 their father had bequeathed them. Even the oldest brother John, a quiet, plain man who married a farmer's daughter, has described the period as "just ten days of hell" during which "we didn't even take our pants off." He has said: "It has taken fifteen years to get even."

Like many Hoosiers, Ralph Gates still dwells on the experience of the early 1930's. The depression probably was no more severe in Indiana than elsewhere, but the state's promise had been so high that the drop seemed farther. In 1934 the largest factory in Columbia City threatened to close. Chamber-of-commerce members hastily raised fifteen thousand dollars and induced it to stay. Ralph Gates was not a leader in this move. He became interested in a subsequent campaign to bring a Cleveland machinery manufacturer, A. J. Weathered, Jr., to town, however; this became the town's largest industry, and Gates became its local attorney and a friend of Weathered. Mr. Weathered has been described as "interested in the labor supply" when he located at Columbia City. Since then the employees, many of whom live on farms, have resisted CIO overtures.

By 1934 Ralph Gates was able to resume his political career. Having reached the top in the state Legion, he once more became Fourth District Republican chairman. The Republican tide began to run in Indiana in 1938 and Gates became a power in state politics. His admirers today describe him as an insurgent, a vote-getting role in Indiana since territorial days. Gates's insurgency, however, appears to have been chiefly that of the outs against the ins. The party battles were complicated and bitter, and they were fought so quietly that one could scarcely see the knives flash. By the summer of 1941 the Republicans had elected nearly every official except Governor and had carried Indiana for Willkie; Gates was the new state chairman, and nearly everyone who had opposed him was in oblivion (and still is).

Working from the precincts up, he built one of the nation's strongest machines. His brother John probably has expressed Ralph's own view: "You can make all the damn speeches you want and if you haven't got that little precinct you haven't got anything." When the 1944 convention met, Gates was nominated for Governor without opposition. Organization did it. Months before the convention, local, county, and district organizations had begun, mysteriously, to announce they would back him for the nomination. One old friend has said: "Ralph Gates first got the idea to be Governor when he was in high school." His Columbia City friends had written letters to their friends, urging his candidacy a year or two before the campaign. His brother

Scott became a precinct chairman, blocked off the precinct house by house, got helpers to make a card file of all voters, alphabetically sorted the cards, took them to the courthouse, went through the registration book, then made sure every Republican was registered and that he voted. (He has since recalled laughing: "I got all but three of 'em out, by God I couldn't get them, hunted and hunted for 'em.") All over the state others were doing the same thing. Gates visited a great many of them. "He saw to it that the job got done, saw to it himself."

Campaigning in June, he spoke three or four times a week; by September he was speaking almost daily, and toward the end he seemed to speak almost without ceasing. He raised the issues of bureaucracy, Communism, veterans' aid, public welfare; he attacked "Browderism and Hillmanism" and the "foreign-born" precepts of "New Dealism"; he pledged an end to the spoils system and a broadened public health program (though he was against "socialized medicine"). A spokesman for the CIO Political Action Committee, Walter Frisbie, charged that Gates "lacks intelligence, integrity and responsibility." Gates was elected, polling about 849,000 votes to his opponent's 803,000. (Dewey led him, with about 876,000 to Roosevelt's 781,000.) At his inauguration January 8, 1945, Gates said: "We must then strive to keep America free from the evils of foreign-born power politics. . . ." He adopted Tom Marshall's pledge—that the right to govern belonged only to the man who "promises to do his utmost to respect the views and protect the rights of alien and citizens alike, and to give to all the people his best in the way of good government, unawed by influence and unbought by gain."

He was determined to make a good record, for he had his eye on higher office. The Governor of Indiana is a large employer; he has about twelve thousand jobs to fill (half, supposedly, on the merit system). Gates adjusted patronage to a mathematical formula. In some instances he fired three Democrats and replaced them with but two Republicans despite pressure. When he discovered that several ex-convicts had been approved for patronage jobs, he upbraided his underlings, who perhaps were less ambitious. He has been a hard-working Governor. "I try to work with all departments. So many things can go wrong." Few people have ever questioned his personal honesty. His legislature outlawed the Ku Klux Klan (as did those of other states). One admirer, a lean, fast-talking Chamber of Commerce man, asked whether Gates was a conservative or a progressive, has said: "O, I'd say very much Ralph's a progressive. Absolutely. I refer especially to state parks, extending public health. This stream pollution thing has to be watched." This man compared Gates favorably with Calvin Coolidge. Actually Gates cannot be said to have accomplished a great deal. He reorganized the Department of Conservation and the State Board of Health. He set up a Department of Veterans' Affairs that has a lot of money but has done almost nothing. (Like many state agencies its functions are largely handled by a Federal agency.) A newspaperman has said: "If there's something good to be done and it'll improve his record and stature and he can do it, he will; if he can't do it, he'll appoint a commission, then take credit for doing it." He always has been extremely conscious of the values and dangers of publicity. Most people thought his first two years as Governor satisfactory; one said: "Things just seem to go along." Oddly enough, when asked if he considered any event in his life a major turning point, Gates himself said: "No, things just seem to go along." About the best his political friends can say of him is that "he hasn't made any mistakes yet." This is high praise among politicians. A political manipulator can hope for little more in this life than a candidate who doesn't err.

The truth is, Gates probably has made several mistakes. He yielded to patronage pressure and allowed the liquor laws to be administered badly, if not corruptly. This aroused criticism by friendly newspapers, gave ammunition to Prohibition advocates who already were planning a strenuous 1947 campaign, and antagonized members of his own machine who didn't profit. He disappointed admirers when he yielded to close advisors and denied Senator Willis, an old friend, renomination. When the CIO struck Standard Oil at Whiting, Elmer Sherwood, a Legionnaire and Gates's adjutant, alerted the National Guard under circumstances that CIO leaders said amounted to mobilization (a politically dangerous move since the 1935 Terre Haute strike). Subsequently, Sherwood resigned. During the General Motors strikes of 1946 Gates refused to call out the Guard, though importuned to do so. The A.F. of L. has seemed friendly to Gates. CIO leaders, however, have complained that they could get in to see him only after having agreed beforehand, in writing, what they would discuss. In the summer of 1946 a number of persons who concern themselves about civil liberties, including Powers Hapgood and Professor Shannon, the Terre Haute teacher who bought the Debs home, petitioned Gates to put the Communist Party on the election ballot. This was done. Soon the Legion asked Gates to investigate Shannon and three other teachers in state schools to determine whether they were spreading subversive doctrines. This was done too.

Elmer Sherwood, a dapper man who is the Legion's American-ism director, remains one of Gates's close personal friends and advisors. Others are an oil executive, a Legionnaire, the Republi-can state chairman, a newspaper editorial writer, Gates's secre-tary, and a manufacturer from Hartford City. Clark Springer, the state chairman, and James Carr, the editorial writer, are prob-ably his closest political advisors. One of his closest personal friends is Forest McKee, a wealthy manufacturer who vacations with Gates in Florida and northern Indiana and who maintains a suite at the Columbia Club which Gates has used frequently. Some people believe that the real power behind Gates's adminis-tration is Robert W. Lyons, who since the Klan's demise is said to have sent a number of Jews and Negroes to college. Lyons, as we have seen, was elected to the Republican National Com-mittee in 1944 when Gates was nominated for Governor, but was quickly dropped. The vehemence with which party leaders since have denied that Lyons still is powerful in the party would seem to indicate that he is at least influential, but there is reason to be-lieve that he is not among Gates's close personal friends, though Gates knows him.

Though Gates has answered questions about his future with becoming modesty—"I just want to go back home and be a country lawyer"—he is supposed to covet the vice-presidential nomination of 1948. He has become a factor in national politics. Though he is yet little known publicly outside Indiana, he is strong in the hotel rooms and his Legion strings reach every-where. His ambitions inevitably have led people to compare him with Tom Marshall. When he was nominated for Governor, his friends at Columbia City said: "Well, when Tom Marshall was nominated and come home on the combination train on the old Vandalia the whole town turned out and yelled their heads off," and so they told Gates's wife to keep him home after Sunday dinner and they formed a parade on horseback and a local party hack donned a stovepipe hat and drove a horse-drawn cabriolet to Gates's house. They took them down to the court house square, and the Legion presented him with a mammoth bouquet, and he spoke to them from the bandstand. From boyhood Gates has admired Marshall. (He is proud, too, that Lloyd Douglas, the author of *The Robe,* came from Columbia City.) About the only things Marshall and Gates have in common, however, are that they both came from Columbia City, both became Governor, both belonged to the Presbyterian Church, and both enjoyed a joke. One man who knew both has said: "Marshall was a Hoosier philosopher. Gates is a Hoosier politician." Stiff-backed, calm, deliberate, of dignified bearing, Marshall was too proud to campaign for the vice-presidential nomination; Tom Taggart, the boss, got it for him. Gates runs. Marshall had a few select close friends and avoided large congregations of people whenever possible; Gates likes everybody, and in large numbers. Marshall thought deliberately and drawled; Gates thinks fast and sometimes tries to talk so fast he stammers. Marshall was a poor businessman, Gates a good one. Marshall was brilliant, irreverent, a splendid trial lawyer. Marshall was poor. During Wilson's illness, the expensive social obligations of the White House devolved upon Marshall; he had spent most of his money campaigning—once a friend saw his roll-top desk in his home-town law office covered with campaign contributions, and Marshall was sending them all back—and after his term was ended he had to go on the Chautauqua circuit. All this is not to say that Gates is a lesser man than Marshall. He is a different man. And indeed the times are different too. In the contrast between Gates the Hoosier hustler and Marshall the Hoosier philosopher, one can read the change that has come over Indiana in forty-odd years.

Like any tourist, Gates genuinely enjoys week ends at state parks. He reads American history, particularly books on Lincoln and the Civil War. He likes Scotch whisky and he is at his best at a party, especially one attended only by men. He does not play poker; cards get between him and people.

In Indianapolis, Gates lives at the Governor's Mansion at 4343 North Meridian Street; the mansion, which originally was fitted with gold-plated ash trays and plumbing fixtures, was built by Jack Trimble, a wealthy oil man and promoter of the 1920's who pioneered the idea of selling gasoline and oil to automobilists through small, scattered filling stations. Gates's son, Robert, after a Navy career similar to his father's, studied commerce and law at Indiana University, where he became head of more extra-curricular organizations than any other senior. Gates took a number of old friends from Columbia City, many of them Legionnaires, with him to Indianapolis—a hotel man, a retired merchant, a couple of lawyers, a school superintendent, a farmer-politician, a judge, a doctor. He still considers Columbia City his home and goes there at least once a month. His home is the same yellow frame house on shaded Jackson Street that he bought when he was married. It is a small house, a story and a half high, with a glassed-in porch and a small lawn planted with spirea and barberry and evergreen. His late father's house close by is a large, white frame house with an L-shaped porch; it looks like a retired farmer's house. Accompanied by a couple of local men, Gates likes to go calling on old friends. He always goes down to the bank and the law office. A color photograph of an airplane, as well as a picture of Gates's father, adorns the walls. Hordes of local politicians pursue him, bringing their problems. Several years ago he cleared everybody out of his office to talk to a young man whose father, a Legionnaire, had been killed in an auto accident; Gates still looks after him.

A man who knows Gates, reflecting on his success, said: "A lot of people wonder why men that go so far in politics come from small towns. Well, they know politics better. They know the precinct. They're down to the grass roots where it all emanates from. My relatives back East couldn't figure out how I could predict that Willkie'd carry Indiana by over 50,000. I told 'em: 'You teach your kids how to read outa primers. In Indiana we begin 'em on a poll book.' "

PART SEVEN

The Conditions That Prevail

Chapter 18

TROUBLED YEARS: THE 1930's
AND 1940's

Tᴏ HE 1930's and 1940's were troubled times in Indiana, as in the nation. We have noted the plight of Banker Gates in the terrible thirties and of Powers Hapgood, picketing in Debs's once-tolerant old home town. About 1933, pictures of Franklin D. Roosevelt and of Paul V. McNutt appeared in newly re-opened saloons alongside the Budweiser pictures of Custer's Last Stand. At the outset McNutt seemed a Messiah as, white teeth and white hair flashing, he stampeded the 1932 convention in Cadle Tabernacle. Previously, he had been a lawyer, Legion-naire, and dean of the Indiana University law school. (As an undergraduate at I.U. he had been active in campus politics with his fraternity brother and close friend, Wendell Willkie.) Elected Governor, McNutt gave Indiana the beginnings of a New Deal before President Roosevelt took office. In addition to social legislation, he shoved through the assembly a law re-organizing the administrative machinery; he did this in the name of efficiency, but it gave him more power than any Governor since Morton. Overriding opposition, he used his power to ac-complish reforms that the state needed and to further his own ambitions. He was another man of force, and the Hoosiers admired the way he got things done. Before long, however, he had sent the troops to Terre Haute; labor, which had thought it had helped elect a "liberal reformer," castigated him; and before long, too, his use of his power, his brazen application of the

253

spoils system, his overweening personal pride and ambition, and his ruthless treatment of those who opposed him had combined to make him seem not so much a Messiah as just another Legion commander with his eye on the White House.

Curiously, to the harried Hoosiers of the early 1930's, John Dillinger seemed a hero, and in their love for him one can read the underdog feeling in the Hoosier character. To most people elsewhere, as to the cop who turned him in on a tip from a whore, Dillinger seemed just another gangster; but to Hoosiers he seemed more like Robin Hood. They were all in trouble, and he was getting his the only way he knew. He was just a boy raised on a farm near Mooresville who fell in with an evil companion and a judge who lacked discernment. The judge sent him to the penitentiary for a long stretch and dealt lightly with the evil companion, and from there it was not far to machine guns and murder. During the months that he played hide and seek with the law, driving a fast car down the back roads with a skill Fred Duesenberg would have admired, walking into a bank and vaulting the six-foot cage and scooping up the cash and roaring away clean, the Hoosiers thought of him as their own. They whispered tales about him: how last night he came home to Mooresville, knocking on the back door of his aging father's farmhouse—not the back door because he was afraid, but the back door because you always go to the back door of a farmhouse—and went into the kitchen to talk awhile, his Thompson gun on the table by the stove, his quick-eyed girl friend silent in the corner. John Dillinger was about all that brightened the early thirties in Indiana, a curious brightener.

Those were the years of head-cracking labor disputes. Governor Cliff Townsend ended the Little Steel strike by persuading union and company to sign an agreement with the state if they wouldn't sign with each other, and people applauded the "Hoosier genius for compromise." But at Anderson vigilantes besieged the CIO hall, and throughout Indiana there was more warfare than reason. Sit-downs and other strikes, Guide Lamp, Little Steel, International Harvester at Richmond, Bendix Products Corporation at South Bend—Indiana's labor troubles were part of the nation's. Disagreement at Detroit could result in a fractured skull for a factory workman only a few months off an

Indiana farm. By and large, labor won here as elsewhere. Businessmen cried: "Outside agitator," but one must remember that an outsider must agitate among workmen already discontented and one should know that Walter Frisbie, state CIO secretary, considers Hoosier workmen easier to organize than most. (The CIO claims two hundred thousand members in Indiana.)

The war gave Indiana industry a powerful boost; Indianapolis factories abandoned since the automakers departed were reopened, new ones were erected. How was it with Indiana during and after the 1941–5 war?

On a Monday night in April 1944 a big, red-necked Indiana farm boy, now wearing khaki and paratrooper's boots, walked down Walnut Street in Muncie, home on furlough with his girl at his side. They were headed for the Rivoli Theater. On Walnut Street near Jackson, in the center of town, a lookout sat by a window up in a second-floor gambling joint. The game was craps and admittance was easy. Nearly all the saloons in Muncie sold tip books, books containing lottery tabs that cost five cents each. Some saloons netted as much as three hundred dollars a day on these books.

Over at the Greek's most of the stools at the counter were occupied by men and young girls drinking coffee. The boy behind the counter had an accent akin to the flat, slurred Indiana speech but less harsh. "Him?" said the newspaperman. "He's one of the hillbillies. Haven't you heard that there are only forty-five states left in the Union? Kentucky and Tennessee have gone to Indiana, and Indiana has gone to hell." He walked through the silent streets of the city. There was a damp chill in the air. Spring was late that year. He said: "A doctor told me the other day that people who used to pay their bills with township orders now are paying them with twenty-dollar bills. And they'll be on the township again." Postwar international affairs? "I never hear any talk about that. People here don't care about other countries. They're strong isolationists. A few people think we'll have to fight Russia some day. You hear a lot of anti-British talk. People think that every time Churchill and Roosevelt get together, Churchill steals something else from him." This was Court Asher's home town. And this was Willkie's home district but he had lost Delaware County in 1940 though he carried Indiana by a narrow margin. One man said: "Oh, nobody paid any attention to what Wendell said. Wendell always did do a lot of talking, but nobody listened to him much."

The county agent's office was cluttered with scientific agriculture leaflets from Purdue University and the U.S. Department of Agriculture. Delaware County's soil was rich, its crops diversified. Corn and hogs—that is the base. The farms looked prosperous with painted barns and mended fences. Like most people in Muncie, the county agent arrived at his office before 8 a.m. He said: "The farmers are much exercised over not being able to get any help." It was the old conflict of farm against city, dramatized in wartime by soaring industrial wages, broken irreplaceable farm machinery, the empty room where the hired hand slept before he went off to war. The farmers were making more money than they had made for many years. Land was worth anywhere from a hundred dollars per acre up, with one sale at $237. But the older farmers remembered the last wartime boom. They were paying off their mortgages and bracing themselves for the smashup.

Late in the afternoon the workmen on the day shift came into the Pig Stand on South Walnut Street, not far from the railroad tracks and catercorner across Walnut from CIO headquarters (which, boldly marked by electric signs, was only four doors south of the Ball department store). Not all the workers were putting their inflated earnings into the sock, some were bellying up three-deep to the Pig Stand bar. The juke box was banging away and the waitresses were on the run from one red-leather booth to another. A grizzled old-time labor man sat with a girl in a red dress; broad-shouldered, gentle of speech, humble but determined, he seemed out of place in the booth. He hunched his shoulders and said: "I can remember the streetcar strike here in 1900. There wasn't any union. They were just men getting twelve and a half cents an hour and they got fed up and struck. They got beat up and they lost the strike. That broke labor in Muncie until the CIO came in. I can remember when I worked for Ball for a five-dollar gold piece and four silver dollars a week. Fifty-four hours a week. But that was in the days when I could take my girl friend to the show at the Columbia—it's tore down now—for fifteen cents."

The windows were steamed over. He ordered a beer for himself and a whisky and coke for the girl in red. She listened to him with respect. He was gray-haired. He clasped his gnarled hands on the table. "I was up in the Calumet making a speech when Little Steel happened, and I was in the Guide Lamp trouble at Anderson, and I was at Richmond too. Richmond was the worst. 1941. You know, after a while we find out we've got to fight for everything we get. If we wanta tell the boss we don't like the way things are going, how can we, unless we fight for it? That's not communism," he said earnestly, "or socialism or anything else. I voted for Hoover and for Landon just like everybody else in Muncie before I finally got some sense in my head and voted for Roosevelt in 1940. It took me all those years, just because my dad was Republican. Well, I heard the fella say two chickens in every pot and two cars in every garage but I never seen it." His brown suit seemed too small for him; he moved uneasily while he spoke, and his voice had become intense. "Take it easy," the girl said kindly.

The old labor man said: "We watch everything they do, we ring doorbells, and by God, like a fellow at the meeting said, we may not win but we're going to scare hell out of a lot of people. What are the soldiers going to come home to? Listen. I was in the last war. I got home January 21, 1919, and I got my first job January 3, 1920. Almost a year. They wouldn't even talk to me. Some guy had got my job while I was in the Army."

The girl said she wanted another drink. He apologized for neglecting her and called the waitress. The juke box was quiet for a minute, and when he spoke again he spoke too loudly and was embarrassed. Then: "What about the average working man, the men up there at the bar—are they thinking about world affairs, about the political future?" He looked at them, at their backs as they stood three-deep. He laughed. He said: "Five years ago they could buy a hog's head and five pounds of beans and that's all. Now they can eat a dollar and a quarter steak. A man can make a hundred and fifteen dollars a week and so can his wife. What the hell do you expect them to think about? They think about spending it." He said: "But maybe if we ring enough doorbells we can pull them with us anyway."

Down at the railroad station a crowd was waitng for the train..

A man and a woman sat uncomfortable with their son in Army
uniform between them. Obviously they were seeing him off to
those wars outside Muncie. They were all dressed up. None of
the three talked much, and the others waiting for the train
avoided looking at them, as people avoid staring at a cripple.
Far away in the rainy night the train whistled, long and lonely.
At the station people picked up their suitcases and brown-
wrapped parcels and went out onto the platform. The train came
from Cleveland, from the East, a long ways off. It was headed for
Indianapolis and St. Louis, but it was a local and it would stop
at several other Indiana towns. Almost all the Muncie passengers
got into the coaches. Nobody but the soldier was going far.

On the streets of Evansville, the old river town, walk Kentuckians from the hills and also businessmen who fly to New York
every week or so. In the McCurdy Hotel lobby Hoosier politicians mingle with Texans in ten-gallon hats, and the talk at the
circular bar of the Coral Room is more likely to be of wildcat
wells in the Smith Mills pool than of crops. Evansville, called
the Pocket City (though not by loyal natives), is the capital of
a tri-state area comprising the neglected tag ends of Indiana,
Kentucky, and Illinois. More than once its isolation has made
Evansville an eddy on the stream of events. Thus, in 1941 Evansville seemed in danger of declining, for, like the railroads so
long ago, the defense boom had by-passed it, and all at once
priorities chopped off the production of auto parts and refriger-
ators to which it had so fondly clung. But its industries converted
to war work, and almost overnight the shipyard came and so
did Republic Aviation. The war boom hit Evansville harder than
anything since the flood of 1937. By January 1944 nearly forty-
five thousand new industrial employees had arrived. That is
nearly half the city's total 1940 population. The boom brought
with it everything you would expect—juvenile delinquency and
girls and soldiers, saloons crowded with warworkers, a housing
shortage that drove new residents to refuge in basements and
attics and trailers, tottering old men in Western Union uniforms,
a swarm of prostitutes and gamblers, and all the barroom anec-
dotes about the lady welder who sailed grandly into a dive

dressed in a dirty housecoat and a five-hundred-dollar fur chubby.

On a November evening in 1944 a newspaperman stood at Third and Main. "The center of the universe," he said and laughed and pointed at the Chamber of Commerce and the National City Bank. Evansville was run by the bank's president and by Louis Ruthenburg, president of Servel—the city's biggest prewar employer, in 1944 the last major holdout against the CIO—a big, tough-minded man with an oblong, poker face, wide, thin lips, and firm jaw. The newspaperman said: "The city of the closed mind and the open sewer. Evansville's built low, so its sewers stink. The people are cold down here. Evansville audiences sit on their hands. Clerks may wait on you in a store or they may not. And that's not just the war."

Down at Nagle's, a big restaurant catercorner across Eighth and Main from CIO headquarters, a CIO man sitting at a white-topped table asked: "Have you seen the booklet the Chamber of Commerce put out? They actually had nerve enough to put out two lists of wages—union and nonunion. Let's go over to the hall. I got a meeting."

Smoke swirled through the big hall. The issue before the union was whether to strike. A bargaining agent had been discharged. Should the union show its teeth? Nearly every seat was taken by a working man or woman. To get the chairman's attention they snapped their fingers and strained half out of their chairs like school kids. There was a good deal of horseplay. Under it was a tension. A few knew some parliamentary procedure. They snarled the others up. The chairman became confused. Voices grew angry. At the back of the room some children fiddled with the slot machines or chased each other or scrambled up to drink from the fountain. Their elders turned to frown at them. The speaking droned on but sometimes it erupted.

"I don't want to strike in wartime. I got two boys in France. But . . ."

"Brother chairman, brothers and sisters," cried the Negro hoarsely, "if you strike they have a legal right to ignore you. They are trying to smash your union. If you strike you will hep them, brothers and sisters."

259

"I have never put the finger on nobody for agitating a strike, I mean a work stoppage."

"What will the International do to us if we strike? Answer me that."

"We are all scared about what's going to happen after the war. We know they are going to try to beat those wages down. If we don't take a stand now, we never can."

"I know there are brothers here with a snootful. I don't believe in strikes in wartime."

"I appeal the decision of the chair. I appeal . . ."

"Sit down—Sit down—Come outside, you yellow-bellied son of a bitch. I'll appeal your ass."

"Brothers and sisters, they are trying to smash your union."

The argument swirled on, late into the night, and the horseplay died and the bitterness mounted, and the sleepy children lay down on long tables and slept.

When Japan surrendered, Indiana went on a binge. At four o'clock in the morning Hoosier men and women, some full-clothed, some half-naked, were still diving into the pool beside the monument in Indianapolis. How much of a war hangover did Indiana have? Indiana's problems, its pressures, were the nation's. People were drifting, bewildered. At the Indianapolis Chamber of Commerce, William H. Book, a small, alert man, said the city's business had come through the war splendidly— and yet, he said soberly: "People are pretty blue. I believe there are people who would like to see an end of the profit system. The strikes are just an effervescence of the underlying causes." The head of the Indiana Farm Bureau said: "We are thoroughly provoked at both management and labor." But these were men at the top level; one bleak, March day at Anderson a haggard, unshaven CIO member who had stayed away from his job at Delco-Remy more than a hundred days, said: "When the telegram come from Detroit last night I had ten cents. I was so damn glad it was over I stood a guy on his head for a fifth of Imperial and I don't remember where I went or how I got home."

In Elwood, Willkie's home town, the move to raise a memorial fund was languishing, and the editor of the newspaper said:

"Most of the people that don't like Willkie think he ought to have done something to help Elwood when we lost the tinplate factory."

Up at Kokomo the Para-dice Cafe was crowded, and so was the furniture store that advertised: "Sells Cheap Sells a Heap." The Army and Navy had closed up Terre Haute's District in 1942 and it had stayed shut, longer than ever before. Respectable people who bought some of the old-time houses were obliged to put signs on them: "Private Residence." The open-cut mines, when not struck, were operating as never before, and the operators, conservation-conscious, were planting trees on the banks of the deep cuts to make wooded lakes out of wasteland. An Indianapolis cab driver was talking about the U.S. policy of sending food to postwar Europe: "I wonder how we're gettin' along fatten' 'em up so they can kill our boys." He was complaining about high prices, saying: "It's the Jews done it." Race questions had been so touchy during the war that newspapers suppressed news of a Negro-white clash at a public park. A housewife said of Eleanor Roosevelt: "I wish she'd get her a nigger husband, she likes 'em so well," and she told with delight a tale of how a large downtown department store closed its tearoom when some Negroes entered, just as a Terre Haute policeman recalled good naturedly a drummer who used to carry in his pocket the preserved big toe of a Negro lynched near the Paul Dresser bridge. A wealthy old man, remembering the good old days of the 1920's, wearing an uncrushed black felt hat and high button shoes—a man who had quit farming in disgust during the war because he couldn't get help, couldn't get gasoline, couldn't get a "decent price"—now said that land had gone too high, labor had gone crazy, everybody was drinking and whoring, and war with Russia was inevitable.

In a political headquarters, the walls covered with black-framed autographed photos of hacks and statesmen, some newspapermen and genial politicians were telling tales—about a ward heeler who, caught with some illegal ballots, chewed and swallowed them; about the time a man asked Senator Jim Watson to get him appointed postmaster at Marion: Watson asked how old he was, and he said sixty-five, and Watson explained he couldn't do it, you couldn't be over sixty-two, or whatever it was, and a few weeks later the man repeated his request and Jim asked: "How old are you?" and, without blinking, the man said: "Sixty-one"; he'd changed his birth record at the courthouse, and Watson got him appointed.

Old ghosts of 1919 and the twenties kept bobbing up. Irvington, an Indianapolis residential section of stiff-backed independence, voted dry. The Anti-Saloon League criticized sale of beer at the State Fair. During a gambling cleanup at New Albany, the mayor shot himself dead and a party hack slashed the executive secretary of the Chamber of Commerce in the face. In the fancy Hotel Lincoln bar at Indianapolis a flashily dressed man in a soft, fawn-colored felt hat was making plans for an underworld fix. The veterans' bonus was a big issue. Albert J. Beveridge's son was campaigning (unsuccessfully, it turned out) for Congress. The Legion parade and G.A.R. encampment were great events, and Governor Gates was on hand for both, hat over heart. Divorce rates rose. Colleges were glutted. Now and then a vigilante group raided a saloon or a gambling joint. In a dingy courtroom at Noblesville old folks sympathized with D. C. Stephenson.

On a Saturday late in the spring of 1946 a college dean, driving through the rainy downtown streets of Muncie clogged with angry traffic, said: "They tell me the streets are so narrow because originally this was a great forest of walnut trees, the hardest trees there are, and so the pioneers only cut narrow paths." He laughed, his eyes twinkling. "It's done something to our thinking, too." After the rain had ceased, farm people and city people not long from the farm sat in cars parked at the curb on Walnut Street and watched the crowds go by. And of what were the people, now at peace, talking? A young fellow in GI khaki pants and a civilian sport coat, with a ruptured duck in his lapel, put one foot on the running board of a parked car and said to his friends: "Christ, I been trying all over to buy a pair of overhauls." Overhead a cloth banner flapped and billowed gently: "Be Sure You Have Enough To Eat *Grow Your Own.*" Leaning against Woolworth's, a fat man in a black hat, his blue coat and vest and black raincoat unbuttoned to reveal a stripe-shirted paunch, was telling his companions: "We need some government. We got no government, we thought we had democracy but we ain't got no government at all, let a man like John L. Lewis run the country." A man in a bar looked up from his paper and said: "Truman reminds me of a story, the fella says: 'I had an uncle played piano in a whorehouse two years before he found out what was goin' on upstairs.'" Out at the Muncie Gear the hiss and clatter was as great as during the war, but shiny outboard motors and solid stokers for civilian homes were coming out of the shipping room instead of "kickless cannon" for the infantry; and only a few women remained standing at the pounding, clashing machines; most had gone back to their kitchens, their husbands had returned from the wars. There were seven thousand people at the basketball tournament. (Hoosiers say: "First you put two peach baskets on posts; then you build your high school around them.")

The CIO clubroom was crowded, and in a booth the union leaders had to talk loudly over the whirr and clash of the bank of eight slot machines. Two years earlier Ed Crago had been just a Muncie man in shirt sleeves who worked at Chevrolet, earnest and burdened with union responsibilities. By 1946 he had become an elder labor statesman. He had spent more time at the dizzy heights in Detroit and Washington than at Muncie. Once he had spoken of the future of the Muncie CIO as a local problem; now he spoke in terms of national politics. He blamed price increases on a strike of capital led by the N.A.M.

In the lobby of the Hotel Roberts you could hear an orchestra playing *I'm A Big Girl Now,* and leaning on the mezzanine railing were sorority girls in formals from Ball State Teachers College. Presently, with the escorts they had invited to their dance, they came down the wide stairs and in their long, white dresses and long, black gloves they looked as fresh and young and lovely as ever did college girls in May. But only a few of the escorts resembled the skinny, awkward small town boys, ill at ease in tuxes, whom you used to see at Indiana college dances. Instead they were older men, and serious-faced, and some had been wounded—how strange it was to see a burly man with a ruptured duck in his lapel and the fragile blue cord of a dance program dangling from his pocket.

Five miles out of town at the Country Club, the first-floor

barroom, with its bare walls and few tables, was filled with loud voices and the whirr and clash of slot machines. Most of the members had arrived about 9 p.m., after cocktail parties at home. A manufacturer was saying: "If we can ever get these damnable strikes over with we can have prosperity in this country undreamed of," but he had come to the bar for change; he quickly went back to get in line and await his turn at the fifty-cent slot. These people were not worried tonight; the war was over; it was no longer necessary to feel guilty about having fun. Upstairs, members were sitting around tables still cluttered with the dishes from dinner; sometimes they danced, though rarely with their own wives. Occasionally some gray-haired woman would sit in somebody's lap, and there was a good deal of laughter, a few off-color jokes, and some talk about fishing trips and the scarcity of nylons.

Many people had thought the war veterans might change things. "Just wait till the boys come home." To see how a town, with a dead hand ever so well-intentioned, firmly presses its own old mold down on the new, the shining, come to the basement room of the courthouse where Muncie's veteran organizations are making plans for Memorial Day. When two men from the V.F.W. arrived, they were the only veterans of the recent war in the room; one, the V.F.W. commander, Oris Fording, had had a wife and three children when he went to the Southwest Pacific. A G.A.R. meeting place, the room was small, stuffy, with smoke-begrimed walls hung with old charters and old gold-framed pictures of heroes in choker collars. The chairman was a white-haired man with nose glasses, representing the Sons of Union Veterans. While he called the roll, one of the V.F.W. men climbed onto a table and opened a window; the chairman remarked the chill night air would soon be too much. Committee nominations proceeded. A stooped, old Spanish War veteran, hard of hearing and with a drooping white mustache, saluted wearily and got to his feet: "Brother Chairman, a motion to close the nominations is not in order." The chairman's apologies were profuse. He asked for a statement of policy: ". . . bands, a parade, speaking, a regular old-fashioned memorial service. Or what?" No one replied. He prodded them. A middle-aged man said the American Legion drum corps had practiced last night and was prepared to parade. The chairman was speaking of committees. "First is decorating the graves and the flags. When we speak of that we think primarily of that old soldiers' plot where the triangle is. These boys [nodding to the V.F.W. delegates] will take care of their own graves, and the American Legion will do likewise." The meeting stumbled on. Most of the women were large, with flowered dresses and bare, muscular arms and thin, determined mouths that turned down at the corners. Adjournment was delayed by a discussion of the courthouse janitor, who claimed he had not been paid. A woman said indignantly: "Sister Vaughan and Sister Peterson and I scrubbed the floor and washed the curtains and dusted all those books and I don't see why we should pay him when he doesn't do anything."

Outside, it was dark and fresh and windy, and the trees on the courthouse lawn were wet. The huge billboard "Honor Roll" loomed white; in front of it was a smaller board bearing a gold star. One of the fellows said: "Jeez, all those women talkin' who scrubbed the place, I thought we'd never get done." They climbed the narrow stairs and Fording unlocked the door to the V.F.W. clubrooms. Most of the men here were middle-aged and the women were heavy, dowdy, though a couple of flashy girls swished around near the blackjack game. Somebody said he'd heard GI's say they intended to go into politics and change a lot of things. Fording grinned. "They forget it damn fast." Up came a meaty-faced veteran of the other war who was a member of the Cooties, the V.F.W. "fun-making" organization; he was wearing a bright-red tie with a white cootie, red sox, and a yellow and red felt hat from which dangled small figurines—a cow, a locomotive, a dog, an outhouse. He wanted to talk to Fording about the size of the parade during the encampment: "You know what we set over there at that table and figured out? 5,300. You know how long that'd make that parade last? You take a hunerd and five steps to the minute," and he calculated.

At lunch in the Roberts the Kiwanians were singing: ". . . and let the rest of the world go by." Yet there could be no question that the world had pressed in upon Muncie. Asking directly about isolationism was like asking about sin—people were against it. It hadn't worked. Something else must be tried. What? Well, there was the United Nations. But what kind of a UN? A white-collar man said: "It is definitely needed. But I don't mean we should surrender our sovereign rights." As for the atomic bomb, it simply was not being talked about. A factory executive said: "Nobody is taking it too serious, I don't think, not in this locality." Most people seemed to expect an economic smashup in seven years or less. Asked about this, a farmer said: "I hope not," and laughed, the same nervous little laugh with which he had commented on the atomic bomb. It was curious how many laughed at mention of depression and the bomb. Were these what they most feared?

Not all Indiana cities came through the war as easily as Muncie. Before the war Charlestown had been a country town on the Ohio River across from Louisville with a population of 891. In the winter of 1940 du Pont and Goodyear flung into it forty-five thousand men to build two gigantic powder plants. Thousands more came later. Somehow, fifteen thousand of these people managed to live in Charlestown itself, and many of the rest overran it: The single liquor store reportedly earned more than one hundred thousand dollars net. What was going on in Charlestown in the spring of 1946? The four-lane highway to it was deserted. You could see where a farmer had had trailers all over his hillside orchard, but now the outhouses were falling in and there was nothing else left but the trailer-rental meter boxes on the trees. The taxi passed the powder plants, the high wire fences and guardhouses, the low saw-toothed buildings, the maze of high-tension lines—all deserted. Not far beyond was Charlestown, its stores and restaurants quiet, the trailers that had housed the whores gone from outside town. VJ Day thousands of war workers hadn't even waited to be laid off; they just piled their mattresses, stepladders, and pots and pans onto their cars and put the kids in the back seat and went back across the river to the hills to stay. But not everybody had left Charlestown. Its population was still five or six thousand. What were all these displaced persons doing? "Loafin', most of 'em," said a large round-faced man at a bar. The juke box began playing *Reconversion Blues*. Where had they all come from? He said:

266

"Everywhere. I come from Maryland." Was he going to stay? "I got no quarters anywhere else. So far, my wife teaches school and I'm a painting contractor and I been doing fine. I'll stay on a year, I guess. But I don't know—I haven't got any business left back there. I wouldn't a come here except you couldn't get no materials back there then. I been here six years now," and he said it as though it surprised him. Going back to Louisville the cab driver, passing the du Pont plant, said: "Some project. Think it'll ever be used again?"

Chapter 19

STRAWS IN THE HOOSIER WIND

A T NOON on a summer day in 1946, working girls came out of the absentee-owned overall factory, one of a few small industries remaining in Brookville, and crowded into a near-by cafeteria. The slight, friendly, graying man at a table was talking about the four and a half million dollars deposited in local banks in 1945 and 1946. "Where'd all come from? Farmers, mostly, I guess. Connersville got some war plants but we didn't. Didn't want 'em." War plants meant union trouble, a disturbing influx of Kentucky hillbillies, and a big boom and a big bust; Brookville would just go along as it was, a peaceful trading center in the Whitewater Valley. Had times changed much since 1900? "Oh my I should reckon. The manner of living is different now," and he was fumbling for words, remembering his youth in the late nineties. "We couldn't get out of town unless we went on a train, so we had different amusements. Now the young folks can get in their machine and go to Richmond or Connersville. But it's more than that. The type has changed. People don't live like they use to; they use to be more neighborly. People don't have time it seems like to develop a character like Old Aunt Mary any more."

Up at Indianapolis that summer the big money was being spent. In the Claypool Hotel bar, packed by 4:30 p.m., a man declined a second drink and waited for his friend to finish, and the bartender picked up his glass, wiped the bar, and told him curtly: "You'll have to step aside for someone else that wants a drink." Ah, the warm Hoosier character of 1946.

> *Wasn't it pleasant, O brother mine,*
> *In those old days of the lost sunshine*
> *Of youth—when the Saturday's chores were through,*
> *And the "Sunday's wood" in the kitchen, too,*
> *And we went visiting, "me and you,"*
> *Out to Old Aunt Mary's?*

Indeed it must have been pleasant. What had happened?

In 1916 Meredith Nicholson had written: "On her one hundredth birthday Indiana may render an account of her stewardship with a good conscience and a pardonable pride. . . . Her citizens have stood steadfastly for sound ideals of government amid many disturbances of the equilibrium. . . . She has contributed men and women of character and genius to every department of human activity. . . . Increasing respect, bordering upon affection, attends the name Hoosier. . . . A typical American state is this Indiana." Local historians writing around 1900 all had reported that "prospects never were more favorable."

But somewhere, somehow, between the beginning of one world war and the end of another, the wonder went out of all the wonderful things of Indiana's past—the magic of Mc-Cutcheon's Indian Summer cartoon and Riley's poems, the boundless promise of natural gas and Elwood Haynes's wonderful machine. Indiana was no longer the fair field Meredith Nicholson had described. A suspicion had arisen that bigotry, ignorance, and hysteria were as much a part of the Hoosier character as were conservatism and steadfastness and common sense. One of Indiana's chief exports had long been ideas, but so many of these had turned out to be wrong-headed, wicked, or useless. Indiana lost its friendly tolerance, its conviction that things would work out, and it by no means fulfilled its magnificent promise. Endless vistas of opportunity stretched before a boy born in Indiana in 1900. He could believe every word of Albert J. Beveridge's advice to a young man: "Be honest with the world and the world will be honest with you." Thus did Beveridge begin *The Young Man and The World*, a book as remarkable as his "March of the Flag" speech. (Senator Beveridge is a widely misunderstood politician; he believed almost nothing very deeply, and nearly everything he did believe deeply was false or base.) He urged men of fifty: "Get yourself into the current of Circumstance—'in the swim,' as the colloquialism has it. . . . People are quick to see, feel, and know that you are in deed and in truth not of the present day. . . . Therefore mingle with men. Don't withdraw into yourself. Don't be a turtle. . . . Growing! Growth! It is only a question of that, after all. . . ." He described a millionaire whose early ventures had failed: "They were the Thor-like blows with which Fate forged the unconquerableness of this man. For unconquerable he has become. . . . look at his brow of power, at the merciless and yet delicate and sensitive lips. . . ." (This was many years before millionaires were discovered to be vulnerable and before mercilessness became a vice, not a virtue.) Beveridge advised: "Another thing. Go you to church. Use clean linen. Wear good and well-fitting clothing. Take care of your shoes. . . . It is an easy process that produces tramps. A few days' growth of beard, the tolerance of certain personal habits of indolence, and your tramp begins, vaguely, but none the less surely, to appear. This is accompanied by a falling off in clear-cut thought, a blurring of the moralities, and a cessation of definite and effective energy. . . . Do not do it. . . . Your problem is not to give way to your weaknesses."

Well, the young men born about 1900 had observed all these rules, and where had it got them by the time they approached fifty in 1947? Hardly where they might have expected, in all probability. With Beveridge's advice clearly in mind, they had been put aboard an A.E.F. transport; it seemed a long time before clean linen was even feasible again. And it proved no guarantee of success anyway. If they came through farm depression and the Klan unscathed—and who did, wholly?—they found themselves in an industrial Indiana full of long lines of unemployed at factory gates. And soon another war began.

Somewhere in those years Indiana, lusty child of the Civil War and pioneer capitalism, lost its way. As the nation and the world shrank, the pressures generated exploded time and again in Indiana. The changes in the nation are beyond the scope of this book; here we shall only inquire into the decline of Indiana. And anyway, Hoosiers can blame only themselves, not the nation, for some of their failures.

There was something noble about a rich railroad owner who could neighbor with a man determined to organize the railroad employees into one big capital-busting union. This capitalist had to know that the organizer was, like himself, just "a man 'at stands." But tolerance is fast disappearing in Indiana. Hoosiers began to chip away at it during the 1914–18 war; German-Americans in Indianapolis had to change the name of Das Deutsche Haus to the Athenæum. (And even earlier D. M. Parry had struck no blows for tolerance.) Billy Sunday and others continued the process during and after the war, and nearly everybody in Indiana joined in during the reign of the Klan. The Klan left scars. The men in the mob that stormed the jail at Marion on the night of August 7, 1930, and dragged out two Negroes and strung them up to the trees on the courthouse square wore no robes or hoods, but who can say what specters stalked their minds? Who can say how many of Court Asher's readers wear mental robes and hoods? None of this has made it any easier for a Jew or a Negro born in 1900 to realize the promise he beheld. Nor, indeed, has it made it easier for anybody else.

And even the material progress of Indiana was arrested. It had seemed limitless in 1900, but it was stunted by some of the very men of vision who had created it—the early capitalists. In almost every small city one can hear tales of how the chamber of commerce discouraged outside manufacturers from building plants there. Why? Because the local magnates, running a low-wage open shop, were afraid an Eastern manufacturer would spoil the workmen, might even bring in labor unions. (This explains why some Indiana cities did not seek war plants after 1940.) Of course, some of these tales are spite stories, but others are true. Why today is not a single automobile made at Indianapolis? True, Henry Ford made Detroit a lodestone and water transport on the Great Lakes is cheap. But there is a widely held belief that local industrialists and bankers discouraged Ford from locating at Indianapolis. Willys, Allison, Fisher, others—they were, as one who knew them recalls, "just poor boys with big ideas, and other people wouldn't put up a dime to help 'em." Indianapolis, until the CIO came along, maintained its reputation as "the open-shop capital" of the United States. And it did not grow much; it stagnated. The doctrines of Mr. Parry had taken hold. Indianapolis had got hardening of the arteries.

Even in Terre Haute the bankers and lawyers administering the estates of the early freebooters felt keenly their obligation to the heirs. They opposed any proposal to raise taxes, for instance. An angry city controller wrote his report for 1945 and quickly resigned: "Over night, practically, in March, 1932, Terre Haute's valuations for purposes of taxation were reduced approximately twenty million dollars [roughly by a third]. . . . none of these missing millions has been restored. . . . So long as real estate valuations are fixed by a local board of review . . . subject in a sense to certain influences . . . glaring inequalities . . . continue. From these inequalities Terre Haute suffers more than any other city of her class in the State. She has the most illy-paid school teachers of any city in the State of comparable size; the most poorly paid municipal employes of any city in the State with the exception of policemen and firemen. . . . We have firehouses where the men are compelled to sleep in quarters the average man would not permit his pet dog to occupy; others have roofs so leaky that when it rains the men have to move their cots; we should have more fire plugs and more street lights, and many other things. . . ." When the combined efforts of management, strikebreakers, local police, and the state militia failed to destroy the unions in Terre Haute, several industries announced they were moving away for good. Sinclair Lewis, making a curtain speech in the Terre Haute Opera House, praised Debs, and, one man recalls: "You could feel the ice creep over" the first-night audience.

Debs had given the workingmen a vision of a world and made them want it, but they had forgotten. The fight for equal rights had got smothered in feather bedding. Labor skates turned William Hapgood's bold experiments into a squabble over wages and hours. Jurisdictional disputes replaced reform. In Evansville the wartime shipyard hired everything—Kentucky sharecroppers, women schoolteachers, retail clerks, salesmen, farmers, businessmen, West Coast construction workers, even a couple of preachers—and the A.F. of L. man who represented them hoped they'd go away after the war. "Hell, a labor organization is a business. You got to have an established revenue. You don't get nowhere recruiting new members. Quittin' time down there, they're like a bunch o' goddam cattle. Awhile back I went down there and I'd of got knocked down and trampled on like a bunch o' cattle if I hadn't got behind somethin'. Where they goin'? All they do is run across the street and drink beer." He sighed. "It's like anything else. You got some o' the best and some o' the worst when you got twenty thousand people."

Many plain people in Indiana blame the politicians most of all for stunting Indiana's growth. There is a saying that every Hoosier baby's first words are: "Although I am not a candidate for any public office, if nominated by the people of my party and elected by the sovereign voters of the great State of Indiana, I will serve to the best of my ability." The overweening interest in politics goes back to the time when an election was held every year, when every voter of good character could become a lawyer, when politics was a diversion of work-burdened pioneers. Today Indiana is full of people who never see the economic or social ends of politics but are fascinated merely by the day-to-day business of vote getting, buttonholing, horse trading, drink buying—all the little trickeries that make Presidents and ward heelers alike. To win a public office is the same as to make a touchdown or to hit a home run, and as devoid of meaning. The bosses advise: "If you got a weak candidate and no issue, wrap your candidate in the American flag and talk about the Constitution." Along with political myopia goes political corruption. As we have seen, there were few months between 1915 and 1947 when some Indiana public official was not under indictment, on trial, or in jail.

Now, a healthy body politic can stand a lot of corruption. But not an endless amount. Healthy Indiana was in 1900. But look what she had to sustain for forty years: breeders of hate and intolerance, capitalists and bankers who thwarted industrial growth, wealth that resisted change and wanted nothing for the community but lower taxes, unions that resisted change and wanted nothing but shorter hours and more money and more

273

dues, politicians who wanted nothing but a treasury to plunder and an office. Nor were they all. For ordinary people also spent forty years in trying to progress backward. Once every small town wanted to be called a city, but now every city wants to pose as a small town, as if to get back to simpler days. Indiana is conscious of its past greatness. There are societies for the preservation of the 194 remaining covered bridges, for the restoration of the Whitewater Canal. Newspaper columnists begin daily: "Good mornin'": they print stories of neighborliness; artists seek diligently for bucolic scenes: sugar camps in Orange County, buggies on back roads, the water wheel in Spring Mill State Park. Newspapers keep reprinting Abe Martin's quips, Hoosiers still keep Riley's mottoes on their dining-room walls, citizens frantically erect bigger signs proclaiming their town the friendly town. They seem to realize that, just as Debs said forty years ago, "There is something wrong." And sometimes in their self-conscious rusticity there is something false, a perverted motive or at least a nervous lack of balance, as when, in a column called "The Farmer's Wife Says" the author writes: "Not long ago I saw a striker picketing his way along the street in front of the struck bus station. Small silo doors attached to his front and rear said 'unfair.' . . . He was the first picket I ever saw unattached to a fence and he looked very silly. I felt sorry for him and would have liked to ask him questions, but I suppose he couldn't stop on picket duty to visit, and since I couldn't possibly walk that slowly, I had to give it up. I am glad farmers don't have to strike. It would be humiliating to parade in front of the barn labeled 'unfair.' The cows might agree and form a meat and milk union, and strike."

Conflicts have sharpened, battle lines drawn tighter. Depression and war raised issues and built fences higher. Outsiders became suspect. In the paternalistic towns people even were afraid to be seen with strangers. Confidence evaporated. In the banquet hall of the Hotel Antlers in Indianapolis, the Kiwanians lunched, but they sang their songs diffidently, absent-mindedly, fumbling with the buttons on their vests—the zest was gone. Somehow a consciousness of guilt had developed in Indiana. Rotarians looked behind the door before slapping each others' backs. Manufacturers—and, of all people, Chamber of Commerce boosters—said nervously: "But don't quote me." Books singing the praise of mighty and benevolent capitalists grew fewer and fewer, and obituaries of rich men became more and more unadorned. The eulogists seemed unsure of themselves. Chamber of Commerce secretaries, as has been said, could offer nothing better than: "We are a self-sufficient community of well-diversified industry and we have enjoyed a slow steady growth." Where is the boundless enthusiasm of the 1890's and the 1920's? Heirs to great wealth seemed strait-jacketed, silenced, lacking in leadership, fooling around with hobbies. Few new businesses had been started since 1930; a white-collar job in a chain store or in the local branch of a foreign corporation awaited a college graduate. Many went elsewhere; one said, as young men everywhere always have: "Indiana is a good place to be from." Almost desperately the chambers of commerce sought solace in the past: "The story of Hulman & Company and other surviving pioneer time firms, is well worth the careful consideration of every one of today. . . ."

There have been in Indiana a number of tremendous family fortunes operating quietly, fighting a rear-guard action, hanging onto what they had inherited, hoping everything would work out, but fearing it wouldn't. They opposed unionism, contributed to good works, made large profits, carried much weight. Sometimes they owned great farms, which they rented out; they lived in the towns they owned. Some manufactured something, others made their money by shuffling papers. (A little-known glass manufacturer of Terre Haute reputedly died the richest man in Indiana, having collected a royalty on every Coca-Cola bottle.) They had been attacked often since the 1930's, these businessmen. Walter Frisbie of the CIO, a quiet, round, determined man who dug ditches in the Calumet after the depression forced him to quit college, has said: "Paternalism is not wholly bad. Neither is slave ownership." These businessmen eagerly supported the political candidacy of Homer E. Capehart, an advertising man and salesman who, having announced "[I am] sick and tired of the New Deal and intend doing something about it," on August 27, 1938, held a mass meeting, widely heralded as a grass-roots conference, on his twelve-hundred-acre farm in southeastern Indiana. He set up about forty striped tents, he prepared to feed chicken and baked clams to 8,500 people, and more than twice as many came. This was a protest meeting. But how different from earlier protests. True, it was played against a farm backdrop, but the protestants were not men like the Grangers; they were, simply, all the Republican precinct committeemen and vice committeemen in Indiana, together with political and business leaders, Capehart's personal guests. Elected to the Senate in 1944, Capehart supported the America First Committee and, when it became more popular, the Indiana Committee for Victory, whose objective was to combat America First. He called every labor leader in the state by his first name, and his foremen fought the CIO's organizing drive in his juke box factory, and businessmen supported him, whatever private doubts they might entertain as to his statesmanship. They had had few spokesmen in recent years, and they had grown afraid. None even cried publicly: "Smash 'em, Mr. Parry, smash 'em"; they lacked their grandfathers' vigor, or they had grown more circumspect or fearful. Now and then they gathered in their clubs to hear a politician, and though they listened politely while he said: "Management and labor must both recognize their responsibilities," they liked better sentences that began: "I am a friend of the workingman but—"; and after the speaking, drinking Scotch at the bar while waiters cleared away the debris of dinner, they told each other what they thought of labor, they wondered peevishly what was wrong with the country.

By 1946 one could scarcely recognize in Indiana the widely held conception of the Hoosier state. One could not escape to the past in the cities. They had changed irrevocably. In individual farm homes, perhaps; but so many farms were "telephone farms," and "town" meant a factory city. True, the southern half of Indiana seemed still bucolic; but Brown County was little more than a widely advertised commodity, with bearded men in the villages neatly arranged as props for the tourists; and many "unspoiled" regions had become nothing but rural slums. Where were the prosperous farm towns of yesteryear? Only a few, like Winamac, remained.

Sometimes Indianapolis seemed a small town, sometimes a city. An Indianapolis department store bought more advertising space in 1945 than any other store in the United States save one (Hoosiers believe in advertising). But people still called the telephone operator "Central." A woman knocked at the door of a home and asked if she could come in and talk about religion for a little while (she could). People still "went to market"; huge Saturday crowds jammed the first floor of old, red-brick Tomlinson Hall. A traveling salesman complained: "This town's deader at night than Kokomo." Central Indiana people regarded the people of the Calumet as foreigners because they wanted to keep their saloons open all night. A waitress from Detroit considered Hoosiers yokels: "They're rude, with all that the word implies." The State Fair was big news in Indianapolis—"the typically Hoosier institution. Folks will flock here from all parts of the state for fun and competition"—and so was the tallest stand of corn grown in Indianapolis. Gardening was not the pastime of dilettantes; it was the joy of a woman who, reared on the farm, remembered her father saying it was so hot in August he could hear the corn grow at night.

The roots of these people go deep and they go to the soil, as even a casual visitor can see. This may be one reason why outsiders still think of Indiana as essentially rural even though it has steadily grown more urban and industrial, a process accelerated by each war, each farm depression. This Indiana idea, this conception of the state as a bucolic place inhabited by pleasant, simple, neighborly folk, contains a good deal of mythology. Like any myth, it has some truth in it; like any myth, it goes back to ancient times, though not until Riley's time did it receive wide currency. And Hoosiers today try to conform to the myth. They are likely to speak, often self-consciously, in rural idiom; they protest that they are only country boys at heart. Some wear this myth like a mask to hide their schemes. A Chicago promoter born in Indiana wishes wearily—and loudly—that he could go back home to Brown County, but he never would seriously consider doing so. Eating a ten-cent hamburger and drinking coffee out of a mug, Dwight Smoker seems the rustic come to the Fair; but he is a rustic worth three hundred thousand dollars. And this he knows. Did

277

he not diffidently buy a valuable farm for almost nothing from a slick Chicago racketeer? Just so, a hundred years ago, O. H. Smith stood mute in his muddy clothing when Cincinnati men said they'd never heard of him; *he* knew he'd just been elected to the U.S. Senate and that his hogs were worth seven thousand dollars. Pretense is fatal to a politician, as James Brown Ray learned; derision of pretense is common to all Hoosiers, the stock in trade of some, like Ade. Hoosiers called Professor Follansbee "Do-se-do" in Civil War times, and their 1947 legislature, essaying a pleasantry, forbade the use of the atomic bomb in Indiana. And this tendency to whittle everything down to Hoosier size goes back to the dim years when "Hoosier" meant a scorned, unlettered rustic. When Hannegan made love to the Queen of Prussia, the home folks were delighted for he had confounded the fops who had laughed at them all; his triumph assuaged their shame. And the scorn of others has also produced in the Hoosiers an underdog's defiance—Court Asher's denouncing his powerful enemies in folksy idiom is kindred to Joseph Gorrell's proclaiming he has voted the "anarchist" ticket for Bryan, to the Hoosiers' love for John Dillinger, to the stubborn independence of Eugene Debs defying the bosses. In 1896 Joseph Gorrell reported that guards at a duck-hunting preserve owned by some Chicago rich men had shot some farmers, and he printed doggerel exhibiting this stiff-backed independence: "I'm an Indiana farmer, and I want it understood that I make an honest living and my reputation's good. Some twenty years or so ago I bought a tract of land and settled down in Tolleston to rough it in the sand. The vegetables I planted took nourishment and grew, and though I've not made a fortune I'm fairly well to do; I trained the vines in summer time to climb the beanpoles tall, and harvested the products and sold 'em in the fall. A more contented fellow never used a hoe or rake in the state of Indiana in the northern part of Lake. When the weather was inclement, and clouds obscured the sun, I hunted in the forest with my tried and trusty gun. Along the sluggish Calumet I set my traps with care, and the mink and muskrats there about were driven to despair; and oftentimes on winter nights I'd build a rousing fire that lighted up the country from Tolleston to Dyer. But alas a day of sorrow came—some money bags from town bought a monster game preserve and paid the boodle down; they ran a fence around the swamp, hemmed in the brooks and rills, and served a notice on the boys to leave the knobs and hills. Perhaps they had a legal right; but darn their dwarfish souls they employed a lot of vagabonds to shoot us full of holes, and that's the reason, stranger, I bought this 'navy six,' and loaded down my pockets with cobblestones and bricks. I don't believe in fighting, but when I'm pressed you bet I ain't afraid of nothing along the Calumet."

Farmers like that, though in grimmer mood, joined the Grange in the 1870's. Farmers like that howled at land speculators, they fought Harrison's autocracy, they curbed the authority of circuit judges, and in our own time they set up co-operatives to get the monopolists off their backs. Unskilled workingmen, ignored by the A.F. of L., found a voice in Debs, and though one can hardly say as yet that the powerful CIO unions are in the great Indiana tradition of protest, they are full of rank-and-filers like the earnest, bent, old man at Muncie. Debs helped to make possible, so soon after the end of the craftsman period in American industry, the CIO and other industrial unions. He raised the issues of the new society, discovering them here in the heart of America. And indeed it can be argued that he was the most influential man Indiana ever produced, though today he is remembered only as a "nutty radical" or as a politician who failed of the Presidency. Certainly he was the most effective of the many protestants who have raged through Indiana's history. He joined the continuing quest for the better life that began in the dim years before statehood. He stands in company with the experimenters at Harmony and Shakertown and Lagrange County and Columbia Conserve. And all this in a state usually accounted one of the "conservative" states of the Midwest, as opposed to the "progressive" ones like, say, Wisconsin.

None the less, neither Debs's doctrines nor those of the farmers in revolt swept Indiana as, for example, Populism swept Kansas. Nor did the farm rebellion of our own time capture control of Indiana as of North Dakota. For always in Indiana a counterforce is operating. Complex Indiana is inhabited by people of such divergent problems that no single solution is a solution for all. Since there are few but farmers in North Dakota, what the farmers wanted the state got; but the farm bloc cannot run Indiana. Just so, in America at large a successful national political party must be a hodgepodge of conflicting interests, a shock absorber for many pressures.

Sometimes in Indiana, opposition to strange doctrine has been only gentle reproof, as when a Republican newspaper termed the Populists "wayward children." A tolerance lies in this, and Eugene Debs of Terre Haute benefited by it. But bigotry has run equally strong through Indiana. As Billy Sunday denounced Debs, so the circuit riders warred on the Shakers. The church has long been powerful in Indiana—poor Dreiser could not rid himself of Puritanism however hard he tried—and usually the church has thrown its weight with the bigots. It attacked liquor and other wickedness before the Civil War, and its minions were among D. C. Stephenson's ablest organizers. The Klan grew fat on ancient hatreds. Court Asher and less noted Hoosiers who today dislike hillbillies, Negroes, and other "outsiders" are but carrying on an unfair fight that was old a hundred years ago when a mob killed a Negro on a downtown Indianapolis street. And were not the Klansmen descended from the Regulators? Indeed, they made good use of the pre-Civil-War law that legalized the Regulators.

To get things done—it is a Hoosier impatience. The link is strong among Oliver P. Morton, Paul V. McNutt, and D. M. Parry. They were men of force. In their view, ends justified any means. More, they were national leaders, men in the forefront of their times. As Morton led the new Republican Party in one holy war, so Parry led the capitalists in another. Albert J. Beveridge, self-righteous and confident, led the American imperialists, just as Hannegan had done earlier. All these men were quick to implement ideas. Ideas—resentment of the money power, of the East, of the British—embraced by the dispossessed pioneer Indiana farmers lay a heavy hand on our own times. And were not those pioneers, journeying over wilderness traces to hear a muster day orator, more eager for ideas than pioneers elsewhere? Here slavery came to issue very early, here the Greenback Party began. And the automotive industry arose in Indiana, and Carl Fisher became almost the archetype of the American promoter of the 1920's.

This state was not plundered by outside corporations as were others. The enterprises of Oliver and Studebaker and Atkins, of Ball and Hillenbrand and Parry, of so many others, were enterprises native to the Indiana soil. The wondrous place that Francis Hulman beheld was the home of the American dream; his success was that dream come true. And in those bright early years it came true for so many others; the promise was constantly renewed. It was the middle class that created capitalism here in the interior of the United States, and in so doing it also created an enraged lower class, just as "self-made" men of mature years always have trampled on those who in boyhood were their equals. The poor who had applauded paternalism in the golden age, when it promised to distribute its fruits to all, came to hate it. And, hated, the capitalists sulked, renounced leadership. And so, belatedly, the foreign corporations moved in. The pattern of native control was changing.

Yet it had left many heritages. Not the least were pride and wonder, the pride and wonder that the Hoosiers, so recently out of the forest, felt in the golden age at their own success. Thus arose the fabled Indiana character, the smug, confident man of middle class who was a match for anyone. Charles A. Beard, the historian, a native Hoosier and one of the first American academics exposed to European Marxism, came home to Indiana and expounded the Marxist faith to his father, an Indiana banker who listened carefully and then said: "Yes, yes, I follow you, the workers rise and take over the property. Now what I want to know is, how soon do the smarties get it back?" Years later, asked why Thorstein Veblen wrote such tortured sentences, Beard replied: "Well, the man never knew where his next meal was coming from and if that lasts long enough it gets into your writing. Me, I've always known where my next twenty meals were coming from. It makes a difference."

Hoosiers, delighted with the inventions and gadgets of the golden age, continued to revere material progress of any sort, as Ned Gorrell does today. Materialism long had been a dominant Hoosier characteristic; had not the early Yankees at Vincennes outtraded the dreamy French, had not later settlers watched unmoved the shameful treatment of Indians who stood in the way of progress? Similarly they countenanced political corruption, and not the laity so much as competing politicians jailed the Sim Coys of the 1870's and the uncounted thieves of the 1920's. A saying runs that every Hoosier baby is born with a ballot in his hand. Beveridge but carried on in the oratorical tradition cherished by Hannegan's admirers. Though today oratory is out of favor, two other political traditions persist from Jackson's time and earlier: the politician as a man of the people, preferably rural (Hannegan's street fighting and Jonathan Jennings's logrolling served the same purpose as the cornfield setting for Homer Capehart's clambake), and the politician as pure professional (Ralph Gates is the spiritual heir to Jennings and O. H. Smith).

Gates meeting the national banking crisis by going round to talk to his friends, Gorrell extolling the virtues of the small town and turning a sharp tongue on city people, a lean, stringy, farm woman with pursed lips determined to get her money's worth in Saturday shopping, Court Asher defiantly telling the U.S. government to "slap it on your sore heel"—these are Hoosiers in action. Gates is a joiner; so is Asher, so is Gorrell. At quilting bees the pioneers learned to love this, their own place; beside them today stand the old folks at the band reunion in Winamac, Asher and his fellow isolationists in the Jurdon hills. Gorrell loves the soil. But he does not grub in it. Riley praised country life, but from a safe distance, comfortable, in the city. The sing-song sadness in a farm woman's voice is attuned to the bathos of Riley's poetry. Does it not comment on Indiana to say that one of the closest friends of Eugene V. Debs was James Whitcomb Riley? They had more in common than love of mankind, too; Riley said he knew an artist who could spit clean over a boxcar, and Debs said he thought he ought to have a veteran's bonus.

It is a century now since Mrs. Maury ascribed the ebullience of Western men to "their remoteness from that peculiar kind of civilization which belongs to sea board and manufacturing districts." A manufacturing district Indiana has become, and her people less ebullient than Hannegan. This is only to say that Indiana has shifted her ground with the nation. As they had to, Hoosiers pioneered in the wilderness, they erected the structure of capitalism after the Civil War, they gloried in a dream come

true around 1900, they turned promoter and Babbitt in the
1920's, they pulled down many an idol in the troubled later
years. They did as their nation did. If it is objected that the
character traits we have examined as Hoosier are really common
to all America, one can only reply that Indiana, as we said at
the outset, is the U.S. in little. Do Hoosiers complain that we
blame them unfairly for a decay common throughout the republic? That the problems which beset Indiana today are the
nation's problems? The proposition can be reversed. Perhaps
the problems that afflict the nation are really Indiana's own,
thrust upon the other luckless forty-seven. For America is full
of people like the Hoosiers, America is a larger Indiana; and if
we knew what had gone wrong—and right—with Indiana we
might well know what has gone wrong—and right—with the
nation. Indiana is a good place to look for clues, the Hoosier
wind carries many a straw. This Indiana is in truth, as one of
Gates's admirers has said of him, "down at the grass roots where
it all emanates from."

Acknowledgments

MANY of the facts in this book came from newspapers and newspapermen, labor organizers, manufacturers, workingmen, chamber-of-commerce secretaries, policemen, politicians, local historians, merchants, press agents, housewives, lawyers, miners, doctors, insurance men, realtors, taxicab drivers, Legionnaires and other veterans, farmers, farm politicians, hotelmen, lobbyists, businessmen, publishers, editors, railroaders, undertakers, professors, Presbyterians, Methodists, Kiwanians, waitresses, retired madames, and other people who need not be classified by trade or faith. I lived in Indiana from 1919 to 1938 and I have since made frequent trips back, gathering material. The people I talked to on those expeditions are too numerous to name here but I am grateful to all of them—they contributed. Much of the best material came from newspapermen; I regret that many of them—including some who supplied information of the highest value—specifically requested that their names be concealed. I am, however, able to thank publicly these people who helped me: Ernest Showalter, the *Brookville American* and the *Brookville Democrat;* Governor Ralph Gates and his brothers, John and Scott Gates, Columbia City; Anton Scherrer, Indianapolis; Clark Springer, Chairman of the Republican State Committee; C. Lester Bush, formerly of Muncie; Paul Ross, Division of State Commerce and Public Relations; Paul Squires, State Department of Conservation; Horace Coats, Secretary, Republican State Committee; Ralph Cheshire, Democratic State Committee; Ned Gorrell, *Pulaski County Democrat;* Powers Hapgood and William P. Hapgood, Indianapolis; Walter Frisbie, Indianapolis; William Book and Carl Dortch, Indianapolis Chamber of Commerce; Howard Friend, Indiana State Chamber of Commerce; Fay Paul, Court Asher, George A. Ball, Ed Crago, Wilbur Sutton, Oris Fording, all of Muncie; Donald D. Hoover, Ed Heinke, Noble Reed, Robert Bloem, Sherley Uhl, all of the

Indianapolis *Times;* Levi P. Moore and Scott Waldron, publicity, Indiana State Fair; H. J. Reed, Tom Johnson and Zenas Beers, all of Purdue University; Richard Forbes and James Benham, Terre Haute *Star;* S. D. Fox and Professor J. R. Shannon, both of Terre Haute; I. H. Hull, Indiana Farm Bureau Cooperative Association; Harry J. Riddick, Columbia City *Post;* B. J. Bloom, Columbia City; Eugene S. Pulliam, Lowell Nussbaum, and Ben Cole, all of the Indianapolis *Star;* Hassil Schenck and Glenn W. Sample, Indiana Farm Bureau; Al Bloemker, Indianapolis Motor Speedway; Herb Hill, the Indianapolis *News;* John G. Coulter, Indianapolis; Gaston E. Marque and Robert Ross, publicity, the Studebaker Corporation; Carl H. Mullen and Edgar A. Perkins, Indianapolis; Howard H. Peckham, Director, Indiana Historical Bureau; Chester Cleveland, Indiana Society of Chicago. I alone am responsible for the use I have made of the material they gave me.

Some of the persons named above supplied photographs as well as information. In addition, I was aided in my search for photographs by these: Ruth W. Bright and Frank Hohenberger, Nashville; John R. Funk, Kentland; Frankie I. Jones, La Porte; J. E. Graf, Smithsonian Institution; Charles E. Randall, Forest Service, U.S. Department of Agriculture; Bancroft Yarrington, U.S. Steel Corporation; Stanley B. Campbell, French Lick Springs Hotel Company; Floyd W. Stoelting, Vincennes Chamber of Commerce; Clarence B. Randall, L. B. Hunter, William E. Geidt, all of Inland Steel Company; Paul Vanderbilt, the Library of Congress.

The map was drawn by Gertrude Burch, Chicago, from my directions.

For suggestions in planning the book I am indebted especially to George R. Leighton, New York, Francis S. Nipp, Chicago, and my wife, Frances Smethurst Martin. In addition, Mr. Nipp, a longtime personal friend and now an Instructor of English at Roosevelt College, read, corrected, and helped rewrite the entire manuscript, rendering aid both technical and as to content; while Mrs. Martin also helped with the research, proofreading, and indexing, and typed the manuscript.

I wish especially to express my gratitude for the intelligent and willing co-operation of Mrs. Marguerite Anderson and Mrs.

Hazel Hopper, both of the Indiana Division of the Indiana State Library at Indianapolis. (Since I did my research, Mrs. Anderson has joined the Detroit Public Library and has been succeeded as Chief of the Indiana Division at Indianapolis by Mrs. Hopper.) It may be worth noting that the newspapers collected at this library are extraordinarily useful since they have been indexed (though incompletely). I also wish to thank Margaret Pierson, archivist, Indiana State Library and P. H. Wolfard, in the same department; and Mary A. Egan, Librarian, Highland Park, Illinois, Public Library, who helped me obtain books on loan from the Indiana library.

Grateful acknowledgment is made to *Harper's Magazine* for permission to reprint the material on D. C. Stephenson, on Court Asher, and on Muncie in 1944 and 1946, which originally appeared there (though, save for Asher, in altered form), and to *Life* for permission to print the material on Evansville in 1944 and on Charlestown and Indianapolis in 1946 which *Life* bought as portions of two articles but did not publish. All these were my own writings.

Grateful acknowledgment is made for permission to reprint the writings of others still in copyright, as follows: To D. Appleton-Century Company, Inc., for permission to reprint selections from *The Young Man and The World*, by Albert J. Beveridge; to The Bobbs-Merrill Company for permission to reprint selections from *Afterwhiles* by James Whitcomb Riley, Copyright 1898, 1926, from *Neghborly Poems* by James Whitcomb Riley, Copyright 1891, 1919, from *Abe Martin's Town Pump* by Kin Hubbard, Copyright 1929 (all used by special permission of the Publishers, The Bobbs-Merrill Company); to Helen Dreiser (Mrs. Theodore Dreiser) for permission to use a quotation from *Twelve Men*, by Theodore Dreiser; to Greenberg Publishers, Inc., for permission to reprint selections from *Eugene V. Debs A Man Unafraid*, by McAlister Coleman; to Harcourt, Brace and Company, Inc., for permission to reprint selections from *Middletown*, by Robert S. Lynd and Helen Merrell Lynd; to Josephine Herschell for permission to reprint a selection from "Ain't God Good To Indiana," by William Herschell; to the Indiana Historical Bureau for permission to reprint selections from *Indiana As Seen by Early Travelers*, edited by Harlow Lindley; to the *Indiana Magazine of History* for permission to reprint selections from "Mrs. Lydia B. Bacon's Journal, 1811–1812," edited by Mary M. Crawford, and from an unsigned review of *The Valley of Democracy,* by Meredith Nicholson, which appeared in the issue of March 1919 (vol. xv, no. 1); to the Graduate School, Indiana University, for permission to reprint selections from *That Man Debs and his Life Work,* by Floy Ruth Painter; to The Lewis Publishing Company for permission to reprint selections from *Greater Indianapolis . . . ,* by Jacob Piatt Dunn; to Lions International for permission to reprint portions of two songs, *The Lions Are Meeting* and *The Fighting Lion;* to Liveright Publishing Corporation for permission to reprint selections from *Debs, His Authorized Life and Letters From Woodstock Prison to Atlanta,* by David Karsner; to the Macmillan Company for permission to reprint selections from *The Hoosiers,* by Meredith Nicholson; to Oxford University Press for permission to reprint selections from *The Growth of the American Republic,* by Samuel Eliot Morison and Henry Steele Commager and from *Indiana, A Guide to the Hoosier State,* by workers of the Writers' Program of the Work Projects Administration in the State of Indiana (American Guide Series); to Parade Publication, Inc., and its photographer, Ike Vern, for permission to reprint a photograph of Ned Gorrell and his family; to Charles Scribner's Sons for permission to reprint selections from *Our Times,* by Mark Sullivan, and from *The Valley of Democracy,* by Meredith Nicholson; to Simon and Schuster, Inc., for permission to reprint a selection from *Reading I've Liked* edited by Clifton Fadiman, Copyright, 1941, by Simon and Schuster, Inc.; to the Socialist Party, U.S.A., for permission to reprint a selection from *Walls and Bars,* by Eugene V. Debs; to The Viking Press Inc., for permission to reprint a selection from the writings of Alexander Woollcott; to The H. W. Wilson Company for permission to reprint a selection from *Twentieth Century Authors,* edited by Stanley Kunitz and Howard Haycraft.

Grateful acknowledgment is made to Edmund C. Gorrell, William P. Hapgood, and George R. Leighton for permission to reprint material from their writings which is not in copyright.

As I have said, this book was not intended to be a history of

Indiana, not even an informal one. In attempting to capture the flavor of Indiana and depict the ordinary people, I have relied for sources more on people, newspapers, and scattered printed material than on standard books, and I have dealt scantily with many large historical events and figures. The bibliography that follows is therefore selective, and at the same time it includes a few works (such as Dreiser's) of which I have not made much use but which anyone who wished to read more about Indiana might find interesting.

Bibliography

BOOKS

Beveridge, Albert J.: *The Young Man and The World.* New York: D. Appleton and Company, 1905.

Blanchard, Charles, ed.: *Counties of Morgan, Monroe and Brown, Indiana.* Chicago: F. A. Battey & Company, 1884.

Bowers, Claude G.: *Beveridge and the Progressive Era.* Cambridge, Mass.: Houghton Mifflin Company, 1932.

Bowers, Claude G.: *The Tragic Era: The Revolution after Lincoln.* Cambridge, Mass.: Houghton Mifflin Company, 1929.

Bradsby, H. C.: *History of Vigo County, Indiana.* . . . Chicago: S. B. Nelson & Company, 1891.

Buck, Solon J.: *The Agrarian Crusade, A Chronicle of the Farmer in Politics.* Vol. XLV, *The Chronicles of America Series,* Allen Johnson, ed. New Haven: Yale University Press, 1921.

Burns, Harrison, ed.: *Annotated Indiana Statutes.* Indianapolis: Bobbs-Merrill Company, 1943.

Cist, Charles: *Sketches and Statistics of Cincinnati in 1851.* Cincinnati: Wm. H. Moore & Company, 1851.

Clark, Roscoe Collins: *Threescore Years and Ten* . . . *Eli Lilly and Company 1876–1946.* Privately printed, 1946.

Clarke, Grace Julian: *George W. Julian.* Indiana Biographical Series, Vol. I. Indianapolis: Indiana Historical Commission, 1923.

Coffin, Levi: *Reminiscences of Levi Coffin, the Reputed President of the Underground Railroad.* Cincinnati: Western Tract Society, 1876.

Coleman, McAlister: *Eugene V. Debs A Man Unafraid.* New York: Greenberg Publishers, Inc., 1930.

Commemorative Biographical Record of Prominent and Representative Men of Indianapolis and Vicinity. . . . Chicago: J. H. Beers & Company, 1908.

Counties of Lagrange and Noble, Indiana. . . . Chicago: F. A. Battey & Company, 1882.

Counties of White and Pulaski, Indiana. . . . Chicago: F. A. Battey & Company, 1883.

Cumback, Will, and Maynard, J. B., eds.: *Men of Progress of Indiana.* . . . Indianapolis: Indianapolis Sentinel Company, 1899.

Cummins, Cedric C.: *Indiana Public Opinion and the World War 1914–1917.* Indianapolis: Indiana Historical Bureau, 1945.

Debs, Eugene V.: *Speeches.* . . . Vol. IX, *Voices of Revolt.* New York: International Publishers Company, Inc., 1928.

Debs, Eugene V.: *Walls and Bars.* Chicago: Socialist Party, 1927.

Debs: His Life, Writings and Speeches with a Department of Appreciations. Authorized. Girard, Kansas: Appeal to Reason, 1908.

Dickey, Marcus: *The Maturity of James Whitcomb Riley.* Indianapolis: Bobbs-Merrill Company, 1922.

Dickey, Marcus: *The Youth of James Whitcomb Riley.* Indianapolis: Bobbs-Merrill Company, 1919.

Dreiser, Theodore: *Dawn.* New York: Horace-Liveright, Inc., 1931.

Dreiser, Theodore: *A Hoosier Holiday.* With illustrations by Franklin Booth. New York: John Lane Company, 1916.

Dunn, J. P., Jr.: *Indiana, A Redemption from Slavery.* Boston and New York: Houghton Mifflin Company, 1916.

Dunn, Jacob Piatt: *Indiana And Indianans.* . . . 3 vols. Chicago and New York: American Historical Society, 1919.

Dunn, Jacob Piatt: *Greater Indianapolis: The History, the Industries, the Institutions, and the People of a City of Homes.* 2 vols. Chicago: Lewis Publishing Company, 1910.

Esarey, Logan: *A History of Indiana.* 2 vols. Vol. I, *A History of Indiana from its Exploration to 1850;* Vol. II, *From 1850 to 1920.* Third edition. Fort Wayne and Bloomington, Ind.: Hoosier Press and Indiana University Bookstore, 1924, 1935.

Esarey, Logan: *History of Indiana from Its Exploration to 1922. Also an Account Of Vigo County.* . . . Edited by William F. Cronin. 3 vols. Dayton, Ohio: Dayton Historical Publishing Company, 1922.

Esarey, Logan, ed.: *Messages and Papers of Jonathan Jennings, Ratliff Boon, William Hendricks.* Indianapolis: Indiana Historical Commission, 1924.

Faulkner, Harold Underwood: *The Quest for Social Justice 1898–1914.* Vol. XI, *A History of American Life.* New York: The Macmillan Company, 1931.

Forker, John L., and Dyson, Byron H.: *Historical Sketches and Reminiscences of Madison County, Indiana.* Anderson, Indiana, 1897.

Foulke, William Dudley: *Life of Oliver P. Morton including His Important Speeches.* 2 vols. Indianapolis: Bowen-Merrill Company, 1899.

Goebel, Dorothy Burne: *William Henry Harrison: A Political Biography.* Indianapolis: Historical Bureau of Indiana Library and Historical Department, 1926.

Goodrich, DeWitt C. and Tuttle, Charles R.: *An Illustrated History of the State of Indiana.* . . . Indianapolis: J. W. Lanktree & Company, 1876.

Griswold, Bert J., ed.: *Fort Wayne, Gateway of the West 1802–1813.* . . . Indianapolis: Historical Bureau of the Indiana Library and Historical Department, 1927.

Hicks, J. D.: *The Populist Revolt.* Minneapolis, 1931.

Howe, Henry: *The Great West.* . . . 2 vols. Cincinnati: Henry Howe, 1851.

Hubbard, Kin: *A Book of Indiana.* . . . Published by Indiana Biographical Association; compiled under the direction of James O. Jones Company. [n.p.], 1929.

Hyman, Max R., ed.: *The Journal Handbook of Indianapolis.* . . . Indianapolis: Indianapolis Journal Newspaper Co., 1902.

Indiana, a Guide to the Hoosier State Compiled by workers of the Writers' Program of the Work Projects Administration in the State of Indiana. American Guide series. Sponsored by Department of Public Relations of Indiana State Teachers College. New York: Oxford University Press, 1941.

Indiana Review. . . . Indianapolis, 1938.

James, J. A.: "George Rogers Clark." Vol. IV, *Dictionary of American Biography,* Allen Johnson and Dumas Malone, eds. New York: Charles Scribner's Sons, 1930.

Johnson, Benj. F., of Boone [James Whitcomb Riley]: *Neghborly Poems on Friendship Grief and Farm-Life.* Indianapolis: Bowen-Merrill Company, 1891.

Johnson, George L. [compiler]: *Commercial History of Rushville and Rush County.* . . . Rushville, 1899.

Karsner, David: *Debs: His Authorized Life and Letters from Woodstock Prison to Atlanta.* New York: Boni and Liveright, Inc.; 1919.

Karsner, David: *Talks with Debs in Terre Haute (and Letters from Lindlahr).* New York: New York Call, 1922.

Kellar, Herbert Anthony: *Solon Robinson.* . . . 2 vols. Indianapolis: Indiana Historical Bureau, 1936.

Kemper, G. W. H., ed.: *A Twentieth Century History of Delaware County Indiana.* Chicago: Lewis Publishing Company, 1908.

Latta, W. C.: *Outline History of Indiana Agriculture.* Lafayette: Alpha Lambda Chapter of Epsilon Sigma Phi (with Purdue University), 1938.

293

Leech, Margaret: *Reveille in Washington*. New York: Harper & Brothers, 1941.

Lindley, Harlow, ed.: *Indiana As Seen by Early Travelers*. Indianapolis: Indiana Historical Commission, 1916.

Lockwood, George B.: *The New Harmony Movement*. New York: D. Appleton and Company, 1905.

Lynd, Robert S., and Lynd, Helen Merrell: *Middletown: A Study in American Culture*. New York: Harcourt, Brace and Company, 1929.

Lynd, Robert S., and Lynd, Helen Merrell: *Middletown In Transition: A Study in Cultural Conflicts*. New York: Harcourt, Brace and Company, 1937.

McCarty, C. Walter, ed.: *Indiana Today*. . . . Published by Indiana Editors' Association; compiled under the direction of James O. Jones Company, New Orleans, Louisiana, 1942.

Major, Noah J.: *The Pioneers of Morgan County*. . . . Logan Esarey, ed. Indianapolis: Indiana Historical Society, 1915.

Maury, Sarah Mytton: *The Statesmen of America in 1846*. Philadelphia: Carey and Hart, 1847.

Morison, Samuel Eliot, and Commager, Henry Steele: *The Growth of the American Republic*. 2 vols. 3rd edition. New York: Oxford University Press, 1942.

Nicholson, Meredith: *The Hoosiers*. New York: The Macmillan Company, 1916.

Nicholson, Meredith: *The Valley of Democracy*. New York: Charles Scribner's Sons, 1918.

Oakey, C. C.: *Greater Terre Haute and Vigo County*. 2 vols. Chicago and New York: Lewis Publishing Company, 1908.

Painter, Floy Ruth: *That Man Debs and his Life Work*. Published under the auspices of the Graduate Council, Indiana University, 1929.

Pierce, Bessie Louise: *A History of Chicago*. 2 vols. New York: Alfred A. Knopf, 1937, 1940.

Reifel, August J.: *History of Franklin County Indiana*. . . . Indianapolis: B. F. Bowen & Company, Inc., 1915.

Riley, James Whitcomb: *Afterwhiles*. Indianapolis: The Bowen-Merrill Company, 1892.

Riley, James Whitcomb [see Johnson].

Roll, Charles: *Indiana*. . . . 5 vols. Chicago and New York: Lewis Publishing Company, 1931.

Root, George F.: *The Trumpet of Reform: A Collection of Songs, Hymns, Chants and Set Pieces for the Grange*. . . . Cincinnati:

John Church & Company; Chicago: Geo. F. Root & Sons [n.d., probably 1874].

Schlesinger, Arthur Meier: *The Rise of the City 1878–1898.* Vol. X, *A History of American Life* in 12 vols. Arthur M. Schlesinger, Dixon Ryan Fox, eds. New York: The Macmillan Company, 1933.

Sells, Allen M.: "Jacob Wetzel, Trail Blazer," pp. 16–18. *Year Book of the Society of Indiana Pioneers, 1945.*

Smallzried, Kathleen Ann, and Roberts, Dorothy James: *More Than You Promise.* New York: Harper & Brothers, 1942.

Smith, O. H.: *Early Indiana Trials and Sketches, Reminiscences by Hon. O. H. Smith.* Cincinnati: Moore, Wilstach, Keys & Company, 1858.

Snedeker, Caroline Dale: *The Diaries of Donald Macdonald 1824–1826.* Indianapolis: Indiana Historical Society, 1942.

Sullivan, Mark: *Our Times: The United States 1900–1925.* Vol. I, *The Turn of the Century.* New York: Charles Scribner's Sons, 1926.

Sullivan, Mark: *Our Times: The United States 1900–1925.* Vol. VI, *The Twenties.* New York: Charles Scribner's Sons, 1935.

Tarkington, Booth: *Alice Adams.* New York: Doubleday, Page & Company, 1927.

Tarkington, Booth: *The Gentleman from Indiana.* New York: Doubleday & McClure Co., 1899.

Thomas, David: *Travels Through the Western Country in the Summer of 1816. . . .* Auburn, New York: David Rumsey, printer, 1819.

Turner, Frederick Jackson: *The Frontier in American History.* New York: Henry Holt and Company, 1920.

Turner, Paul C.: *Some Contributions of the Indiana Farm Bureau Co-operative Association to Indiana Agriculture.* Indianapolis: Indiana Farm Bureau Co-operative Association, 1946.

Who's Who and What's What in Indiana Politics. Indianapolis: James E. Perry, 1944.

Woodburn, James A.: "Albert Jeremiah Beveridge," Vol. II, *Dictionary of American Biography.* Allen Johnson, ed. New York: Charles Scribner's Sons, 1929.

Woollen, William Wesley: *Biographical and Historical Sketches of Early Indiana.* Indianapolis: Hammond & Co., 1883.

PAMPHLETS, MANUSCRIPTS, AND GOVERNMENT
DOCUMENTS

American State Papers. Class X, Misc. Vol. I. Washington: Gales and Seaton, 1834.

Appleton, John B.: *The Iron and Steel Industry of the Calumet District.* . . . Urbana: University of Illinois, 1927.

Burns, Lee: *The National Road in Indiana.* Indianapolis: Indiana Historical Society, 1919.

Carter, Clarence Edwin, compiler and ed.: *The Territorial Papers of the United States.* Vols. II, III, VII, and VIII [Northwest Territory and Indiana Territory]. Washington: Government Printing Office, 1934, 1939.

Constitution of the State of Indiana. . . . Issued by the Legislative Bureau, State House. Indianapolis: William B. Burford Printing Company, 1939.

Correspondence and announcements relating to the Columbia Conserve Company. (In possession of the company at Indianapolis.)

Cost Reports of the Federal Trade Commission, Coal, No. 5, Ohio, Indiana, and Michigan Bituminous. Washington: Government Printing Office, 1920.

Debs, E. V.: *Riley, Nye & Field.* . . . [n.p., n.d., probably about October 1915.]

Documents, Legislative and Executive, of the Congress of the United States, in relation to The Public Lands. . . . Vol. I. Washington: Duff Green, 1834.

Dunn, Jacob Piatt: *The Word Hoosier.* Indiana Historical Society Publications. Vol. IV, No. 2. Indianapolis, 1907.

Esarey, Logan: *Internal Improvements in Early Indiana.* Indianapolis: Indiana Historical Society; 1912.

50 Years of Progress and Achievement Golden History 1890–1940 United Mine Workers of America District Number 11. [n.p., n.d., probably Terre Haute, 1940.]

Francis, Gerald M.: *Cooperative Purchasing by Indiana Farmers.* Farm Credit Cooperative Research and Service Division, Bulletin No. 38. Washington: Government Printing Office, 1940.

Gorrell, Edmund C.: *Breadfruit and Bittersweet.* . . . Unpublished manuscript. Winamac, 1941. (In possession of Gorrell at Winamac.)

Hapgood, Norman: *The Columbia Conserve and the Committee Of Four.* [n.p.], 1934.

Hapgood, William P.: *The Columbia Conserve Company, Indianap-*

olis, Indiana, An Experiment in Workers' Management and Ownership. [n.p.], 1934.

Henry, W. E.: *Some Elements of Indiana's Population.* Indianapolis: Indiana Historical Society, 1908.

Hodgin, Cyrus W.: *The Naming of Indiana.* Papers of Wayne County, Indiana, Historical Society. Vol. I, No. 1. Richmond, 1903.

Holliday, John H.: *Indianapolis and the Civil War.* Indianapolis: Indiana Historical Society, 1911.

Hollingsworth, J. H.: *Eugene V. Debs, What His Neighbors Say of Him.* [n.p., n.d., probably Terre Haute about 1915.]

Indiana Biographical Scrapbook. Compiled by Indiana State Library. 27 volumes in 1946.

Indiana Labor, Annual Publication of the Indiana State Federation of Labor, 1937. Indianapolis, 1937.

Investigation of Concentration of Economic Power, Temporary National Economic Committee . . . Monograph No. 26 Economic Power and Political Pressures. . . . Washington: Government Printing Office, 1941.

Investigation of Concentration of Economic Power, Temporary National Economic Committee . . . Monograph No. 36 Reports of the Federal Trade Commission on Natural Gas and Natural Gas Pipe Lines in U.S.A. . . . Washington: Government Printing Office, 1940.

Investigation of Concentration of Economic Power, Hearings Before the Temporary National Economic Committee, Congress of the United States . . . Public Resolution No. 113 (Seventy-fifth Congress) . . . Part 2, Patents, Automobile Industry, Glass Container Industry. . . . Washington: Government Printing Office, 1940.

Investigation of Railroads, Holding Companies, and Affiliated Companies, Additional Report of the Committee on Interstate Commerce United States Senate . . . S. Res. 71 (74th Congress) . . . Alleghany System—Sale by George A. Ball; Tax Avoidance Through Charitable Foundations. Report No. 25, Part 6. Washington: Government Printing Office, 1940.

Investigation of Railroads, Holding Companies, and Affiliated Companies, Additional Report of the Committee on Interstate Commerce United States Senate . . . S. Res. 71 (74th Congress) . . . Alleghany System—Midamerica Corporation: Its Uses As a Holding Company. Report No. 25, Part 25. Washington: Government Printing Office, 1940.

Jones, Frankie Irene: *Edward A. Hannegan.* Unpublished M.A. dissertation, University of Chicago, 1935.

Knollenberg, Bernhard: *Pioneer Sketches of the Upper Whitewater Valley.* . . . Indianapolis: Indiana Historical Society, 1945.

Pamphlets and other documents pertaining to State Fair, various years.

Pamphlets, leaflets, correspondence, notes, and other material, some unpublished, relating to Eugene V. Debs in possession of Professor J. R. Shannon, Terre Haute, Indiana, and of the Indiana State Library, Indianapolis.

Parry, David M.: *David M. Parry To Organized Labor, Being A Reply to Questions Put to Him by the Central Labor Union of Indianapolis.* Indianapolis, October 24, 1903.

Past, Present, Future of Indianapolis Industrial Employment. . . . Indianapolis: Indianapolis Committee for Economic Development, 1944.

Progress of Pulaski County . . . Souvenir Program and History. . . . Winamac: Pulaski County Centennial Association, Inc., 1939.

Publications of the Agricultural Experiment Station, Purdue University, Lafayette, Indiana.

Publications of the Indiana Historical Society, various numbers [see separate listings for publications especially used].

Reports of the Department of Public Instruction. Various years. Fort Wayne.

Reports to Governor Gates of various state departments. Unpublished manuscripts, 1946.

Shannon, David Allen: *Anti War Thought and Activity of Eugene V. Debs 1914–1921.* Unpublished Master of Philosophy thesis. University of Wisconsin, 1946.

Shannon, David Allen: *Social and Economic Thought of Eugene V. Debs, the Socialist, 1897–1916.* Unpublished manuscript, 1946.

The Wabash Valley Remembers. . . . [n.d., n.p., probably Terre Haute, 1938.]

Winslow, Hattie Lou, and Moore, Joseph R. H.: *Camp Morton 1861– 1865.* . . . Indianapolis: Indiana Historical Society, 1940.

Year Book of the State of Indiana. Various years.

PERIODICALS

Brown, E. R.: "Reminiscences." *Pulaski County Democrat.* (Beginning February 9, 1922, these informal reminiscences of a pioneer settler ran irregularly through issues of 1922 and, though not used extensively in the present work, should interest students of pioneer life in northern Indiana.)

Carleton, William G.: "The Money Question in Indiana Politics, 1865–1890." *Indiana Magazine of History,* Vol. XLII, No. 2 (June 1946), pp. 107–50.

Chicago *Record;* Chicago, Illinois.

Chicago *Tribune;* Chicago, Illinois.

The Columbia Cauldron; Indianapolis. (Official organ of The Columbia Conserve Company; in possession of the company.)

Cottman, George S.: *Indiana Scrapbook Collection.* (Newspaper clippings compiled by Cottman in several volumes and presented to the Indiana State Library.)

Crawford, Mary M., ed.: "Mrs. Lydia B. Bacon's Journal, 1811–1812." *Indiana Magazine of History,* Vol. XL, No. 4 (December 1944), pp. 367–86.

Eley, Fred W.: "The Whitewater Canal." *Indiana History Bulletin,* Vol. XVII, No. 2 (February 1940), pp. 69–75.

Ewbank, Louis B.: "Building A Pioneer Home." *Indiana Magazine of History,* Vol. XL, No. 2 (June 1944), pp. 111–28.

Fesler, Mayo: "Secret Political Societies in the North during the Civil War." *Indiana Magazine of History,* Vol. XIV (September 1918), pp. 183–224.

Harbison, Winfred A.: "Indiana Republicans and the Re-election of President Lincoln." *Indiana Magazine of History,* Vol. XXXIV, No. 1 (March 1938), pp. 42–64.

Hoosier Farmer; Indianapolis, Indiana.

Indiana History Bulletin, various issues [see separate listings for articles especially used]. Indianapolis: Indiana Historical Bureau, State Department of Education.

Indiana Magazine of History. Published quarterly by the Department of History of Indiana University in co-operation with the Indiana Historical Society. [see separate articles especially used.]

Indianapolis *Journal;* Indianapolis, Indiana.

Indianapolis *News;* Indianapolis, Indiana.

Indianapolis *Sentinel;* Indianapolis, Indiana.

Indianapolis *Star;* Indianapolis, Indiana.

Indianapolis *Sun;* Indianapolis, Indiana.

Martin, John Bartlow: "Beauty and the Beast." *Harper's Magazine,* Vol. CLXXXIX, No. 1132 (September 1944), pp. 319–29.

Martin, John Bartlow: "A Gentleman from Indiana." *Harper's Magazine,* Vol. CXCIV, No. 1160 (January 1947), pp. 66–75.

Martin, John Bartlow: "Is Muncie Still Middletown?" *Harper's Magazine*, Vol. CLXXXIX, No. 1130 (July 1944), pp. 97–109.

Martin, John Bartlow: "Middletown Revisited." *Harper's Magazine,* Vol. CXCIII, No. 1155 (August 1946), pp. 111–19.

McCarty, Carlos T.: "Hindostan, a Pioneer Town." *Indiana Magazine of History*, Vol. X, No. 2 (June 1914), pp. 54–62.

Muncie *Morning Star;* Muncie, Indiana.

Pulaski County Democrat; Winamac, Indiana.

Rawley, James A.: "Edward Eggleston: Historian." *Indiana Magazine of History*, Vol. XL, No. 4 (December 1944), pp. 341–52.

Robinson, Oliver W.: "The Shakers in Knox County." *Indiana Magazine of History*, Vol. XXXIV, No. 1 (March 1938), pp. 34–41.

Scherrer, Anton: "Our Town." Indianapolis *Times* (daily column).

Steffens, Lincoln: "Eugene V. Debs on What the Matter Is In America and What To Do About It." *Everybody's Magazine*, Vol. XIX, No. 4 (October 1908), pp. 455–69.

Stewart, Ernest D.: "The Populist Party in Indiana." *Indiana Magazine of History*, Vol. XIV, No. 4 (December 1918), pp. 332–67.

"The Valley of Democracy," unsigned review of book by Meredith Nicholson. *Indiana Magazine of History*, Vol. XV, No. 1 (March 1919), pp. 78–9.

Uhl, Sherley: Obituary on Booth Tarkington. Indianapolis *Times;* May 20, 1946.

Whicker, John Wesley: "Edward A. Hannegan." *Indiana Magazine of History*, Vol. XIV, No. 4 (December 1918), pp. 368–75.

Wynn, Margaret: "Natural Gas in Indiana." *Indiana Magazine of History*, Vol. IV, No. 1 (March 1908), pp. 31–45.

Index

i

Engels, Friedrich, 34, 35
English, *see* British
English Hotel, 71f., 92
English, William H., 76
English's Opera House, 76, 95
Erie Canal, 37, 44
Erie Nickel Plate Railroad, 76
Erie Railroad, 82
Evans, Hiram Wesley, 189, 190, 194
Evansville, 8, 9, 89, 136, 137, 151, 181, 182, 189, 258–60, 272

Fables in Slang, 108–9
Fadiman, Clifton, quoted, 109
Fairbanks, Charles W., 103, 111, 130
Fairbanks, Crawford, 134, 138
Fair, State, 3–7, 18–20, 42, 56, 66, 105, 262, 277
Fallen Timbers, Battle of, 25
Farmers, 6–7, 14, 65–6, 89, 168, 218–19, 222, 224, 228, 238, 256, 262, 266, 268, 270, 274, 277, 278–9; in politics, 37, 44, 64, 66–74, 242, 276, 282, 279–80; *see also* Co-operatives; Farming; National Grange of the Patrons of Husbandry; Smoker, Dwight
Farmers' Alliance, 69ff.
Farmers' Mutual Benefit Association, 69ff.
Farming, 10, 18–20, 104–9, 216, 225–6; about 1860, 56; at close of Civil War, 65–6; before 1800, 23–4; depression of 1920's, 180–1; pioneer, 33; today, 182, 220, 224–5, 256, 276; *see also* Farmers
Fascism, 171
Federal Bureau of Investigation, 212
Federalist, 42
Field, Eugene, 143
Findlay, Ohio, 75

Finley, John, 103
Fisher, Carl, 16, 113, 117–21, 122, 123, 271, 280
Fishing, 15, 229, 234, 237–8
500-mile Race, *see* Indianapolis Motor Speedway
Flatboat trade, 36
Flat Rock Creek, 12
Fletcher family, 113
Florida, 119, 120, 121, 181, 182, 190, 204, 223, 247
Fontanet, 136
Ford, Henry, 116, 271
Fording, Oris, 264–5
Forsyth, William, 96
Fort Wayne, 15, 27, 28, 30, 44, 89, 242
Fort Wayne & Pacific Railroad, 92
Fortune, William, 93
Foster, William Z., 154
Fountain County, 43
4-H clubs, 4, 19
Fourier, François, 35
Fowler, 225
Franklin County, 223; *see also* Whitewater Valley
Fraternal orders, 96, 208, 237; *see also* Kiwanis Club; Lions Club; Masonic Order; Rotary Club
Fremont, John C., 51
French, 23–4, 25, 26, 281
French Lick, 10
French Lick Springs Hotel, 10, 102
Frisbie, Walter, 245, 255, 275
Front Page, The, 206
Fur Trade, 8, 15, 23, 24, 25, 27, 57

Gambling, 97, 98, 135–6, 255, 258, 262, 264, 265
G.A.R., *see* Grand Army of the Republic
Garfield, James A., 92
Garland, Hamlin, 96

Roosevelt, Eleanor, 261
Roosevelt, Franklin D., 81, 111, 168, 202, 207, 208, 209, 210, 211–12, 243, 245, 253, 255, 257; *see also* New Deal
Roosevelt, Theodore, 125, 130, 239
Rose, Chauncey, 56, 76, 134
Rotary Club, 177, 237, 241, 274–5
Rush County, 11
Rushville, 10, 11, 123
Russia, 153, 155, 156, 165–6, 180, 261; *see also* Communism
Ruthenburg, Louis, 259

Sacco, Nicola, 166
Salem, 10, 32
St. Ange, 24
St. Clair, Arthur, 25
Saint Joseph River, 15
St. Louis, 9, 12, 42, 51, 69, 98, 137, 182, 258
Santa Claus, 229
Scarlet Empire, The, 127
Scherrer, Anton, 98
Schmidt, Matt, 167
Schram, Emil, 14
Servel Company, 259
Shaffer's restaurant, 97
Shakers, *see* United Society of the Believers in Christ's Second Appearing
Shannon, J. R., 170–1, 247
Shelburn, 76, 136
Shelbyville, 12
Sherman Act, 143
Sherwood, Elmer, 246, 247
Shirkieville, 136
Shoals, 10, 31, 62
Shrewsbury, Charles Lewis, 56
Simmons, William J., 189
Sinclair, Upton, 127
Slavery, 26, 35, 47, 58–9, 280
Slocum, Frances, 33

Small town life, 13–14, 56, 89, 91, 92, 134–5, 136, 177, 189–90, 191, 192, 217–24, 225–6, 230–2, 237–9, 240–1, 274
Smith, Alfred E., 195
Smith, Asa J., 189, 195–6
Smith, Gerald L. K., 202, 209
Smith, Gypsy, 179
Smith, O. H., 38–42, 59, 66, 278, 282
Smoker, Dwight, 4, 18–20, 277–8
Smoker, Jim, 3–4, 18–19
Socialism, 127–8, 144, 146, 149, 154, 159, 162, 163, 179
Socialist Party of America (and predecessors and Socialist Labor Party), 128, 140, 145, 146, 148–9, 150–1, 152–5, 156, 157, 165, 168, 170, 171, 180, 236; *see also* Debs, Eugene V.; Socialism
Social Justice, 209
Songs, 58, 99, 136, 147, 155, 156, 201, 220–1, 239, 263, 266; Grange, 67–8; Lions, 177
Sons of Union Veterans, 264
South Bend, 15, 16, 76, 89, 116, 122, 153, 181, 182, 192, 254
Southern Tenant Farmers Union, 170
South, influence of, 10, 11, 24, 25, 45, 55, 60, 182, 205–6, 210–11; *see also* Hillbillies; Kentucky
Sparks, Will M., 196, 197–8
Speedway, *see* Indianapolis Motor Speedway
Speedway City, 120
Spink, E. G., 181
Spink-Wawasee Hotel, 15, 181
Spiritualism, 13, 55, 96–7
Spring Mill State Park, 274
Springer, Clark, 247
Springer, Raymond, 208, 210
Squatter Sovereignty, 26, 58
Stagecoach, 9, 13, 37